Praise for

THE ONLY GAME THAT MATTERS

"Harvard-Yale has always occupied a unique place in the American sports pantheon. Regardless of who wins or loses the games, the stories revealed in *The Only Game That Matters* about the people who play in them are well worth hearing, whether you are a graduate of the schools, a football fan, or merely someone interested in the human condition."

—John Feinstein, bestselling author of *A Civil War, The Last Amateurs,* and *Caddy for Life*

"In 1894, Harvard President Charles Eliot claimed football was 'unfit for colleges' and condemned the game as 'more brutalizing than prizefighting, cockfighting, or bullfighting.' Happily, his view didn't prevail over the long run, or else we'd not have *The Only Game That Matters,* a celebration of such worthies as Pudge Heffelfinger, who, as a forty-eight-year-old volunteer coach, nearly demolished the Yale team just to demonstrate that he could do it, or Joe Walland, who took the field with a temperature of 103 and quarterbacked Yale to a win. There may be some stories about tough and heroic Harvard players in this book as well, but I don't remember them."

—Bill Littlefield, Yale '70, author of *Fall Classics* and host of NPR's *Only a Game*

"The Harvard/Yale game is the mother of all college football rivalries. Corbett and Simpson chronicle this ancient competition, beginning when these teams dominated college football and tracking how The Game and therefore the sport are built on tradition and culture. To understand Ohio State/Michigan, Florida/Florida State, and USC/UCLA, you need to understand Harvard/Yale. *The Only Game That Matters* is a great place to start."

—Lee Corso, college football analyst, ESPN

"I was delighted at how the pages of *The Only Game That Matters* evoked the sense of competition and camaraderie that marks these great events, for they are about much more than just a football score. This book is a joy to read for anyone who appreciates the real values of college football."
—Jack Ford, Yale '72, news anchor and correspondent

"When these two schools first started playing each other, Ulysses S. Grant was in the White House. Harvard/Yale was the first great rivalry, and it remains the most important annual sporting event in New England. In *The Only Game That Matters*, Bernard M. Corbett and Paul Simpson capture both the spirit of this rivalry and the true spirit of the sport. I tell every real fan of college football I meet that they must see a Harvard/Yale game before they die. If they can't make it to Cambridge or New Haven they can do the next best thing and read *The Only Game That Matters*."
—Beano Cook, college football analyst, ESPN

THE ONLY GAME

THE
HARVARD/YALE RIVALRY

THAT MATTERS

BERNARD M. CORBETT

PAUL SIMPSON

Forewords by

Senator Edward M. Kennedy and Governor George E. Pataki

THREE RIVERS PRESS • NEW YORK

Library of Congress Cataloging-in-Publication Data
Corbett, Bernard.
The only game that matters : the Harvard/Yale rivalry / Bernard Corbett and
Paul Simpson.
1. Harvard University—Football—History. 2. Yale University—Football—
History. 3. Sports rivalries—United States. I. Simpson, Paul, 1969–
II. Title.
GV958.H3C67 2004
796.332'64'097444—dc22   2004006189

ISBN 1-4000-5069-3

Printed in the United States of America

Design by Leonard Henderson

10 9 8 7 6 5 4 3 2 1

First Paperback Edition

For my parents, Donald and Marilynn Simpson; and in memory of Bryan Harrison Porter (May 25, 1956–December 29, 2003), a courageous man of immeasurable strength and spirit who knew what mattered most.

—Paul Simpson

This book is dedicated to the memory of longtime Boston newspaper columnist, writer, bon vivant, and quintessential Harvard man George Frazier.

Frazier was a favorite of my late father, Mitchell. I had the opportunity to become familiar with Frazier's work at a tender, impressionable age. His 1960 *Esquire* magazine piece "Harvard Versus Yale: The Best of Everything," served as an inspiration.

The Game never strayed far from the irascible Frazier's thoughts as evidenced by an incident from his final days. While on his deathbed in Cambridge's Mount Auburn Hospital—on the opposite bank of the Charles River from Harvard Stadium—the curmudgeonly scribe had the following exchange with a particularly patronizing nurse.

Slowly, painfully succumbing to lung cancer, a withering Frazier suffered the additional indignity of frequently being talked to "as if he were a child with a cold."

On a particularly painful day close to the end of his life a nurse was having difficulty getting George to agree to a blood test.

"But we must have one, mustn't we?" persisted the nurse.

"I don't want one," persisted George.

"Well, aren't we here because we are sick?" asked the nurse.

"No," replied George Frazier wearily, summoning for the last time the quick wit that had marked his whole life and spontaneously fashioning what remains his most telling epitaph. "I'm just here for the Yale game."

May this tome be worthy of a toast from on high—a bit of libation shared between my father and Frazier.

—Bernard M. Corbett

Contents

Foreword

Senator Edward M. Kennedy

THE CALL ALWAYS COMES in November. Every year. Like clockwork. When I hear it's from the *Crimson*, I know it can only be about one thing: The Game. "What is your prediction?" I'm asked, and "What will be the final score?" The memory comes flooding back, and I glance at an old photograph on the wall of my office that shows a young Harvard football player holding up the ball he has just caught in the Yale end zone. I hardly recognize myself now, but I still remember the thrill of that magical moment in my life. The memory would be even sweeter if we'd won the game!

Catching that touchdown pass was a dream come true for me, especially since my father and my brothers were in the stadium that day. Dad took us all out to dinner that night, and everywhere around us people were glum about the loss, but I was walking on air. Bobby kept my head from swelling by reminding me that I'd missed a tackle that would have prevented a long Yale gain. I can still see that halfback putting the move on me.

In this book about the remarkable football rivalry between Harvard and Yale, Bernard Corbett and Paul Simpson capture the unique intensity of this famous game as felt by the teams who go all out on each play, and by the families and the alumni in the stands who live and die by each touchdown. The authors take us into the middle of the action at both universities during the tense week leading up to The Game. They remind us of the excitement on campus, and occasionally even the attention of the national press. Their vivid description of Harvard Yard brought me once again into Leavitt &

Peirce to see the game ball from the famous comeback to a 29–29 tie in 1968.

The tactics used by the coaches to prepare the teams, the personalities of the players, or the loyalty of the past players and alumni who make the annual pilgrimage to Cambridge or New Haven for The Game—they're all here. The traditions, the great games, the festivities, and even the pranks are a colorful part of this extraordinary in-depth look at the meaning of this historic competition. I found myself not only remembering the games in which I'd played, but fascinated by the behind-the-scenes descriptions of games and players I'd only heard about.

Whenever I can, I try to gather with old college friends and teammates to attend The Game when it is played in Cambridge. It's always a wonderful reunion, and even better when Harvard wins! Victory is never a sure thing regardless of how well a team has done during the season. Past victories go out the window, because The Game brings out a level of concentration and effort that always make a win possible for the underdog. As a player, you point to it all year. You work even harder in practice, and you can feel the electricity on the field and in the locker room. Trick plays are learned and memorized. Bumps and bruises are ignored. Sleep is hard to come by. On game day, the very air smells special. You know a losing season can be salvaged by a victory in The Game. There's the sudden feeling of goose bumps as the Little Red Flag is carried into the stadium by an honored alumnus, and you realize the importance of tradition and responsibility it represents. All the waiting is over. It's time to play. The kickoff comes and the first collisions with Yale players clear your mind. All that matters is the next play. The wind is cold. The ground is hard and often wet. Win or lose, it is the love of the game that is always there. When victory finally comes, the memory is savored for a lifetime, and so are the bonds of friendship, commitment, and teamwork that are the essence of this great tradition. Players on both sides quickly learn that The Game is good training for the game of life.

But when the *Crimson* calls again next year, I'll still pick Harvard to win!

Foreword

Governor George E. Pataki

LIKE MOST AMERICANS, I love sports—football, base-ball, the Yanks, the Knicks. But Yale football is my abiding passion.

Too often, however, when we turn to the sports pages, the inspiring stories we love about athletic achievement get lost in squalid stories about courtrooms, drug abuse, potential strikes, or academic fraud. Restoring the concept of "student-athlete" to its rightful position of prominence and respect in college sports is more than an urgent goal of the NCAA—it's the ardent hope of millions of Americans who yearn to have positive feelings about our heroes once again.

That hope, that quest to regain a lost spirit, is reason alone to read *The Only Game That Matters*—the story of a true student-athlete contest—the Yale-Harvard football rivalry. Here, we read of and exult in a rivalry the equal of any, a tradition surpassed by none, and a contest which for fans like me remains "the only game that matters."

I know people more familiar with Michigan vs. Ohio State, Alabama vs. Auburn, or some other "BCS" relevant game are probably thinking: *There they go again . . . those Yale and Harvard guys . . . trying to convince themselves that their football game actually counts.* Well, it does.

For Yale-Harvard represents a time, an afternoon, when fans of college football, whether rabid like me or more casual followers, know that the passion for excellence shown on the field is matched by passion for excellence in the classroom, that talent and character come together in a way that seems all too rare.

The first time my parents took me to a Yale-Harvard game, I was a high school sophomore and my older brother Lou was in the Yale band. For me, like so many other Catholic kids from my hometown, Notre Dame was the only football team that mattered. But why miss Notre Dame on television to see Yale live? I wondered. And then I saw.

The first thing that amazed me was the crowd. The tens of thousands of people in the stands were not just typical football fans. Mixed among the crowd were many older, distinguished alumni and friends, in their tweeds and sweaters, looking as if they had just exited their Park Avenue offices or suburban commuter trains. But once in the stands, these seemingly rational people were transformed into passionate fanatics given to adorning their outfits with odd accessories like plastic hats in the shape of a bulldog or obscene buttons calling on their despised enemy to have some woeful misfortune.

Elderly men, clearly eminent and admired by their peers, were risking instant death from stroke or heart attack by screaming mercilessly at the referees over a perceived bad judgment on the field. All of a sudden, I began to feel there was a reason these fans called this contest "The Game."

There *is* something different about the Yale-Harvard football rivalry that sets it apart from other athletic contests. Bernard Corbett and Paul Simpson have done an excellent job, not only capturing key elements from The Game itself, but capturing the intensity and feelings of the players, coaches, students, supporters, and alumni as the tension builds on this particular afternoon.

The book captures great moments that are still vivid in my mind: the powerful Yale teams of Brian Dowling and Calvin Hill, Brian Dowling's last-minute pass to Del Marting to win the '67 game for Yale, Eric Johnson's catch of Joe Walland's end zone pass "inches" off the ground to win the '99 game with 29 seconds left, as well as other games when the noble Blue were able to snatch victory from the clutches of the hapless Harvards.

On the other hand, to this day I do my best to forget attending the '68 game, which remains a dark cloud for me and other Yale alumni more than thirty-five years later. And this brings me to the only shortcoming of *The Only Game That Matters:* Historians more faithful to the enduring truth of Yale superiority would have ignored this historical aberration. Like all Yale fans, however, I take some solace in the knowledge that Harvard considers a tie with Yale to be its greatest "victory," while Yale considers the tie with Harvard to be its worst "defeat." How appropriate.

As you read this book, it becomes clear how The Game differs from other notable athletic rivalries. On this day of the Yale-Harvard football game, almost every student and faculty member (and many alumni, regardless of where they are) give their full attention to a game and a sport that for the rest of the season they follow only remotely, if at all. Unlike other universities where football is the unquestioned center of student and institutional identification (or still others where there is never a meaningful game), in this contest, for this one time, victory transcends everything else for nearly everyone at both schools.

Two of the greatest universities in the world, whose alumni compete for success and recognition in so many fields—whether politics, medicine, academia, science or the corporate world—focus that competition on a rectangular patch of green occupied by twenty-two true student-athletes. One afternoon every fall, the alumni's personal drive for excellence in the real world is transported to the field of play.

The otherwise unspoken desire for victory that dwells in the competitive hearts and minds of Yale and Harvard alumni around the world is, on this one afternoon, given full voice for all to hear in a place where they will be forgiven their momentary lack of personal decorum.

And for this one day and this one afternoon, fine athletes who make enormous sacrifices and endure year-round training in virtual anonymity gain the attention and glory that regularly follow their fellow football players at other campuses.

The Only Game That Matters lets Yale and Harvard football fans relive some of their great memories and experience again the anxiety and excitement this contest always provides. For everyone, including those who have never attended The Game, it vividly illustrates how top-flight athletes at our best academic universities can reaffirm our belief in the student-athlete and the true meaning of amateur sport.

For the past decade, my family and friends, former roommates and classmates, including a number from that lesser institution in Cambridge, have gathered each year to make a weekend of The Game. We get together from across the country and overseas beginning as early as Thursday night. On Saturday we take a bus, Elis and Harvards together, to either Boston or New Haven to cheer on our respective squads. It is perhaps a sign of maturity that after thirty-five years, we can sit together and act civilly toward one another both before and after the game. But we know better than to sit together during The Game itself.

Maturity and experience may have put The Game in perspective, but they do not diminish its importance. There are perhaps a cynical few who might think the book's title a tad overblown. But *The Only Game That Matters* does a great job of explaining why Yale-Harvard football is The Game—one that does matter, and should matter more. It is a shining example of what college football and amateur sports should be.

1

The Tie That Binds

THE COLD STING OF a brisk New England morning slapped Neil Rose in the face as he exited Dillon Field House. His breath caught a little as the icy air numbed his lungs. He had no doubt that the crisp football field would be near empty save for himself, fellow Harvard quarterback sophomore Ryan Fitzpatrick, and Todd LaFountaine, a freshman quarterback who'd followed Rose from Honolulu to Harvard. Even after four years in Cambridge, Rose still wasn't used to these hellish winters. The native Hawaiian sure wouldn't miss the weather when he returned to Oahu after graduation.

As cold as it was, Rose had no intention of changing the pregame ritual that had brought him so much success on the gridiron. He wore only mesh crimson shorts and a white T-shirt, and when he reached the field he kicked off his socks and shoes. Growing up in Hawaii, the kids always played football in the schoolyard barefoot. Rose needed to feel the grass and dirt with his bare feet, even if it crackled and crunched underfoot.

As far as football went, this was it for Rose. The 6′2″, 220-pound quarterback appeared on the tail end of some draft lists after leading his team to perfection in the 2001 season, but the NFL wasn't really a consideration. Intelligent and creative, Rose had other aspirations and though he loved the game, he wasn't sure that football alone would fulfill him. Nonetheless, he wasn't eager to see the last seconds of the fourth quarter dribble off the clock in the 119th play-ing of the Harvard-Yale game. He didn't want to hear the referee's whistle signaling the end of his playing days.

Rose looked high to the stadium roof at the three flags flapping and snapping in the steady November wind. The first, atop one side of the horseshoe, bore a white *H* outlined with a thin black band against a field of crimson. The second, in the middle of the horse-shoe's curve, was the American flag, the flag at which he would be staring during the national anthem as he reflected on his football career and made final mental preparations for the game. The third flag, directly opposite his school's on the other side of the horse-shoe, was that of Harvard's archrival, the Yale Bulldogs. A simple white *Y* on a dark blue background. The wind whipped the flags taut on the flagpoles, causing them to snap straight as if they had been dipped in the icy waters of the Charles River and left to freeze overnight.

The three flags collectively signified an incredible history. Long before the founding fathers turned back the redcoats so that they could proudly fly the red, white, and blue over a sovereign nation of their own, Harvard and Yale nourished a budding rivalry that had exploded onto the football field in 1875 and became the most important in the sport. Every player, coach, and fan that looked toward the sky today would be reminded of the more than century-old skirmish that they held dear. If the wind continued its violent thrashing, the flags might be reduced to a few frayed threads by game time. It would not be a good day for throwing the pigskin, and that didn't bode well for the Crimson's all-time passing leader on a day when he needed to be his sharpest. The weather didn't matter to Rose, though. The team had always performed well in bad weather. They were better than the weather.

Rose threw some passes to LaFountaine, testing the wind. He sent the freshman on an outside hard post—Rose's favorite route—and dropped back in slow motion, counting out his footsteps. *One, two, three, four, five. Plant the back foot. Fire.* Rose hit LaFountaine twenty yards out amid a visualized Yale defense. The defense always gave up something against Harvard's multiple-threat offense, and Rose exploited the weakness. He'd stare down the free safety and watch him cheat just a little left or a little right, reluctantly providing the ideal situation for a completion, especially if the intended receiver was Carl Morris. LaFountaine tossed the ball to Fitzpatrick, and Fitzpatrick mapped his own steps before hurling it back to Rose. The sophomore needed to test the wind himself in case he had to relieve Rose at quarterback.

Rose would miss the pregame routine more than anything else about being a football player. In the still of an empty stadium, with the grass between his toes, Rose was never more at peace with himself. Never more confident in his abilities or more certain of what was to come. Rose prolonged this final ritual for fifteen minutes before the trio headed back to the locker room to avoid hypothermia. The senior settled into one of the metal hot tubs in the training room to take off the chill and warm up his fragile back muscles. He prayed that his frequently injured back wouldn't betray him in his last game.

While Rose warmed in the hot tub, Yale senior captain Jason Lange got off the team bus and sauntered to the visitor's locker room. On the way he glanced overhead, getting his playing instructions for the day from those same three flags flying high above the stadium. The Bulldogs' coaching staff had prepared two defensive game plans—one for Harvard's passing quarterback, Neil Rose; the other for Harvard's scrambler, sophomore Ryan Fitzpatrick. Lange, a nearly three-hundred-pound nose tackle, was the anchor and heart of the Yale defense, and he realized that the wind was sending him into a fight against an attempted ground attack by the Crimson. He would spend the day bulldozing his way into the backfield, clogging and collapsing holes in the defensive line, and trying to wrap his arms around Harvard's slippery and elusive running back, Nick Palazzo. At 5'4" with a low, balanced center of gravity, Palazzo darted like a cat—often streaking past a stunned defensive line before it could react and leaving the tough tackling job for the secondary. Palazzo missed the 2001 game with injuries, so Lange had not had the chance to face him prior to this last game for both young men.

At least Harvard's defensive line would be able to sympathize with Lange. Yale also had a sensational running back who wore the number 22, the same as Palazzo. Sophomore Robert Carr had proven early in the season that he was a big-game player, and there was no game bigger than Harvard-Yale. At 5'6" and with blazing speed, Carr often left opposing defensive linemen staring at the back of his uniform. The Crimson had just as much, if not more, to worry about in terms of defending the run. And if the winds let up, the Harvard defense would have to be concerned with Yale's passing game as well. Quarterbacks Alvin Cowan and Jeff Mroz combined for sixteen touchdown passes on the year, the same as Harvard.

The weather didn't bother Lange. He grew up playing outside of the Windy City in Hoffman Estates, Illinois. Cold, rain, and wind gave Lange a mental edge. Players unaccustomed to intemperate conditions lost their focus in bad weather, and Lange took advantage of it.

The senior was ready for anything or anyone Harvard could throw at him. He welcomed a challenge, and not just on the football field. Lange was planning to take the spring semester off from school to work full-time in Yale's development office. He also had his sights set on earning a spot on another fabled Yale team, the singing troupe known as the Whiffenpoofs. He thought maybe his tenor could take him around the world. He would get to the West Coast by bike, though—for the following summer Lange had scheduled a biking trip across the country with two teams of college students to raise money for Habitat for Humanity International. However, for the time being Lange focused on the challenge at hand, the biggest and last game of his football career, and how his defense would stop the Crimson offense.

Lange prepped for the Harvard game as he had for all of his others. He slept for precisely eight and one-half hours. He fortified himself with eggs, bacon, French toast, two bowls of raisin bran, and some fresh fruit. He let head athletic trainer Chris Pecora tape his delicate, injury-prone ankles. (Lange's right ankle had weathered five sprains and his left ankle seven.) He dressed in the same order, starting with his socks (left foot first, then right) and ending with his number 97 jersey. Finally, until the call to stretch he listened to music that got him pumped up for the game, Eminem's "Lose Yourself" and Drowning Pool's "Bodies." Only then was the captain ready.

When Yale's defensive coordinator Rick Flanders saw the flags at the stadium, he knew unquestionably which defensive scheme the Bulldogs would use. The forty-four-year-old veteran coach breathed a little easier—the wind indicated that Harvard's prolific pass attack would take a backseat to the run, and Flanders liked his chances of stopping the ground game. Even so, Flanders remained worried and wary. The coordinator had developed Yale's secondary into a solid unit, but his defensive backs had found mixed success earlier in the 2002 season against challenging receivers like Cornell's dependable Keith Ferguson, Brown's playmaker Chas Gessner, Princeton's track star speedster Chisom Opara, and powerhouse Penn's Rob Milanese. They had yet to see their biggest challenge: Harvard's record-breaking receiver and defending Ivy League Player of the Year, Carl Morris, who would be playing his last college football game on this blustery day. Morris was remarkable, plain and simple, and Flanders nursed private fears over what kind of antics the Morris-Rose combination had saved for their farewell home performance. Flanders hoped for continued gusts. He was counting on the stubborn cold front and favorable jet stream to foil the Crimson aerial assault.

The fierce gales didn't take sides, though. Strong winds struck fear into the heart of both special teams units. Harvard's place-kicker Anders Blewett and punter Adam Kingston and Yale's place-kicker John Troost and punter Ryan Allen were sure to play a major role in the game, and the weather conditions were killing their confidence. As kickers they had a relatively thankless position. Aside from a sparse opportunity to boot a game-winner in the final minute, like Harvard's Mike Lynch did in the 1975 Harvard-Yale game, there was little chance for glory. Solid punts, long kickoffs, and chip-shot field goals were taken for granted at times, mostly by fans but sometimes by coaches and teammates as well. On a frigid, blustery day that featured the most important game of the year, however, all bets were off. It didn't take an Ivy League scholar to realize that the goat-to-hero probability ratio leaned conspicuously in favor of the former under toe-numbing, windswept conditions. The impending ground game ahead of them posed more challenges to first downs than the preferred pass-filled contest, and Kingston and Allen would be faced with a good number of fourth downs where they would be responsible for establishing starting field position for their opponent.

Possibly the only factor unaffected by the categorically seasonable weather was the attendance figure. Neither rain nor snow nor sleet nor hail ever kept fans from their precious Harvard-Yale game. By ten o'clock in the morning the Friends of Harvard Football parking lot just outside the stadium's ivy-covered walls was a sea of celebratory cooking. Although the casual fan got by with a simple spread (hot dogs and burgers cooked over the glowing coals of a hibachi, washed down with ice-cold Budweiser drawn from a quarter-keg), the most dedicated tailgaters had lugged lavish four-star comforts to the pavement: card tables draped in white linen, dainty candelabra, spiral-cut glazed ham garnished with pineapple slices and maraschino cherries, cold cuts, calzones, and rolls, and a beverage buffet of red and white wines, fresh juices, soda, and coffee.

Fans of all stripes lined the lot. One group slowly sipped steaming coffee and huddled around the bed of a pickup truck, trying to keep out the chill. They were parked next to a showroom-clean black Saab with physician's plates, which sported a Harvard 1957 banner on the dashboard next to a softball-size button that shouted "Go to hell Yale!" A trio of Yale supporters passed by the car and chuckled at the button's message. They didn't return the sentiments; after all, they were deep in Crimson territory.

Most of the Yale fans warmed their insides in the parking lots near the outskirts of campus. The host team always got the prime tailgating real estate, and the Yale faithful happily deferred. They'd have their day at the Yale Bowl next year and show the Harvard fans how tailgating was done. After all, Yale football fans *invented* tailgating—though Princeton and Rutgers folk think that the honor belongs to them—and they thought they had the festivities down pretty well by now.

The London family, however, would stack their tailgate against that of any Yalie.

The long London family love affair with Harvard football started with Lauren Cohen. Cohen wrote letters to his nephew Abe London while serving in World War II, mesmerizing the child with stories of 1930s legends like Harvard star quarterback Barry Wood and his equally talented counterpart at Yale, Albie Booth. Cohen promised to take the boy to the Harvard-Yale game when the war ended. Cohen kept his promise, and Abe London fell in love with Harvard at first sight. London graduated from Harvard in 1957, eventually becoming a doctor with children of his own.

Dr. London passed on his love of Harvard football to his son Jon. "He begged me to take him to the football games as soon as he started speaking," Dr. London recalled years later. The doctor finally relented and took young Jon to a game versus Columbia in 1973. Like his father, Jon fell under Harvard's spell, and as a six-year-old held his first season ticket. Jon followed his father's path to Cambridge and graduated from Harvard in 1988. He wed and had children as well, and continuing in the family tradition Jon's daughters, ages three and five, became season ticket holders for Harvard football.

After Jon graduated, he and his closest friends from Quincy House decided to make the Harvard-Yale game the backdrop to an informal reunion. Harvard didn't have an official homecoming and they all planned on attending the game every year Harvard hosted Yale anyway, so it was a natural fit. Three or four of London's housemates and twenty or thirty friends attended the first biennial London tailgate in 1988.

At least seventy people were expected in 2002. At half past seven in the morning Jon arrived to set up the feast in the parking lot, assisted by a few of his housemates who flew in from Seattle, Miami, and California. Although London planned well (he organized the contents in a Microsoft Excel spreadsheet to make sure he didn't forget anything), it took them about ninety minutes to arrange the buffet. Tablecloths, turkey breasts, and tenderloins. Cheese, crackers, chili, and chowder. M&M's, mustard, mayonnaise, and Maalox. With so many years of experience, London and company came prepared. For its attendees, the London tailgate at the stadium every other year is a can't-miss event, though sometimes other obligations keep one or two of the housemates out of the lineup. Those that *do* miss their biennial chance to catch up with friends had better have a damned good excuse, as Steve Bilafer discovered the hard way.

Bilafer, now Massachusetts District Attorney Tom Reilly's chief of staff, told London he'd be unable to attend in 1992. Bilafer wouldn't divulge the reason. His parents attended London's tailgate that year, however, and leaked his whereabouts to the gang. While his housemates partied in Cambridge, Bilafer went to a craft fair and pottery show with his wife. Not an acceptable excuse when over the years people have flown in from places such as London, Stockholm, Australia, and Hong Kong. Armed with cell phones, the partygoers barraged Bilafer with harassing calls. He hasn't missed the event since. His friends will never let him live it down, especially when others not even affiliated with Harvard show up time and again— including a contingent from the Great White North.

One of London's housemates lived in Ottawa the year after he graduated and brought his Canadian roommates with him to the first London tailgate. The group has shown up unannounced each year since, with or without London's roommate. They rent a van or motor home, bring a traveling bar, set up a table, and commence with drinking games. After the game they pile in and drive home. No one at London's tailgate has any other contact with them.

The most difficult part of the tailgate is getting the revelers to actually stop the partying long enough to go to the game. London, a rabid fan and former radio color analyst for Harvard football, bolts for his seat at game time—he has always witnessed the opening kick-off. His father also wouldn't think of missing a down. After all, the traditional wardrobe would go to waste otherwise.

Each year Dr. London dons his Harvard hat, scarf, and boxers, and a wool overcoat that his uncle made for him when he was a student at Harvard. The pockets of the overcoat, which he only wears to the Yale game, overflow with ticket stubs. Dr. London's pants are unremarkable—only because the Crimson pants he used to wear split long ago. To top off the outfit, he wears two pins on his lapels. One says, "Go Harvard!" The other, "Go to Hell Yale!" Since 1945, Dr. London has missed only five Harvard-Yale games due to military service and medical residencies, but he almost missed the 2000 game for another reason.

While traveling in France that summer, Dr. London fell—hard. He suffered a torn rotator cuff that eventually led to surgery, which occurred the day before the Harvard-Yale contest. The operating doctors ordered Dr. London not to go anywhere, including the football game. But there was simply no way that was going to happen. Dr. London rationalized his planned attendance at The Game by saying that he thought it would actually *help* with his recovery. Jon London refused to drive his father to the stadium, wanting no responsibility for disobeying doctor's orders. Dr. London persuaded his wife to drive instead, and while in the car feeling began to return to his paralyzed arm. Though his physician thought otherwise, a trip to The Game seemed to be just what the doctor ordered.

The Harvard-Yale game has always been a family affair, and not just for fans. Peter and Dan Mee, two brothers who played for Harvard, nursed their own sibling rivalry when it came to playing

Yale. The teams Peter Mee played on in 1974 and 1975 both defeated Yale. Dan lettered in 1979 and 1980 but won only one game against the Bulldogs. It was bad enough that his older brother gloated about the Ivy League championships won by the Crimson teams on which he played. But if the Harvard teams Dan played on had lost to Yale both years he never would have heard the end of it. Fortunately Dan's 1979 Harvard team upset Yale 22–7 at the bowl. "We had no business winning that game. We didn't even belong on the same field as them," he said. "But we played like giants that day and somehow pulled it out." The 1979 Harvard victory prevented Dan from a lifetime of torment from Peter, and it demonstrated that anything can happen when the two teams meet, regardless of which team is better on paper.

Arch O'Reilly, who played for Harvard in the early 1960s, felt there was no sense in trying to predict a winner. He had seen enough Harvard-Yale games as a former player and during his thirty years as a fan to know that the team who wanted it more usually won— despite the weather or any other outside factors. O'Reilly, weaving in and out of tailgate parties and warding off the late November chill in a red ski parka zipped to his chin, was proud to say that the Harvard teams of which he was a member never lost to Yale.

But he relished more than just the action on the field. O'Reilly loved what The Game was all about, and his thoughts on playing football in the Ivy League could be neatly summed up by a fond memory involving one of his teammates. Joe Jurik, a 6'6", 270-pound lineman, once spent the night in O'Reilly's dorm room after taking the exam for organic chemistry, said to be the most difficult course at Harvard. Jurik spent the entire evening berating himself for getting a particular question wrong. He hadn't failed; he'd simply missed one question that he thought he should have known. "When you play behind a big, huge lineman who was eventually drafted by the Patriots, and his big deal is that he actually got a question wrong in the hardest course at Harvard, *that's* what it's all about," O'Reilly said. "You feel that the guys who are playing football are playing for no other reason than they want to play football. And that's why it's worth coming to this game."

Even those who don't love the sport jam into the stadium whenever Yale comes to town, and November 23, 2002, was no exception. The tickets sold out earlier in the week. Over thirty thousand people would fill the seats, more than doubling Harvard's highest home game attendance for the season. Harvard and Yale students support their football teams during the season, of course, but this isn't Michigan or Notre Dame. No one is competing for a national championship and no one kids themselves that football is the schools' main draw. A cynical person might liken it to lining up on the fairways to watch two golfers shoot one hundred. On Harvard-Yale game day, however, you'd think it was the Rose Bowl. After all, it isn't just a game—it is The Game.

The nickname originated with Yale athletics official Charlie Loftus. Syndicated sports columnist Walter "Red" Smith called Loftus in 1959 to let him know that he wouldn't be able to make that year's Harvard-Yale game. "What?" Loftus asked incredulously. "You're going to miss THE Game?" Smith thought the moniker extremely fitting and used it in his column. But the name didn't really take hold until 1960, when Harvard sports information director Baron Pittenger splashed the title across the program for the Yale game. Each of the programs for the other games at Harvard was titled according to the opponent: The Dartmouth Game, The Princeton Game, and The Penn Game. When Yale came to Cambridge that year, the program simply read "THE Game." The name stuck. Harvard and Yale fans love it. At the same time it provokes college football fans nationwide who feel that the title is pretentious, snobby, and inaccurate. They think many bigger, better games take place around the country on what is traditionally college football's Rivalry Day.

But to Harvard and Yale, The Game represents much more than just a couple of mediocre teams battling for position in the bottom half of the nation's football landscape. It is living history—two of the country's most storied schools defending their honor. The rivalry certainly swells beyond the boundaries of the gridiron, and examples can be found wherever Harvard grads or Yalies have the opportunity to take a swipe at their rival. For instance, alumni writers from *The Harvard Lampoon* frequently have landed jobs writing for such shows as *The Late Show with David Letterman, Late Night with Conan O'Brien, Saturday Night Live,* and even *The Simpsons,* and lines mocking Yale have curiously found their way into dialogue. In one episode of the Springfield series, the curmudgeonly Montgomery Burns returned from a Harvard-Yale football game in which Yale lost. "Harvard can have its sports and academics," Burns sneered. "Yale will always be first in gentlemanly club life."

From dysfunctional animated families to America's First Families, however, the subject always comes back to football. Since 1940, in presidential election years the outcome of the game has paralleled the vote. If a Democratic candidate wins, Harvard wins. If a Republican candidate wins, Yale wins. The only exceptions were Kennedy's 1960 victory (Yale, 39–6) and Carter's win in 1976 (Yale, 21–7). Even the most recent election in 2000 followed suit despite the recounts, hanging chads, and court battles. During most years, the Harvard-Yale game takes place after America knows the results. But because of the controversy surrounding the 2000 election, a winner hadn't yet been determined at game time. Yale won the 117th playing of The Game, and history repeated itself when Republican and former Yalie George W. Bush took over as the nation's leader.

Tradition clearly cloaks all aspects of The Game, the years having molded antics into hallowed rituals. One of the oldest and most revered of these is Little Red Flag. A crimson pennant adorned with a black *H* and attached to a walking stick, Little Red Flag came to New Haven in 1884 with Harvard graduate Frederick Plummer, who was then a freshman. The flag has been carried to every Harvard-Yale game since. The honor of waving Little Red Flag used to belong to the Harvard man who had been to the most successive Harvard-Yale games, but the criteria changed in 2001 when Harvard Varsity Club Executive Director Bob Glatz had trouble coordinating the delivery of the flag to then ninety-three-year-old curator Burdette Johnson. Glatz formed a committee and together the group selected alumnus Bill Markus.

Markus had witnessed only twelve consecutive Harvard-Yale games, but the committee felt that he was more than worthy because of his dedication to, support for, and promotion of Harvard athletics. Markus lives in Pittsburgh and has traveled to all of the Harvard football games since 1986 in venues from Cambridge and New Haven to Ithaca. His devotion to Harvard isn't limited to the gridiron—Markus has watched nearly all of Harvard's forty-one varsity sports teams in competition. The only sports he hasn't watched so far are golf, skiing, cross-country, and sailing, but no one would be surprised to see Markus in a dory on the Charles rooting Harvard's fleet of Larks on to victory.

Markus hardly slept the night before the 2001 Harvard-Yale game. The fact that a Harvard win over Yale would mean an undefeated season for the Crimson only magnified the honor of carrying Little Red Flag. A relative of Markus's picked him up at the Harvard Club of Boston early on the Saturday of The Game. On the way to New Haven, the inertia switch in the Ford Explorer broke and the two were left stranded on I-95. They frantically made two phone calls—the first to a towing company, the second to a taxi company. Markus requested a cabbie that had a few hours of free time, and before long he resumed travel. So preoccupied with worry that he wouldn't make it in time, Markus didn't notice the cab driver miss a critical split in the highway. Instead of heading south toward New Haven on I-95, they began racing south on I-93 toward Cape Cod. Ten miles later the driver corrected the mistake. He barreled down I-95 and deposited a thankful Markus at the Yale Bowl an hour before the game started. The ride cost around $150, but Markus would have paid double.

The committee asked Markus to carry Little Red Flag again in

2002, and he made his way to the stadium without incident after a good night's rest at the Harvard Club of Boston. As the kickoff time of half past twelve approached, Markus took his seat alongside Harvard's President Lawrence H. Summers and his family at the fifty-yard line. Markus happily shared the honor of waving Little Red Flag with Summers's kids.

Outside the stadium, hopeful last-minute drivers clogged the streets. Police and security banished most of them to the distant satellite parking lots, forcing them to walk several blocks through the cold just to park their behinds on the stadium's concrete bleachers. Experienced fans opted for public transportation and walked to the stadium from the Harvard Square subway stop, crossing over the Lars Anderson Bridge.

The bridge spanned the Charles River—whose waters were churned into a whitecapped frenzy by the howling winds—and connected Boston with Harvard Square a few blocks away. Harvard Square teemed with spectators seeking shelter until the last possible minute. Even the street musicians who normally gathered in "The Pit" outside the stairway to the Red Line T stop had turned tail on the cold, taking their competitive cacophony inside.

In the eyes of those who come to Cambridge only in conjunction with attending the annual Harvard-Yale game every other year, the square has evolved considerably over the years. In the 1960s, Harvard Square was synonymous with antiestablishment rhetoric and a pervasive climate of rebellious protest. It became a gathering place for the peace-loving flower child crowd. They filled the coffeehouses to listen to the likes of Joan Baez repopularize the folk music movement, and beatniks sat on benches in the square and penned poems or read Kerouac. Abbie Hoffman and Timothy Leary led demonstrations against the Vietnam War and protesters leafleted the area. The 1960s square was a prickly adolescent extension of its austere Ivy League parent campus, but it has begun to mellow with age. The area's younger adults still post signs on telephone poles and in shop windows, although protesters share the landscape with a diverse crowd. Panhandlers shake Styrofoam cups at men and women in business attire carrying briefcases as they emerge from the subway. Preppy students shop at The Gap and Abercrombie & Fitch. Street musicians play instruments ranging from electric guitars to violins to overturned five-gallon plastic buckets.

Like the square's prevailing antiestablishment mood, the shops, restaurants, and bars that had contributed to its unique fabric gradually faded. Eateries like the Wursthaus, the Hayes Bickford, and Elsie's (home of the roast beef special and a four-meat sandwich called the "fresser's dream") closed their doors. Familiar franchises like Starbucks, Dunkin' Donuts, and Au Bon Pain set up shop in the empty storefronts. Fortunately a few establishments like Mr. Bartley's Burger Cottage and the Tennis and Squash Shop stayed, both preventing the square from becoming a glorified strip mall and reminding shoppers that this is not Anytown, USA. And no business works harder to keep the "old" Harvard Square alive than Leavitt & Peirce.

The door in Leavitt & Peirce's facade is not really a door at all. It is a portal to the past. In addition to pipe tobacco, cigars, and cigarettes, Leavitt & Peirce sells nostalgia, straight up. Shaving kits for the steady-handed, with straight razors and brushes for applying mug-mixed shaving cream. Hand-carved cherry pipes. Backgammon, mah-jongg, and chess sets. Tin windup toys. Upstairs, two dollars an hour buys you a table in the chess room, where cigars push slow-looping curls of smoke to the ceiling. It's a true throwback—a haven for smokers, society's latest pariahs.

Leavitt & Peirce began a unique relationship with Harvard athletics over one hundred years ago. Though ownership has changed hands several times during that span, the management has always kept a museum-quality tribute to Harvard athletics, especially the crew and football squads. Several pairs of heavily lacquered oars are fastened to the walls, dated in paint on the blades with the oldest from 1883. Framed newspaper stories heralding Harvard's success on the water and sepia-toned photographs of rowing teams line the walls. Medals on faded ribbons, the spoils of victories, hang from nails. For over sixty years, until the advent of e-mail, one of the only places the daily rowing schedule was posted was in the window of Leavitt & Peirce. Lazy crew team members frequently called the store instead of walking down to the square to check the schedule.

The store helped the football team as well. Before the creation of the Harvard Athletic Association, Leavitt & Peirce served as the de facto ticket agent in the square. Until 1893 it was the only place patrons could buy tickets. Due to ticket demand for the Harvard-Yale game, a second entrance had to be installed—not because there wasn't enough room in the store to handle and process ticket trans- actions, but because of some unscrupulous fans. With tickets in hand, satisfied patrons would file out of the store past the long line of customers hoping to get seats. So desperate were some people to ensure that they would get into the Harvard-Yale game—which was a guaranteed sellout—that they snatched tickets from the departing customers. The second means of exit in Leavitt & Peirce alleviated this problem by sending those with tickets in hand out the newly installed door.

Leavitt & Peirce's football memorabilia is equally as impressive as its homage to Harvard crew. Ticket stubs tacked to the walls date back to 1884. Photos from the 1919 Rose Bowl team adorn one sec- tion. Thirteen footballs used in Harvard-Yale games sit side by side, each painted with the date and score. From the bloated, balloonish sphere used in the 1908 game to the familiar shape and material of today's pigskin, Leavitt & Peirce charts the evolution of the ball. Twelve of the thirteen represent a Harvard win. The thirteenth ball, the crown jewel of the collection, reads 29–29, the score of the most famous Harvard-Yale game of them all. The date was November 23, 1968.

At Yale in 1968, football was religion, Brian Dowling was God, and his followers believed. The charismatic quarterback and captain of the Bulldogs enjoyed an iconic status at the New Haven campus and beyond. Students held candlelight vigils beneath Dowling's dorm room window, similar to those that might occur when zealots spot a likeness of the Virgin Mary in the grain of a wooden door. When rain poured down on the fans at one game they chanted for Dowling to make it stop. After the season's first game, a helmeted football player named BD who wore number 10 appeared in a *Yale Daily News* comic strip called *Bull Tales*, drawn by Yale sophomore and budding cartoonist Garry Trudeau (who later turned *Bull Tales* into *Doonesbury*). Dowling's on-field exploits even drew comparisons to Frank Merriwell, the fictional hero of a hugely popular turn-of-the-century dime novel serial. Dowling, however, was flesh and blood, and ever since arriving at New Haven he had given his followers reason to believe that something special would undoubtedly happen when he was on the field.

A nationally recognized superstar whose legend grew exponentially from week to week, Dowling became a unifying spirit during a chaotic time. In other years the posters that read "God Wears #10" might have prompted letters to the *Yale Daily News* about worshipping false idols, but that autumn the students had bigger issues on their minds. Reeling from a series of mind-numbing tragedies and turbulence that tested the mettle of all America, the country teetered precariously on the precipice of tragedy and disaster in 1968.

The specter of the Vietnam War cast a constant pall over the calendar, from the Tet Offensive in January all the way to a volatile election campaign that culminated with the election of Richard Nixon in November. Within a two-month period in the spring, the assassinations of two of the century's most galvanizing and compelling figures, civil rights activist Martin Luther King Jr. and Senator Robert F. Kennedy, thrust the country further into an abyss of despondency.

All across America people were taking to the streets. The race riots that ravaged urban America in the long, hot summer of 1967 were revisited in many cities as a result of King's murder, and the antiwar movement gathered momentum as America sank deeper into the quagmire of Southeast Asia. The college campus morphed into an epicenter of protest. With their generation directly affected and their peers dying thousands of miles away in support of America's foreign policy, it was the nation's college students who reacted the most vociferously, and sometimes violently, to what they viewed as the indiscriminate life-and-death decisions of the elder generation with regard to a war that was increasingly perceived by the American public as unjust.

Every college campus needed something positive to rally around in 1968. At Yale, Dowling was it.

Dowling came to Yale having not lost a football game in which he started at quarterback since the seventh grade. When he was recruited out of St. Ignatius High School in Cleveland, Yale was not his only suitor. In choosing to play in New Haven, Dowling disappointed over one hundred college football coaches, including those at perennial powerhouses Notre Dame and Ohio State. He turned down a punched ticket to the pros, respecting his father's wishes that he play at Yale so that he'd have a good education to fall back on if he didn't make the NFL. Only one man was not sorry to hear of Dowling's selection: Yale's new head coach, Carm Cozza.

The thirty-five-year-old Cozza, one of his predecessor John Pont's assistants, took control of Eli football fortunes for the 1965 season when Pont decamped for Indiana and the Big Ten conference. Cozza's roots extended back to Ohio, the core of football country. A native of Parma, a Cleveland suburb, Cozza had played for a pair of coaching legends at Miami of Ohio: future Notre Dame coach Ara Parseghian and Ohio State coach Woody Hayes.

The link to the legends was no help in the beginning, though— Cozza's career as Yale head coach began most inauspiciously. In his first game the Blue did the unthinkable: they lost to the lowly University of Connecticut for the first time in history. The loss shook the foundation of the Yale football community, and the head coach felt the tremors most acutely. A telegram sent to Cozza from an irate alumnus read, "There's a train for New London at 5:40PM: Be under it!"

Cozza also gained no favor with alumni supporters by losing to Harvard in his first two years as coach. Not only was Yale defeated, but the Bulldogs failed to score a single point, losing 13–0 and 17–0.

The mood in 1967 was different. Cozza's first recruited players, the outstanding Class of 1969, were now juniors. Led by Dowling and running back Calvin Hill (who would become the father of Duke University and NBA star Grant Hill), the Bulldogs proceeded to steamroll through their Ivy League schedule, scoring 191 points and giving up just 58 while winning five straight games. The roll included an emotional, decisive Ivy League title-clinching victory at Princeton. With the league crown secured, Yale looked to end their season on the highest note possible, a win over Harvard. It wouldn't be easy.

From 1964 to 1966 Harvard held sway over Yale. The Bulldog defense was simply never able to solve the mystery of Harvard running back Bobby Leo. Beginning with a dramatic 46-yard dash to the end zone in the fourth quarter of the 1964 game, the pride of the Boston suburb of Everett scored the winning touchdown versus Yale in three consecutive seasons.

But in 1967 Leo was gone. A sun-splashed fifty-degree day at the Yale Bowl attracted a crowd of 68,315, the largest since the Ivy League began formal play in 1956 and the biggest since Army's visit in 1954. The teams rewarded fans with a dramatic seesaw battle, and Dowling tipped the scales in Yale's favor for good on a 66-yard touchdown pass with time winding down in the fourth quarter. A Yale fumble recovery with two minutes remaining secured the win. The Elis were Ivy and Big Three champions (Harvard, Yale, and Princeton) and, most important, victors in The Game. Dowling had completed only five of nineteen passes for 153 yards and was intercepted four times, but he'd made the plays that spelled the difference.

Less than forty-eight hours after the game at the Yale Bowl passed into history, Harvard and Yale each announced to the media the 1968 captains of the Crimson and Blue, a tradition that ensured a sense of leadership continuity. Vic Gatto would lead the 1968 Harvard squad. Expectedly, it was Brian Dowling for Yale.

Still smarting from the painful loss to Yale, Harvard's Vic Gatto made a bold pronouncement. "We came so close this year (against Dartmouth and Yale), I don't see any reason why we can't go 9–0 next year."

Dowling didn't comment on the forthcoming season. He didn't need to. His actions had spoken louder just two days before. There wasn't any reason for 1968 to be anything but better.

Dowling wasn't the only one who felt this way. Despite the graduation of several key seniors from the previous year's championship team, including five players who had achieved All-Ivy recognition, the expectations for the 1968 Yale football team could not have been higher. The return of running back Calvin Hill and a healthy Brian Dowling at quarterback were all the Elis needed to build around. The Blue faithful could not help but think that something good would happen, as long as Dowling was on the field. Thankfully, good things happened even when he wasn't.

Dowling missed his first four varsity games due to a wrist injury, but Yale managed without him until he got his first start. Then the Bulldogs took off. Through the first seven weeks of the season, only Cornell came within two touchdowns of the Big Blue machine. With each passing week the Dowling legend grew larger.

At Harvard, preseason expectations were considerably lower. Despite the opinions and presence of captain halfback Vic Gatto and several experienced defenders, the consensus prognostication of the sports media called for a middle-of-the-pack Ivy League finish for the Crimson. Gatto had set the bar with his previous comment, however, and his teammates had listened.

Featuring a diverse group of seniors, including Vietnam veterans and members of Students for a Democratic Society, the Crimson got off to a strong start with a pair of nonleague victories. They didn't have a prolific offense, but they made up for it with an emphasis on defense. Dubbed the "Boston Stranglers," the Harvard defense allowed just twenty-seven points over the next five weeks of the Ivy League schedule. Three defensive players—safety Pat Conway, linebacker John Emery, and defensive end Pete Hall—made the All-Ivy team. On the less heralded offensive side Gatto was joined by a two-hundred-pound guard from Plano, Texas, a roommate of future vice president Al Gore and a talented aspiring actor named Tommy Lee Jones.

The Crimson and Bulldogs plowed through their respective schedules, setting up a potential battle of two unbeaten and untied teams facing each other in Cambridge in the last game of the season. Harvard and Yale needed only to beat their respective opponents in the final game before their annual showdown. Yale did its part, routing Princeton for the second straight year, 42–17, before an enthralled, jubilant crowd of sixty thousand at the Yale Bowl. Calvin Hill scored three touchdowns to set an all-time Yale record for career touchdowns. The Yale student rallying cry of "Squeeze the Orange" even attracted the pregame participation of Yale President Kingman Brewster. The Crimson stepped up with their best offensive performance of the season, defeating Brown 31–7. The *Boston Globe* front-page headline on November 17 said it all: "The Stage Is Set." Yale would travel to Cambridge 8–0–0. Harvard would defend the hallowed ground of the stadium turf standing 8–0–0. For the first time since 1909 both teams would enter The Game undefeated and untied.

The buildup to game day was unprecedented. Not since the last of the three head-to-head clashes between Harvard's Barry Wood and Yale's Albie Booth in the 1930s had a Harvard-Yale game completely captured the imagination of the sporting public, and the saturated media coverage constantly trumpeted the matchup.

The *Boston Globe* had a man in New Haven. The *New Haven Register* had a man in Cambridge. Television and radio reporters jostled elbow-to-elbow with print journalists from regional newspapers and national magazines, all trying to get the goods on each team's preparation. For two squads of gridiron combatants that were destined to become stockbrokers, investment bankers, corporate lawyers, and doctors, this was a taste of what it was like to play in the Super Bowl.

The 1968 Harvard-Yale game may have been slated for the stadium, but the players were living in a fishbowl.

The pregame hype escalated with each passing day. Gordon Page, the longtime Harvard University ticket manager, became a sought-after celebrity. Disgruntled alumni shut out from the forty-thousand-seat capacity stadium cursed his name. In all, Page estimated that the Harvard community alone requested more than seventy thousand tickets. Twenty years earlier Page could have accommodated almost all the ticket requests, but since then over twenty thousand seats at the open end of the horseshoe-shaped stadium had been removed. Page theorized that his office could have realistically sold a hundred thousand tickets, a big-time number usually seen at the likes of Michigan Stadium.

Though neither Yale nor Harvard had contended for the national title since the 1920s, the 1968 game qualified as big-time football. Harvard and Yale were far from obscure on the national landscape. Behind Dowling, Yale led the nation with fifteen straight victories. Mentioning the two schools alongside the likes of Oklahoma, Penn State, Tennessee, and Notre Dame in discussions about the nation's best football programs wouldn't draw looks of confusion or laughs of ridicule. People around the country other than Ivy League fans recognized the names of players on those teams, especially Dowling. The ticket requests came from far and wide.

Given the inadequate seating capacity, Harvard officials established ground rules for obtaining tickets. No Harvard alumni after 1949 were eligible, and exceptions were made only for faculty and Varsity Club members. Harvard offered fifteen thousand tickets to the Yale contingent, a number that was less than one-quarter of the Yale Bowl's capacity. Countless Dowling disciples went ticketless, forced to watch the game on television or listen to it on the radio. Home field provided no advantage for many Harvard fans either. Harvard graduate Andre Sigourney '51 nearly missed his first Harvard-Yale game since 1938, but the depths of his school spirit gained him and his wife two tickets.

Sigourney, who played on the junior varsity squad while an under-grad, always enjoyed the festivities of the Harvard-Yale weekend, especially the freshman game the day before the varsity squads squared off. While at the 1968 freshman game someone introduced him to Harvard captain Vic Gatto's father. Sigourney told Gatto how much he admired his son's play. In a moment of overwhelming Crimson spirit, Sigourney then told Gatto that he and his expectant wife—due any day—would name their child Victoria after the Harvard captain if the young couple had a baby girl. "Mr. Gatto was so moved by my decree," Sigourney said, "that he reached into his pocket and gave me tickets for two great seats!"

Sigourney arrived early at the stadium the following day. He and his wife, Jean, told their obstetrician that the two planned on going to the game and asked him what they should do if Jean went into labor. The obstetrician, Dr. David Kopans (who was a former Harvard football star), told the Sigourneys not to worry. Kopans had tickets also and told them he'd deliver the baby in Dillon Field House if necessary. Baby Sigourney didn't arrive until the following Wednesday but the couple kept their promise, even though they had a baby boy. The Sigourneys named him David (after Sigourney's father and Dr. Kopans) VictorGatto Sigourney. The Sigourneys paid a unique price for their tickets, but they were lucky to get them at all. Most people came up empty regardless of the creative means they pursued to get into the game.

Between the ticket crunch and the media microscope, both squads felt the pressure mounting the week before the game. Steve Lalich, the father of Harvard quarterback George Lalich, concocted ways to keep the stressed Crimson team loose. The South Side Chicago native and former professional boxer got the fun started by handing out Al Capone gangster-style soft hats to the entire Harvard team in the locker room. On the brim of each was a card that read, "Rub Out Yale."

The stunt was only the beginning for the elder Lalich. He printed 1,500 wanted-poster-style handbills that pictured each of the eleven members of the Crimson starting defense and one of the team managers helped him post them around Harvard Square among the anti-war rally bulletins:

WANTED
For Massacring Yale's Offensive Football Team
On Saturday November 23, 1968
Warning
These men are considered the most dangerous defensive team in the NCAA
REWARD
Free Trip to Sing Sing

Despite Lalich's efforts, the hijinks failed to fully distract the Crimson underdogs. Injuries to running back Ray Hornblower, linebacker Gary Farnetti, cornerback Neil Hurley, and safety Pat Conway weighed heavily on Harvard coach John Yovicsin. "We need to play our absolute best," he stated matter-of-factly. He knew that his Crimson team could ill afford the absence of key performers.

Yale reported much better health. Their only concern was kickoff-return man Bob Sokolowski's rib injury. Dowling had shown his versatility by volunteering to step in for Sokolowski the previous week, and he likely would do so again if necessary. When informed that the Ivy League coaches had made his team the unanimous consensus favorite, Carm Cozza said, "Well, I guess I have to agree with them." The oddsmakers concurred and set the line with the Bulldogs as seven-point favorites.

Anything was possible, of course, but Cozza hoped the predictions came true. During the media frenzy a reporter asked the Yale coach if he'd be satisfied with a scoreless tie and a share of the Ivy League crown. Cozza replied, "Why, that's like kissing your sister."

The pregame media hype continued to focus on the irresistible force of the Yale offense attempting to move against the immovable obstacle of the Harvard defense. For the media, the most immovable object appeared to be Harvard sports information director Baron Pittenger. With nine thousand spectators already given clearance for standing room accommodations on the roof of the stadium, Pittenger faced the unenviable task of somehow finding room for all the media members who hoped to cover the game. Safety regulations limited the number of media spectators to 350, which included representatives of a staggering forty-six daily newspapers. Pittenger solved the problem with a special closed-circuit presentation of the game at three locations around the Harvard campus, a small gesture to those (including reporters) who couldn't get into the stadium.

After all, since Ivy League play began in 1956 only one other season had featured two undefeated teams battling for the title, and whether media or med student, all of Cambridge wanted to be there. Everybody, everywhere was making plans. A telegram arrived from Al Bergin, an All-Ivy offensive guard who played through the bitter disappointment of the game the previous year and who was stuck in Oxford, England. "I'll hear the game via trans-Atlantic cable in the Harvard Club of London. Give 'em hell," he wrote.

The day prior to the game featured a Crimson sweep of the six football games between Harvard and Yale houses. The junior varsity game ended in a 7–7 tie, foreshadowing the varsity contest. After practice on Friday night, the varsity Crimson players returned to Dillon Field House and a lusty serenade of Harvard fight songs by the band. Burning flares surrounded the field. The pomp and circumstance underscored the fact that a Crimson win would end the Eli dreams of a perfect season, as it had in 1921 and 1937. And an undefeated season would be the Crimson's first in forty-eight years.

The weather cooperated on Saturday, a bright sun presiding over a calm forty-five-degree day. Harvard Square teemed with Crimson and Blue, old and young, all intent on witnessing history. Tickets with face values of $6 now cost $100 in the ever-escalating pregame economy, an amount equal to $520 in 2002. In final comments to the media, both coaches proclaimed their team's readiness. The only thing left to do was play.

The game started cautiously. Late in the first quarter, Yale's Mark Bouscaren recovered a Harvard fumble at the Yale twenty. Dowling promptly engineered an eighty-yard touchdown drive highlighted by a thirty-two-yard inside reverse run by Norman Davidson. Dowling covered the final two yards himself on a quick option run. Early in the second quarter the Bulldogs visited the end zone again as Dowling tossed a three-yard touchdown pass to Calvin Hill, who broke the all-time Yale record for career points on the play.

The Yale onslaught continued midway through the second quarter, when a blocked Crimson punt led to a five-yard touchdown pass from Dowling to one of his favorite targets, Del Marting. The heroic combination from the 1967 game hooked up again for a two-point conversion play. Yale 22, Harvard 0. Dowling's scrambling, unorthodox throwing style and improvisational skill had the vaunted "Boston Stranglers" befuddled.

When Yale's next series ended with a Hill fumble at the Harvard thirty-six, Harvard coach John Yovicsin went to his bullpen and summoned unheralded backup quarterback Frank Champi. Starter George Lalich had been the junior varsity quarterback as a sophomore and the number three quarterback as a junior, but he just wasn't a reliable signal caller. Erratic throughout the 1968 campaign, Lalich had completed only fifty-three passes in Harvard's eight victories for just 666 yards and three touchdowns. Lalich was faring no better in his final outing versus Yale. Yovicsin needed a change and Champi fit the bill.

The second-stringer from nearby Everett, Massachusetts (the hometown of three-time Bulldog slayer Bobby Leo) quickly engineered a twelve-play, sixty-four-yard drive capped by a fifteen-yard touchdown pass to Bruce Freeman. A missed extra point sent the teams to the locker room with Yale leading 22–6. The late Harvard touchdown did nothing to faze the sense of Bulldog invincibility. The only question that remained was the margin of Yale's eventual victory.

Crimson momentum carried over to the second half, however,

once again initiated by virtue of Bulldog generosity. Yale's Bouscaren gave the ball back, fumbling on a punt return after a hit by Bob Jannino. Freeman pounced on the ball at the Yale twenty-five-yard line.

Champi returned to the Harvard offensive huddle. After losing a yard on the first play, Champi threaded a perfect throw to tight end Pete Varney for twenty-five yards. On the next play, the Crimson offensive line blasted open a gaping hole for fullback Gus Crim to rumble in for the touchdown. Left-footed soccer-style kicker Richie Szaro, who had made his varsity debut the previous week, successfully converted this time. The Crimson had closed the gap to 22–13.

The Elis dominated play for the remainder of the third quarter, but fumbled away two more offensive opportunities. First, fullback Bob Levin coughed one up at his own forty-six. Later in the quarter Calvin Hill fumbled for the second time at the end of a long run. It was the first scoreless quarter played by Dowling and his Big Blue offensive machine in the last twenty-six.

Dowling took matters into his own hands on the next Yale possession. Beginning the first fourth-quarter drive at midfield, Dowling had the Bulldogs in the end zone in seven plays, again calling the option run to cover the final five yards on his own. The Yale lead stretched to 29–13. Approximately five thousand of the forty thousand fans in attendance packed up and headed for the exits. The remaining Yale faithful taunted the Harvard fans by waving handkerchiefs and chanting, "You're number two!"

Despite the Elis' frustrating habit of losing the ball at the most inopportune times, Dowling had been spectacular, and directly responsible for twenty-six of Yale's twenty-nine points. It was Dowling who had the stranglehold on the Harvard defense, and it appeared that he wasn't quite finished. The masterful field general marched the Yale offensive unit deep into Harvard territory again. But with just three and one-half minutes to play, fullback Levin had the ball wrestled from him by a Harvard defender at the Crimson fourteen-yard line. From that moment on, all rationality departed the proceedings on the stadium stage.

Champi led a battered Harvard offense back on the field. Injuries to captain Gatto and the other starting halfback, Ray Hornblower, resulted in the insertion of another backup, halfback John Ballantyne. On second and twelve, Ballantyne scooted seventeen yards on a reverse. A pass attempt by Champi to Ballantyne fell incomplete, stopping the clock. The next play ended with Champi sacked for an apparent twelve-yard loss back at the seventeen-yard line, but the referees called a defensive-holding penalty. It was a Harvard first down at the Yale forty-seven-yard line, the spot of the infraction, and the Crimson's first major break.

Champi then threw an incomplete pass aimed at Bruce Freeman. On the next play he looked for Freeman again, this time finding him for a seventeen-yard gain. First down at the Yale thirty-yard line. On first down, Champi threw incomplete to fullback Crim. The Yale pass rush trapped Champi in the backfield on the next play, netting an eight-yard loss.

Faced with third and eighteen and less than a minute remaining, the Yale defense again trapped Champi. Under intense pressure, the increasingly resourceful Champi shoveled a lateral pass toward Fritz Reed, a converted end. Reed fielded the ball and rambled twenty-three yards to the Yale fifteen. First down. Reed, an offensive tackle, had made the longest Harvard run from scrimmage of the afternoon. The bizarre play unnerved the Eli defense. Champi didn't let them gather their thoughts. He wasted no time on the next down, rolling out and finding Bruce Freeman. The junior end hauled in the ball at the Yale five and battled his way into the end zone for his second touchdown of the afternoon, and only his eighth catch of the season. The Crimson's first attempt at the all-important two-point conversion ended as Champi's pass to tight end Pete Varney was knocked loose. But then disaster struck for Yale in the form of a flag. Pass interference on the Elis. On the second chance for two, the Crimson decided to keep it on the ground. It proved a good decision. Fullback Crim followed the block of guard Tommy Lee Jones into the end zone. Incredibly, Harvard was within striking distance: Yale 29–21.

Forty-two seconds remained. Harvard's only hope was an onside kick. They knew that the only way to win was to keep doing what they had been doing for the past 2:49—keep the ball out of the hands of Dowling. The Yale captain had proved his versatility, returning a punt earlier in the game and now acting as a deep safety on the kick-off team. But he should have lined up near midfield. That's where all the action took place.

All season long Harvard had practiced for just such an opportunity. Their regular kickoff man, Tom Wynne, lined up the ball as usual, but at the last second defensive back Ken Thomas sneaked in from the right and deftly bunted the ball across the field in the direction of the Yale sideline. A wild scramble ensued as Yale guard Brad Lee bobbled an opportunity for the recovery, and Crimson number 27 fell on the ball on the Yale forty-nine-yard line. Several seconds passed before sportscaster Don Gillis found the name of the Harvard hero: sophomore Billy Kelly.

"We had practiced those onside kickoffs all year," Kelly recalled. "The key was to kick the ball on the top so it would bounce twice on the ground and then into the air. The kickoff came to my side but it didn't bounce right, and I thought, 'Uh-oh, this isn't what we practiced.' Then the Yale player fumbled, and I saw the ball lying on the ground with no one around it. I thought, 'This is amazing. All I have to do is fall on it.'"

On the first down of Harvard's final drive, under heavy duress, Champi scrambled out of trouble for fourteen yards around the left end before Bouscaren collared him right in front of the Yale bench. A flag flew once again. A face mask penalty was called, despite the protests of the Bulldog coaching staff. A Yale fan just behind the bench grabbed his hair in clenched fists and screamed, buckling in anguish while the officials tacked on fifteen crucial yards. First and ten at the Yale twenty.

Thirty-two seconds.

Champi momentarily lost his magic. Two pass attempts fell incomplete, the first to Bruce Freeman and the second to Jim Reynolds.

Twenty seconds.

Gatto, the Crimson captain and heart and soul, miraculously hobbled into the Crimson huddle with the next play call. He promptly split out wide to the right, attracting considerable attention from the Yale defense. Just what Harvard wanted. The call, a fullback draw play, a flashback from 1967, broke wide open. This time the Crimson executed perfectly and fullback Gus Crim gained fourteen yards.

"We were in the same situation the year before in New Haven," Vic Gatto later recalled. "In 1968, we called the same play." The results were dramatically different this time. Instead of Yale running out the clock, the Crimson found themselves first and goal at the Yale six.

Fourteen seconds.

Champi scrambled frantically again on the next play as seconds ticked off the clock. The Yale defense sacked him for a two-yard loss. From the bottom of the pile Champi screamed for Harvard's last timeout.

Three seconds.

There was time for one more play. One more opportunity for Champi to position the Crimson for a miracle comeback. "Flank Vic left," Coach Yovicsin told Champi, "then roll right and throw back to Vic."

The Harvard quarterback, who had played a total of twenty-two minutes prior to that fateful afternoon, took the final snap from scrimmage as a hush descended over the stadium. Champi dropped back to pass again, and the Yale defense swarmed. Champi rolled right but he couldn't find Gatto on the other side of the field. The sound of the final gun broke the silence of a moment frozen in time. Champi scrambled for what seemed like an eternity. For a split second he thought about lateraling again but instead wiggled free from a defender's grasp, spied a man in the corner of the end zone, and threw to a wide-open Gatto. The captain collected the prize. Touchdown! Harvard trailed 29–27.

"I remember just this tunnel of noise," Gatto recalled, "and it was as if time had slowed down. I knew I was free but I didn't want to wave because I didn't want to call attention to the fact that I was open. Then Champi threw to me, and the ball came so slow and big."

The throngs around the perimeter of the stadium turf mobbed the field. As officials and police cleared the gridiron, Champi checked the Harvard sideline. Coach Yovicsin relayed the play for the two-point conversion attempt: a curl-in pass to tight end Pete Varney—a big target at 6'3"—over Yale defensive back Ed Franklin, a player that Yovicsin had said earlier in the week could "jump like a kangaroo" despite his height of 5'9".

Champi took the final snap.

Again he immediately found himself under heavy pressure from the Yale defense. Backpedaling all the way to the fifteen-yard line, Champi spotted Varney positioned perfectly in front of Ed Franklin just inside the goal line and hit him right in the numbers. Harvard 29, Yale 29.

"The stadium exploded," reported *The Harvard Alumni Bulletin*. "Strangers embraced, full professors danced, and the Yale people put their handkerchiefs to the use they were intended for."

Dowling had pleaded with coach Cozza to enter the game on defense, but Cozza declined, not wanting to embarrass any defender who had played at his position all season long by sending in Dowling as a replacement. Forced to helplessly watch Frank Champi's Warholian fifteen minutes with the thirty-five thousand fans that remained, Dowling finished his brilliant career on the Yale sideline. Still undefeated, yet crushed by a heartbreaking tie.

Out of all the dejected Yale players, fans, and coaches, none was more distraught than Brad Lee. Lee carried the weight of the botched onside kick recovery like Atlas. He couldn't bear to face his teammates, so he skipped the bus ride back to New Haven and spent the night alone in a Boston hotel room. "That was the worst feeling of my life," Lee said in 2003. "It still hasn't left."

Frank Champi received an unusual reward for his laudable contribution. In order to earn the varsity *H* a player needed to have at least ninety minutes of varsity game experience. Champi had a mere twenty-two minutes under his belt prior to the Yale game. Even after receiving "double credit" for his exploits in the Yale game from the Harvard Athletic Association, Champi's total remained at sixty. The HAA issued waivers under special circumstances, and bringing the Crimson back from the grave against Harvard's archrival certainly qualified as special. Champi received his letter.

The media coverage following the 1968 game rivaled the pregame buildup. Within five minutes of the game's completion, a special extra edition of the *Crimson* was handed out to amazed spectators as they left the electric celebration inside the stadium. It was the headline on Monday morning's edition of the *Crimson,* however, that truly summarized the 1968 game. It read, "Harvard Beats Yale, 29–29!" The author of the headline remained anonymous. The Crimson photo editor at the time, Tim Carlson, suggested it to night editor Bill Kutik, but Carlson credited a drunken Harvard undergrad who slurred the phrase to him in the end zone during the wild celebration.

On Sunday, November 24, the previous day's events were rebroadcast by Boston's CBS affiliate, soothing those not fortunate enough to see the miraculous comeback in person—as well as for the five thousand fans who left prematurely. Those who witnessed the game firsthand must have gathered around their sets as well, just to make sure they hadn't been dreaming. The replay captured the attention of New England, garnering ratings similar to a State of the Union address. The streets in and around Boston, all the way to Manchester, New Hampshire, were reportedly desolate during the broadcast. Two weeks later, Boston's CBS affiliate aired *42 Seconds,* a documentary about the 1968 game and Harvard's season. Hosted by Don Gillis, a Boston sportscaster who pioneered the sports-reporting segment during the nightly news and provided the play-by-play for the television broadcast of the 1968 game, the show featured clips of the action and commentary from Harvard players and coaches.

In 1978, however, both sides of the story found screen time. Producers selected the 1968 Harvard-Yale game as a topic for *The Way It Was,* a nationally televised show hosted by legendary broadcaster Curt Gowdy and Dick Enberg. The game was in good company—the show had previously featured roundtable discussions with key figures from momentous sporting events, including the New York Giants–Brooklyn Dodgers 1951 playoff game that spotlighted Bobby Thomson's "Shot Heard Round the World," and the 1967 "Ice Bowl" NFL championship game between Dallas and Green Bay.

Ten years after the unforgettable 1968 game, Frank Champi, Vic Gatto, and Bruce Freeman took the stage for Harvard; Carm Cozza, Brian Dowling, and Bob Levin for Yale. As the game film rolled, the reactions of the participants were shown inside a cutout at the bottom right of the screen. Vic Gatto's ear-to-ear Cheshire-cat grin contrasted sharply with Carm Cozza's disbelieving stoic gaze. It was the first time Cozza had seen the footage since the grim events of November 23, 1968, and it was obviously not any less painful.

Gowdy told Champi, the reluctant hero, that his play was nothing short of inspirational. The compliment did not, however, soften Champi enough for him to elaborate on why he walked away from Harvard football the following fall after two games. Champi also seemed a tad disgruntled at the way he was portrayed at the time, insisting that he was no Cinderella story. Like Dowling, Champi couldn't recall losing a game in which he started, including freshmen and junior varsity games at Harvard.

Gowdy and Enberg concluded the special by asking each of the men if they felt Harvard won the game. Not surprisingly, the answer was a resounding yes from Champi, Gatto, and Freeman. Dowling, who had moved to the Boston area, said that he never met anyone who said it was a tie. Levin joked that after seeing the game footage again, he now realized that it was *Yale* who had won on that day. He wasn't able to say it with a straight face, garnering laughter from the panel. Cozza said it best: "The score read 29–29, Curt, but, I admit, it was the worst loss of my career."

It seemed that no form of media failed to preserve the magic afternoon of November 23, 1968. Fleetwood Records of Revere, Massachusetts, put broadcasting hall-of-famer Ken Coleman's radio call of the entire game onto an album. The 1968 Harvard-Yale game became part of the company's series of sports recordings that also featured the Boston Celtics, Boston Bruins, and Boston Red Sox.

The popularity of the 1968 game as one of sports history's most dramatic finishes has not faded. Ted Mandell, author of *Heart Stoppers and Hail Marys: 100 of the Greatest College Football Finishes (1970–1999)*, included the 1968 Harvard-Yale game as number one on his list as the founding father of miracle finishes in college football. Sportswriter Al Silverman went a step further in his 2002 book *It's Not Over 'Til It's Over*, where he selected the 1968 game, along with such events as the 1980 Olympic U.S.-U.S.S.R. hockey game and Ali-Frazier I as one of the thirteen most unforgettable sports moments of all time.

For good reason the 1968 Harvard-Yale game, "The Tie," has become the most renowned chapter in the football rivalry. Of all the times the two schools have met, never has The Game's outcome been so reviled by one side and so rejoiced by the other, despite the fact that *nobody won*. The tie gives Crimson faithful an edge in arguments over which school has the better team: Harvard's come-from-behind equalizer often is tough to top.

🏈 🏈 🏈

If Neil Rose had his way, there would be no debate after the 119th playing. Rose fully planned on emerging victorious. At the traditional team dinner on the Thursday preceding the Yale game, each senior addressed his teammates. Rose spoke last, thanked his coaches, and offered simple advice to the team. *Never give up.* Rose had had to prove himself over and over to the coaches during his Harvard football career, especially in 2002, and he wanted the younger players to remember this. He sometimes had wondered whether he would be as good or as accomplished as he wanted to become, and questioned whether he had the strength. "No matter what I do or accomplish in life, I will always consider being a Harvard football player—being one of you—my greatest honor and accomplishment," the captain said to an emotional, teary-eyed room.

Crimson Head Coach Tim Murphy said nothing special to his team on the morning of The Game. In fact, Murphy offered little in the way of advice or encouragement during the preceding week. He didn't have to. The players knew how critical a win over Yale was to the team and its supporters.

Yale head coach Jack Siedlecki felt the same as Murphy. By the time the Harvard game arrived there was nothing left to say. Siedlecki had ingrained into his players the necessity of a win over the team's main rival all season long. A few sentences before the game weren't needed to inspire his players to go out and get it done.

Jason Lange, like Rose, wholly intended to leave Cambridge with a win in his final game as a player. The Ivy League had instituted overtime in 1981, so a finish like that of the 1968 game wasn't possible. Something had to give. Lange addressed his teammates in the lobby of the Marriott Hotel the night before and reminded them of the Harvard game's importance. "Ten or twenty years from now you'll only remember a handful of moments from your football careers. The Game will definitely be one of them."

Harvard took the field first for a pregame celebration to honor its seniors and their contribution to Harvard football. Siedlecki knew from experience that the ceremony always ran past the time allotted, so he kept his players inside the locker room longer than usual. Let the opponent stand out in the cold. He'd keep his team as warm as possible prior to kickoff. Any advantage, no matter how slight, could make the difference.

When the Harvard senior ceremony came to a close, Yale took the field. The Bulldog fans erupted with applause, and students representing each of Yale's houses waved giant flags. The Harvard fans countered, trying to drown out the enemy rallying cries. Rose and Lange met the referee at midfield for the coin toss. The two captains shook hands, the last cordial act until the game's end. Icy wind carried the cresting wave of crowd noise into the Cambridge streets. The referee flipped the coin with his thumb, and the captains' eyes followed the shimmering circle upward against the cold, gray sky.

Anatomy of a Rivalry

BEAT HARVARD . . . BEAT HARVARD . . . Beat Harvard . . . Beat Harvard. Like a pounding heartbeat, the scrolling words on Coach Jack Siedlecki's computer screen reveal an unrelenting inner drive. They say everything that needs to be said about Yale football. Sure, there's more to the program than The Game. But there's nothing more important.

After all, the annual goals never change: Win the Ivy League and wallop the Crimson. Accomplishing both makes for the best kind of Yale football season, but performing the latter will compensate for not achieving the former.

And at the beginning of the 2002 season it looked like defeating the Crimson would be the only way the Bulldogs could scrimp together a semblance of success. In the eyes of the pundits, Yale wasn't a legitimate contender. The media predicted a lackluster sixth-place Ivy League finish. Out of eight teams. Siedlecki, fifty-one, couldn't really blame them. He had suffered through the growing pains of rebuilding his program in 2001 and posted a 3–6 record. Undaunted, Siedlecki took the poll results in stride. In fact, he thought they provided a great motivational tool that would whip his team into shape. He had a knack for turning negatives into positives.

The poll also didn't factor in an invaluable intangible Siedlecki enjoyed as Yale's head coach: more than three decades of coaching experience perched on his shoulder.

Siedlecki operated under the watchful eyes of his predecessor, Carm Cozza. Cozza concluded his thirty-two-year tenure as Yale's head coach in 1996 but still attended practice a couple of days each week to prepare for his duties as color analyst on the school's radio broadcasts. As the long-standing patriarch of Yale football, Cozza was revered in New Haven and respected throughout the Ivy League and beyond for his skill as a coach and his dedication to collegiate football. He led Yale to 179 victories and ten Ivy League titles during his three-decade turn at the helm. In 1996 Cozza retired as a legendary figure in Yale football annals, placing him alongside the likes of the sport's most influential figure Walter Camp, Heisman Trophy winners Larry Kelley and Clint Frank, and folk-hero quarterback Brian Dowling.

Cozza's segue into retirement gave him the rare opportunity to help select his successor. The grizzled veteran coach met with each of the handful of finalists individually to provide a recommendation, and he gladly endorsed Siedlecki.

"He really knew the Ivy League and was familiar with many of the coaches," Cozza said. "He seemed to be a good fit."

Many coaches might resent the daily presence of the team's previous coach, especially one who is a newly inducted member of the College Football Hall of Fame, but Siedlecki saw the value in Cozza's vast storehouse of experience. Cozza, however, carefully stayed an arm's length away from the coaching staff. "I don't generally assist Jack with any game plans or X's or O's," Cozza said, preferring to lend a hand with things like alumni relations. Once in a while, however, Siedlecki asked Cozza a football question. After all, any Yale coach worth his weight in Rhodes scholars uses any and all avenues available to help his team beat Harvard.

And in 2002 Siedlecki would take anything he could get. True, he did have confidence in the depth and skill of the team's defensive front seven, especially the on-field leadership and talents of his captain, nose tackle Jason Lange. Siedlecki expected Lange's roommate and fellow senior Luke Mraz, a starter in 2001, to help anchor the defensive line, which was probably Yale's strongest overall unit on the team.

But Siedlecki's prospects at the all-important position of quarterback weren't so bright. He had lost both the players who took all the snaps the last two seasons. The leading contenders to fill the void were junior Alvin Cowan, the only candidate with any snaps taken at the varsity level, and junior varsity veteran sophomore Jeff Mroz. Cowan had lettered the previous year as a special teams player and completed two of four passes, all from punt formation on trick plays. Mroz, candidate number two, saw all of his action in junior varsity games the prior season. Siedlecki watched the two spend the preseason squaring off, and Cowan believed all along that he'd win out over Mroz. It had nothing to do with his chief competitor—it was just Cowan's confident Texas swagger. In his mind he came to Yale his junior year as the starter. When Siedlecki made the decision and announced Cowan as the starter, the junior saw it as a mere formality.

A rough-and-tumble player as eager to scramble for a few crucial yards as to launch a Hail Mary, Cowan had shown every indication of being the type of flamboyant leader that could elevate Yale's inexperienced offensive unit. Blessed with blond, All-American looks and an accurate arm, Cowan starred at Austin's Westlake High, a longtime bastion of Texas high school football excellence. (Drew Brees played his prep ball at Westlake before starring at Purdue and going on to start at quarterback for the San Diego Chargers.) An affable and articulate young man fond of strumming his guitar to unwind after practice, the tenacious quarterback couldn't help but notice the sparse turnout at many Ivy League games. The thin crowds were a noticeable contrast to the roaring fans who watched him play high school football in the schoolboy world of "Friday Night Lights."

One negative aspect of playing for such a renowned high school program was the depth chart. Most of the college recruiters started looking at players as juniors, and Cowan spent much of his junior season riding the pine behind starting quarterback Adam Hall, who went on to start at quarterback for San Diego State. As a result, recruiters had no prior knowledge of Cowan when he moved to the starting spot his senior season. Cowan brushed off any concerns about his visibility. He knew he'd play college football. He just didn't know where.

Though the Austin native always felt he would play at the Division I-A level at a school like Texas, he kept the Division I-AA Ivy League in the back of his mind. His best friend's brother, Jeff White, played linebacker at Westlake and saw action at Yale. White spoke so highly of Yale's program that Cowan decided to visit New Haven. He also looked closely at Columbia and Dartmouth. Harvard, however, was not an option. Though the Crimson coaching staff initially expressed interest in him, Cowan thought they did so halfheartedly. The feeling was mutual—Cowan knew a couple of players from Westlake who hated their Harvard experience. One of them even quit the team altogether. Cowan, who felt he was cut from the same cloth as many Westlake players, didn't think Harvard would have made him happy.

Cowan also considered walking on at a Division I-A school—he figured he could have made the roster on many programs at that level. In the end, however, he couldn't get past what it would be like to look back at age forty and wonder what would have been if he'd attended an Ivy League school. He couldn't allow himself to squander the opportunities and advantages such an education could offer him, and he chose Yale. He later confessed that if a Division I-A academic powerhouse like Duke or Stanford had shown interest in him, he would've passed over Yale. Luckily for the Bulldogs, Cowan slipped under their radar.

Despite Cowan's confidence, Siedlecki didn't lose sight of his new quarterback's inexperience. He was counting on a solid ground game and diligent blocking by the offensive line to help with Cowan's adjustment period. At the running back position, hard-charging Jay Schulze was returning for his senior year and the health of speedster Robert Carr would provide a vital link in offensive success. Quarterback pro-

tection duties fell to three-year starters guard Kyle Metzler and center David Farrell, the most veteran players on the offensive line.
Inexperience, however, wasn't limited to Cowan. A string of preseason
injuries, including one to cornerback Steve Ehikian, had weakened
the defense, which pushed raw recruits up to the line of scrimmage.
Siedlecki depended on one individual to step up his game to
strengthen the secondary.

In his sixth year in New Haven as the Eli defensive coordinator,
Rick Flanders had proven that Siedlecki could trust him. Over the
previous three seasons Flanders guided the Yale defense to two first-
place Ivy League rankings and one second-place ranking. Prior to
arriving at Yale, Flanders coached the Penn defensive backs to a number one national ranking in pass efficiency in 1994. Flanders knew of
what he spoke—the forty-four-year-old logged time as a defensive
back at the University of Maine. He remembered well the adrenaline
rush of not giving up an inch of grass and he kept himself lean and
in shape, the better to get his hands dirty and demonstrate drills to
his players. He would need to draw from his considerable intelligence
to provide the defense with the proper schemes that would contain
such wildly differing threats as Princeton's track star Chisom Opara,
Brown's sure-handed Chas Gessner, and the total package, Harvard's
Carl Morris.

With the exception of free safety Barton Simmons, Flanders didn't
think he had any healthy individual players who could match up one-
on-one with the league's top receivers. Simmons was as good as anyone Flanders had coached in twelve years, but he found the
remaining seven players comparable to one another. No superstars,
but no slouches either. The coordinator planned on building around
Simmons and frequently rotating the remaining defensive backs.
Could the defensive mishmash work? Flanders's success would play a
huge part in determining whether the Bulldogs could prove the polls
wrong. And, of course, whether they could trounce the boys from
Cambridge. Time would tell. They had the whole season to gear up
for The Game.

The Crimson started the season in a slightly different place. Five rows up in the poll, atop the Ivy heap.

"I'd like to thank the members of the media who voted for painting the bull's-eye on our chest," Coach Tim Murphy told the audience at the 2002 Ivy League Media Day in August. Murphy disliked the mantle of preseason favorite. He should have been prepared for it. His Crimson racked up a perfect record in 2001, its first such accomplishment since 1913, an eighty-eight-year span that saw the likes of some of Harvard's all-time greats, including coaching icon Percy Haughton, drop-kick specialist Charlie Brickley, and the gifted Barry Wood.

Flattering indeed, but the poll results put immediate and unnecessary pressure on his players. Murphy had to find a way to make it clear to the team that last season was just that—*last* season. The perfect record. The Big Three title. The Ivy League championship. The victory over Yale. Last year's season was as ancient as Harvard's first. The Crimson had a blank slate, and whether the team could pile up such gaudy accolades again would be determined one game at a time. One game at a time. One game at a time. Murphy planned on drilling this mantra into his players before opening day.

In his ninth year as the Crimson head coach, Murphy, forty-five, didn't have to look back too far in the history books for an example of what can befall a team the year after winning a championship. His first Ivy championship team in 1997 slumped to a mediocre .500 the following season. Of course this year's Crimson wanted to stay on top. But just wanting it wasn't enough.

"Our goal is definitely to win an Ivy League championship and our goal is to win every football game we play," Murphy said. "And you know what? That was our goal last year and we were undefeated. And it was our goal the year before when we were a 4–6 team and had some very narrow losses."

This season would hinge on the roster's reliability.

The coach felt confident about his solid band of returning players, but he couldn't fight off an undercurrent of uneasiness. One of the major contributing factors to accomplishing a perfect record the year before had been the defense, but Murphy lost seven defensive starters to graduation, including six All-Ivy selections. He needed to rebuild a depleted offensive line as well. But the refreshing strength of the offensive core calmed the coach's nerves a bit. With quarterback Neil Rose's calm field generalship and wide receiver Carl Morris's explosive ability to single-handedly alter the course of a game, Murphy knew that his offense had the potential to carry the team to another stellar season.

Murphy described Morris as a "super highly motivated elite athlete" and Harvard's top offensive threat, and he wasn't propping his best player up on a pedestal. In fact, Murphy knew that he was damn lucky to have the kid on his team.

It was hard to miss Carl Morris. Movie star good looks and a constant, radiant smile made him a natural for a Wheaties box cover. Tall with lean muscles, there was a graceful smoothness to the way he moved, especially when he ran. While at Episcopal High School in Sterling, Virginia, Morris attracted attention from seven of the top twenty-five football colleges in Division I-A. Besides football, he excelled at basketball and baseball, and the University of Washington, West Virginia, Virginia Tech, the University of North Carolina, North Carolina State, Northwestern, Rutgers, William & Mary, and University of Richmond all offered him scholarships in at least one of the three sports. As Morris fielded these options, the thought of attending an Ivy League school never entered his mind. His father, however, made the high school senior promise to fill out a Crimson questionnaire. Then Morris discovered that one of his second cousins had enrolled, causing serious Ivy considerations to creep into the picture. Hearing the cousin chirp happily about Harvard convinced Morris to burn one of his NCAA visits on a trip to Cambridge. He almost didn't make it.

Snow pelted Washington, D.C., that Saturday, trapping a miserable Morris and his mother in the airport as they dejectedly watched flight after flight get cancelled. But someone was watching out for Tim Murphy's Crimson. "Fate intervened," Morris said. "My mother and I got seats on the last flight to leave D.C. for Boston." During Morris's abbreviated visit, the students he met shattered the stereotypical image of snobby, WASPY intellectuals. Morris figured that he'd encounter preppies in navy blue blazers with crests on the pockets, peppering their speech with Latin phrases and speaking through clenched teeth à la Thurston Howell III. They turned out to be, well, just regular people. As did the players, who managed to win him over. "They had one of the closest teams I had ever seen," he said, "and that was what sealed the deal."

By 2002, Morris possessed almost all of Harvard's single-season and career receiving records. His devastating combination of speed, pure athleticism, competitiveness, and exceptional hands translated into seventy-one receptions for 943 yards and twelve touchdowns during the Crimson's 2001 run to perfection. As the Crimson headed into his senior season, the 6'3", 205-pound Morris was a modern day Ivy League football aberration: a bona fide NFL draft prospect at a skill position. Not bad for someone who didn't even start playing football until his junior year in high school.

The senior's capabilities drew national attention from the moment he started catching passes for the Crimson in 1999, and Morris's wideout accomplishments fueled a four-year furor. In the summer of 2002, the Sporting News Network rated Morris as the top receiver in Division I-AA and listed him as a likely finalist for the Payton Award (the Division I-AA Heisman Trophy equivalent). Morris was also among those selected in the 2002 preseason to play in both the East-West Shrine and Hula Bowl postseason all-star games in January 2003.

Morris's exploits in two games in particular illustrated his amazing prowess. In the sixth game of the 2001 season, Harvard trailed an unheralded but inspired Dartmouth team 21–0 in the third quarter.

Dartmouth appeared headed for its biggest victory over Harvard since spoiling Harvard Stadium's grand opening in 1903. But the 1903 Harvard team didn't have Carl Morris.

Down by three touchdowns, Morris took over the game. He began by throwing a thirty-five-yard flanker option touchdown pass to fellow wide receiver Sam Taylor. The big play breathed new life into the Crimson's flailing hopes of keeping the winning streak alive. After Harvard recovered a Dartmouth fumble on the ensuing kickoff, Morris made a remarkable leaping catch off a Rose aerial for a thirty-two-yard touchdown. Following a Dartmouth three-and-out on its next offensive series, Morris returned a Big Green punt for fifteen yards. His subsequent forty-yard reception put Harvard on the one-yard line, and running back Nick Palazzo punched into the end zone. Game tied. Harvard tacked on another touchdown for the win, dragged from a 21-point deficit to an eventual 31–21 victory by Carl Morris.

At Harvard Stadium two weeks later, in a showdown between two unbeaten teams, Harvard and Penn, Morris elevated his game once again. With Harvard trailing 14–7 in the third quarter, Morris snared a twenty-yard touchdown pass from Rose. Minutes later, after an interception by Harvard cornerback Willie Alford, Morris made one of the most spectacular plays in Harvard football annals. His fully extended sixty-two-yard catch and sprint to the end zone clutching a Neil Rose pass became the signature moment of the season, and the Crimson slapped the Quakers with a 28–21 loss.

Having the luxury of a receiver like Morris also boosted the offense indirectly. Defenders had no choice but to key in on the standout receiver, which opened the door for the running game. Murphy's productive tailback Nick Palazzo made the most of each opportunity. Palazzo heard countless cracks about his height (5′4″) but he used his size to his advantage by running low to the ground. Blink for an instant, and a blur would streak by just below your field of vision.

Palazzo counted on brawny blockers to distract the defense, and with the loss of four 2001 offensive line starters to graduation, he hoped Murphy would find new giants to protect him. Palazzo felt confident that the abilities and bulk of bookend 300-pound tackles 6'4" Jamil Soriano and 6'6" Jack Fadule could anchor an inexperienced group, but if he was calling the shots, he'd make sure the new guys were mean slabs of solid muscle.

Coach Murphy would add a burly, battle-tested defense to Palazzo's wish list. The loss of seven starters, six of them All-Ivy selections, forced Murphy to make do with green freshmen. Despite the overall inexperience on his defense, Murphy counted on one very imposing given in the middle. Junior linebacker Dante Balestracci, a 6'2", 235-pound heat-seeking missile, had the potential to affect a game on every play.

A relentless performer with an appetite for mayhem, Balestracci, who had been recruited by several Division I-A schools, had been an All-Ivy and All–New England performer in each of his first two seasons. Murphy felt fortunate when Balestracci decided on Harvard. "He just does things on the field that you can't coach," Murphy said. "He's obviously the backbone of our defense physically, emotionally, every way."

Although Murphy could have done without the added pressure of being the preseason favorite, after reviewing his roster and contemplating his squad's depth he couldn't truly disagree. In a perfect world he would have tweaked a player here or there or beefed up the team's experience, but the bones of the championship Crimson remained. Maybe reporters were right. You wouldn't catch Murphy frowning if the poll standings matched the real standings when the dust settled from The Game at season's end.

Although a full schedule loomed before their annual showdown, both Murphy and Siedlecki didn't deny that thoughts of a blustery November afternoon at the stadium were never far from their minds. To Harvard and Yale, The Game is the Rose, Sugar, Fiesta, and Orange bowls rolled into one glorious face-off, a starched New England epic fraught with history, honor, and a hoary, proprietary blend of intellectualism and intensity. Let the Division I-A teams aspire to one of the ever-multiplying bowl bids to games like the Motor City Bowl and the Continental Tire Bowl, their overall significance diminished by the sheer proliferation of games. Those schools don't even know where or whom they may play. The hatred has no time to accumulate, the fever no time to rage, the fans no time to travel. Not the case in Cambridge or New Haven. The battle lines are always clearly drawn. The Bulldogs and Crimson know who the enemy is and when he will be met. They know that they will play before the largest crowds of their careers—perhaps fifty thousand fans or more. They know they'll have a chance to see themselves on national television in highlights featured on ESPN. They know that win, lose, or tie, the game will shadow them the rest of their lives. The unprecedented tradition marches on.

♦ ♦ ♦

The Harvard-Yale rivalry began long before the two schools fielded football squads. It all started with an Atlantic crossing two centuries earlier, and it had absolutely nothing to do with sports. Although pride and glory were a factor, Harvard and Yale competed for much higher and very different stakes. The colleges played a major role in furthering the churches that were at the very heart of the Massachusetts Bay and New Haven colonies, and they vied for pre-eminence in education. Providing that education, however, was predicated on generating enough cash to keep the colleges afloat.

Established first, Harvard often received first dibs on money over its Connecticut counterpart. Second place to Harvard in both founding and funding rankled the Elis. So did the irritating fact that Yale had its nemesis to thank for its very existence—it was born out of changes and evolution at Harvard.

Both colleges christened themselves after prominent donors, although ironically neither John Harvard nor Eli Yale had much to do with the founding of the schools that bear their names. Both simply made significant financial contributions. Yale, the governor of the English trading post in Madras, died twenty years after the school was founded in 1701, never having seen the Yale campus. John Harvard did frequent Harvard, but apparently he wasn't very memorable.

A plaque on the statue of Harvard erected in 1885 on the Cambridge campus in front of Harvard Yard reads: "John Harvard. 1638. Founder of the college." Wrong, wrong, and wrong. The school was founded by the Great and General Court of Massachusetts, not John Harvard. The year was 1636, not 1638. And the model for the statue wasn't John Harvard. No portraits of the young minister could be found, so the face is reportedly that of Sherman Hoar, a Harvard student chosen at random by the sculptor, Daniel Chester French.

Harvard and Yale were both founded on the platform of the Puritan church, and Harvard also educated its young men in business and trade. For the eighteenth-century students, these endeavors nurtured the spirit and expanded the mind. They didn't, however, provide much in the way of an escape valve to blow off steam. While the faculty at both schools constantly barraged students with weighty, intellectual material, they didn't bother with athletic competition and physical development. With no way for students to feed their natural instincts for both exercise and competition, the rigid campus life often pushed the boys into aberrant behavior. All work and no play made Jack (or John or Eli) a drunken, brawling, antisocial boy. The buttoned-up students let loose by executing pranks that escalated into vandalism. They snipped ropes in the bell tower, defaced books in the library, and hurled bricks through windows. They indulged in football-like contests of casual violence, tossing balls and smashing into one another in the name of winning games. Without more than mental exercise and classroom competition, the country's cream of the crop—the government of the future!—was slipping down into mayhem and petty lawlessness. The faculty fretted about how to save the young nation's soul.

The sport of crew first filled the void when Yale started its boating club in 1843. The following year Harvard purchased an eight-oared boat, christened the *Oneida*. While both schools participated in local regattas around Boston and New Haven, they did not compete against each other. The seeds for the first Harvard-Yale boat race, the first intercollegiate sporting event of any kind, were planted in an unlikely place by Yale student James Whiton and an entrepreneurial train conductor named James Elkins.

Drained from intense studying and in need of rest at the end of his junior year at Yale, Whiton returned to his family home in the New Hampshire mountain region in June 1852. On his journey he encountered Elkins. While passing through the Lake Winnipesaukee area, Whiton, a member of the Yale Undine boating club, suggested that a regatta should be held at the venue. The number of potential customers needing his trains to travel to a boat race captivated Elkins, an ambitious young man. He offered to pay all the bills for the competitors if Whiton would organize a regatta between Harvard and Yale on Lake Winnipesaukee. Whiton agreed and challenged the Harvard crew, which accepted. The sports rivalry between Harvard and Yale was born.

As promised, Elkins provided free transportation, lodging, meals, and entertainment to the participating clubs. Dinner, dancing, and drinks at Lake Winnipesaukee hotels would follow the contest. In turn, the B, C, M Railroad offered half fare to anyone who wanted to travel to New Hampshire for the event. Elkins, banking on his hunch that many Harvard and Yale supporters would make the trip, hired a brass band and secured an appearance by General Franklin Pierce, the Democratic candidate for president.

On the perfect summer morning of August 3, 1852, intercollegiate athletics began on the calm waters of New Hampshire's biggest lake. The *Oneida* slid across the finish line first, two lengths ahead of the *Shawmut* and four lengths ahead of the *Undine*. Despite Yale entering two boats into the one and one-half mile race, Harvard had won the regatta. The envious Yale rowers watched future president Pierce award the Harvard team a pair of black walnut oars ornamented with silver. The oars would have been nice, but the Elis didn't care about the trophy. Yale had finished second, *again*. Even if Yale managed to beat them a hundred times in a row in the future, Harvard would forever be known as the victors in the first intercollegiate competition.

Even though the Harvard-Yale boat race succeeded, and rowing gave students a sport in which to release physical aggression, it didn't end the rash of violent games played informally on both campuses. Boats had only so many seats, and the remaining students still engaged in the more spontaneous early versions of football.

At Harvard the first references to football dated back to 1827, in a humorous epic poem titled "The Battle of the Delta" (the Delta being the area of Harvard Yard where, on a Monday each year, freshmen and sophomores played a game closely resembling rugby). The lighthearted poem recounted the contest, but it didn't accurately portray the nature of the game. The violence and resulting injuries were more the stuff of Homeric battlefields than rugby playing fields. Players expected scratches, scrapes, and bruises. They tolerated the commonplace broken bones, shattered teeth, and concussions. They often had to be carried off the field. The brutal annual clashes soon deservedly earned the apt title of "Bloody Monday."

By 1858 Bloody Monday had grown into a spectacle worthy of modern-day tabloids. Hordes of freshmen and sophomores gathered on Cambridge Common. Before the game even began, veins stood out in their necks as they screamed insults at one another with a vocabulary better suited to dockworkers than elite intellectuals. The freshmen took the brunt of the abuse when the game finally began. The contest technically had rules, but it mostly amounted to a nearly literal version of the modern schoolyard game "kill the man with the ball." Each time a player touched the ball, the opposing class summarily swarmed him until they knocked the ball loose, body parts be damned. As players threw elbows, kneed groins, and gouged eyes, the violent scrum left a wake of injured players strewn about the common. Newspaper correspondents from New York and Boston related tales of the unbridled bedlam, delighting in the juxtaposition of brutal battle with an institution more readily associated with academia and prestige. The event even captured the interest of artist Winslow Homer, who depicted the carnage of Bloody Monday in a drawing by the same name.

Harvard prided itself on its genteel, learned reputation, however, and the administration didn't appreciate the attention the unruly event generated.

By 1860, the Harvard faculty was fed up with the violent melees and abolished the game on its campus. Some of Bloody Monday's survivors, demonstrating a peculiar distress at the lack of future bloodbaths, mourned the administration's ban of the game by burying one of the balls used in the contest on the Delta. They lowered the ball into the faux grave and marked the site with two black boards, one at the head and one at the foot. The epitaphs stated that football dated back some sixty years at Harvard, apparently evolving from class wrestling matches of the eighteenth century.

Cambridge wasn't the only site where students participated in dangerous games. Yale had a similar chaotic free-for-all masquerading as a game called the "Annual Rush" that began prior to 1840. The rules of the game differed from those in Bloody Monday, but the injuries were all too similar. The Annual Rush consisted mainly of kicking the ball. In the beginning, the freshmen connected with the ball at a much higher rate than the sophomores. On errant kicks the sophomores' feet often landed squarely against the shins, knees, and thighs of the freshmen. When a freshman fell to the ground, the sophomores pummeled his upper extremities. It didn't take long for the freshmen to realize that the game had more to do with hurting the school's newcomers than scoring goals, and the contest quickly devolved into a ritualistic battering.

The Annual Rush took place in both the college yard and on the New Haven town green before administrators and town officials banned it in 1858 from both venues because of the escalating violence. With the repeated school shutdowns of the sport and the intervention of a violence all too real in the form of the Civil War and America's bloodiest days, football faded from college campuses and did not experience a revival until the early years of the post–Civil War era.

The football resurgence at Harvard began in 1871, over a decade after the Bloody Monday game's ceremonial burial. Several Harvard students who had played a blend of soccer and rugby known as the "Boston game" as schoolboys growing up in the area resurrected the game and began to play on Cambridge Common in the fall of 1871. Since the college prohibition regarding the freshman/sophomore football activity directly referred to Bloody Monday, the Harvard administration did not oppose this casual athletic affair. The sport caught on, and soon the men held games almost every afternoon with ten to fifteen players to a side participating on informal teams. By the spring of 1872 students organized class teams and competed against one another, and the success of the competition led to the formation of the Harvard University Foot Ball Club later that year. To truly prove the Boston game's worthiness and longevity as a legitimate sport, however, Harvard needed to test it against other schools in intercollegiate competition. Unfortunately, no other schools knew how to play.

While Harvard players battled among themselves on Cambridge Common, Yale had already started playing against other colleges. Yale, Columbia, Princeton, and Rutgers played a kicking-only game that vastly differed from the Boston game. When Yale heard about the new Harvard University Foot Ball Club, they immediately tried to bring the Crimson into their league's fold. Yale enjoyed competing against Princeton, Columbia, and Rutgers, but no competition was truly worthwhile to the Elis unless Yale had a shot at crushing the Crimson. After all, beating Harvard was, is, and always will be the yardstick by which joy is measured in New Haven.

Yale organized an October 1873 meeting held at the Fifth Avenue Hotel in New York City, the purpose of which was to devise a uniform set of rules under which the schools could compete. Henry R. Grant, the captain of the Harvard University Foot Ball Club, rejected even Yale's invitation to attend the meeting—forget about joining the league. Harvard simply didn't like Yale's game, which bore little resemblance to its Cambridge counterpart. The Elis wouldn't let the offensive players pick up, carry, or throw the ball, or pass it to a teammate if pursued. The defenders couldn't tackle an opponent to prevent him from catching the ball. And if the player did catch the ball, the defender couldn't take it away. Harvard couldn't imagine a game hamstrung by these rules—one of the reasons for the game's popularity in Cambridge was the significance of individual skills such as running, catching, kicking, and tackling. Keeping these elements in the game outweighed Harvard's growing interest in competing on an intercollegiate level.

Yale perceived Harvard's rejection as outright aloofness. The Crimson refusal to send delegates to a meeting dedicated to establishing a set of common football rules seemed strange and snobbish, especially for a school that prided itself on defeating everyone in everything. It was going to be difficult to claim the championship of a sport that no one else played. But to Grant and Harvard it simply boiled down to numbers. Clearly Yale, Princeton, Rutgers, and Columbia had a vested interest in the kicking-based game that they already played. The outcome of any vote concerning rules would be 4–1 with Harvard on the short end. The Boston game would die unceremoniously in a New York City hotel meeting room, and Grant wouldn't be party to such an execution. Grant and the Harvard players enjoyed the Boston game, and they weren't about to give it up just to join some football league. If Yale wanted to play Harvard so badly, they could play by Harvard's rules.

Yale and the other schools held the meeting without Harvard, drawing up the first intercollegiate football rules in America. Grant's worries about what might transpire at the meeting were well founded. Yale, Columbia, Princeton, and Rutgers unanimously adopted the London Football Association's (LFA) rules, the rules by which they essentially had been playing all along. The most glaring pronouncement of the rules was really an omission—there was no mention of allowing a player to pick up the ball during play. In reality, Yale, Princeton, Rutgers, and Columbia pledged an oath to what is now commonly referred to in America as soccer.

Harvard paid a price for preserving the sanctity of the traditional Boston game. If the school wanted to play intercollegiate matches it had to either wait for the other schools to warm up to the Boston game or look for a challenger elsewhere. And Harvard wasn't about to solicit opponents. It would wait for worthy teams to come to Cambridge. Thanks to some neighbors from the north, the Crimson didn't have to wait long.

David Rodger, the captain of the McGill University team from Montreal, sent a letter of invitation to Harvard captain Grant proposing a series of matches between the two schools. McGill played a slightly modified rugby game, so the two schools settled on a two-game series—one rugby rules match and one Boston game match. McGill studied the Boston game in Montreal while Harvard prepared for the rugby game in Cambridge, and the two worked out the details of the rules through extensive correspondence. This initial study of the rugby and Boston game principles laid the groundwork for the eventual blending of the two and the development of modern football.

McGill suggested that each school host the match featuring its game, but the Harvard faculty wouldn't authorize the trip to Montreal during school time. Instead, Harvard and McGill played both matches in Cambridge in May 1874.

On May 8, 1874, a notice in the *Magenta* (the Harvard student newspaper that preceded the *Crimson*) advertised the upcoming game between McGill and Harvard at Jarvis Field. Admission fees of fifty cents per spectator would fund the postgame entertainment, which included a champagne-drenched banquet for the visitors. (The Harvard football team didn't answer to any official university authority, so the gate receipts were theirs for the taking.) A crowd of roughly five hundred spectators turned out, a big number considering that it was a sport that most of the crowd had never seen. Harvard and McGill played the Boston game first. Though the rules allowed from ten to fifteen players per side, McGill's slim roster of eleven players made that the maximum number of men per team. It soon became obvious that McGill hadn't done enough homework. Harvard swept the match 3–0.

The following day Harvard and McGill took to the field for the rugby-rules match using an English oval, a rubber bladder covered with leather. The ball's circumference of thirty inches matched that of the round leather ball Harvard used in the Boston game. After three and one-half hours of play, the match ended in a scoreless draw. True to form, Harvard had studied well. And the players learned something else in the bargain—this rugby game wasn't so bad. Perhaps they were being a bit stubborn in refusing to sway from the Boston game.

By the fall of 1874, when Harvard made the trek to Montreal for a rematch, the Crimson were infatuated with the rugby-rules game. When the Crimson upended the team that had taught them the game 10–0, Harvard all but abandoned future plans for the Boston version as an intercollegiate sport. Upon returning from Montreal, the Crimson sent notice to nearby Tufts University that a previously scheduled matchup for the spring of 1875 was off. Unless Tufts wanted to play McGill's game, that is. Tufts obliged.

The student beat the teacher in the Harvard-McGill matches, and so it went with the Harvard-Tufts game. In June 1875, Harvard lost to Tufts, 1–0, in the first U.S. match played by the rugby rules. Ever the precedent-setter, even though Harvard lost it still notched another first. Dressed in matching white shirts and pants with crimson trim and stockings, Harvard became the first team to compete in full uniform.

The Harvard-Tufts matchup ignited Yale's interest in the rugby-rules game. Despite the comfortable kicking-based game arrangement with Columbia, Princeton, and Rutgers, Yale still itched to play Harvard. Any other school would have been stopped short in trying to persuade an existing football association to switch to a different game. But this was Harvard, and when Harvard led, others followed. And besides, Yale desperately wanted to defeat its rival.

Arthur Ellis, the captain of the 1874–1875 Harvard team who had led the team at McGill, revisited the concept of a football game with Yale. The school didn't feel the need to play Yale in order to legitimize the rugby-based game, but the two schools already competed in rowing and baseball. It would be a feather in the Crimson cap to trounce the Elis across the board. Harvard challenged Yale and suggested a set of rules that could form a middle ground between the two games. Like two war generals hammering out terms of surrender, on October 18, 1875, two delegates from each school met at the Massasoit House in Springfield, Massachusetts.

The meeting evolved into a tit-for-tat affair with each school gaining its share of concessions from the other. Yale had never handled a rugby ball, so Harvard agreed to use a leather-covered round ball thirty inches in circumference instead of the regulation oval-shaped leather rugby ball of twenty-seven inches. The shape didn't bother the Crimson—the team would have agreed to play with tennis balls. By that time in the rules-making process, Harvard had already achieved its major coup. Players would be allowed to run with the ball. Harvard won on another big point when Yale agreed to allow tackling.

When the meeting adjourned, the ecstatic Crimson couldn't imagine losing. The newly inked rules tilted heavily in their favor. Even if the Bulldogs managed to figure out how to effectively run with the ball prior to the game, they wouldn't be prepared for the body blows Harvard would dole out once they started carrying the ball down the field. What's more, the Crimson held a decided mental advantage. Yale's agreement to play Harvard under concessionary rules after Harvard had spurned an invitation to join their formative league proved that Yale needed Harvard more than Harvard needed Yale.

Years later Yale captain William Arnold recounted the negotiations with Harvard, as discussed in Tim Cohane's *The Yale Football Story*. One of the delegates from Cambridge (more than likely Harvard's Nathaniel Curtis) asked the Yale men, "Why not play the Rugby game? It is a gentlemen's game."

"He must have been a humorist," Arnold recalled, "because a reporter for a college weekly had witnessed a practice game and intimated it was a game for roughnecks equipped with armor."

Neither team wore armor on November 13, 1875, a calm, windless, slightly overcast day at the racing oval that was New Haven's Hamilton Park. The Yale team sported dark trousers, blue shirts, and yellow caps, while Harvard took the field clad in crimson shirts and stockings with knee breeches. On the morning of the game, the Yale hosts offered their Harvard counterparts an extensive sightseeing tour of their campus and New Haven points of interest. Had Yale known what lay in store on the field it might not have been so hospitable. Despite a relatively steep admission charge of fifty cents (although Harvard fans had paid the same fee for earlier games, this was twice the price of a ticket for the Rutgers-Yale kicking-based match the previous week) a crowd of 2,000 New Haven citizens and about 150 Harvard students from Cambridge turned out to witness the clash at Hamilton Park.

Harvard won the toss and Yale kicked off. Nathaniel Curtis, the Harvard captain, began running toward the Yale goal. Moments later Herbert Leeds scored the first Harvard goal followed by William Seamans, who scored the second after Yale's Oliver Thompson was thwarted in his bid for a touchdown. After the first half hour (the game was divided into three half hours of play) Harvard held a 2–0 advantage. During much of the early going the perplexed Yale contingent froze at a standstill, baffled by the concessionary rules.

In the second half hour, Harvard's Benjamin Blanchard dropkicked a goal on the run and Hayward Cushing made another touchdown. The final half hour witnessed an awakening for the home team as Thompson did some effective running that almost resulted in Yale getting on the scoreboard. After using two-thirds of the time to adjust to the rules' vagaries, Yale played their best during the game's most intense and exciting final third. Despite their progress, the last half hour was all Harvard; Blanchard scored another touchdown and Augustus Tower added a goal. The final score: Harvard 4, Yale 0. Harvard kicked three of their four goals from the field while the fourth was made by a conversion after touchdown. The score could have been worse. Harvard scored three other touchdowns but failed to convert the kick after crossing the goal line. (Touchdowns had no point value, only giving the offense a chance to kick a goal for a point.)

In an inversion of today's pregame tailgating, the postgame festivities featured food, drink, and song in the college yard with players and fans from both teams. A midnight train returned the Harvard men to Boston, but not before they got into some mischief. A *New Haven Register* item the following day noted that "seven Harvard students were arrested in this city Saturday night for creating disturbances by hooting and singing in the public streets. They all gave fictitious names and deposited their watches and other articles of jewelry as security for a fine of $5.29 in each case."

This first installment of The Game revolutionized intercollegiate athletics. Two smitten Princeton observers returned to New Jersey and successfully converted their Tiger brethren to rugby. The kicking-based game fell to the wayside as the Yale, Princeton, Columbia, and Rutgers alliance crumbled under the weight of Harvard's argument that the future of college football was in the rugby-rules game. In the autumn of the following year representatives of Harvard, Yale, Princeton, and Columbia met, inaugurating the Intercollegiate Football Association and initiating the formalization of new football playing rules among the colleges.

Football was taking tiny steps toward becoming the sport we know today, and one architect of its modern development had been keenly watching the first version of The Game. He was a student in his final year at the Hopkins School, located next to Yale's campus in New Haven. He planned on enrolling at Yale in the fall and hoped to join the Bulldogs football team. His name was Walter Camp.

He would help Yale prevent further losses at the hands of the Crimson, much to the delight of the Bulldog faithful. Losing to the Crimson, even in this baby-fresh game, stuck in the craw. Beat Harvard . . . Beat Harvard . . . Beat Harvard. The goal is simple.

Even more than a century later.

Friends or Enemies?

HARVARD QUARTERBACK Neil Rose and Yale nose tackle Jason Lange seemed slightly out of place loitering outside venerable Dillon Field House. After all, the two captains represented teams associated with decades of fierce gridiron contests. They should have been tearing at each other's throats, not smiling and chatting like reunited frat brothers.

Sweat glistened on their brows. Dressed in full pads, the two felt every degree of the stifling record-breaking heat of a mid-August morning. Both players wished the photo shoot for the program cover of the 2002 Harvard-Yale game had been taken in the customary conditions of a pleasant May day, although Rose had no one to blame but himself. When the fifth-year senior headed back to his native Hawaii for an internship after walking with his classmates in the 2002 graduation ceremonies, the schools shuffled the shoot to late summer. Despite the suffocating humidity, Rose and Lange gladly represented their squads. Sweat—along with blood and tears—was an essential sacrifice required of every player who prided himself on upholding the standards of his Ivy League uniform. Neither captain would let himself wilt in the face of the traditional photo shoot.

Begun four decades ago, the ritual dictates that the two players meet and pose at the home team's venue. Nowadays both Harvard and Yale use photographs for the program covers, but for many years Yale commissioned an artist to capture the captains in a portrait. Whether the scene is rendered on film or canvas, the event offers a unique opportunity for the rivals to interact at a time and place far removed from the intensity of the field of play. It's an opportunity not afforded to the captains of well-known college football rivals like Ohio State–Michigan, Georgia–Georgia Tech, and Army–Navy. Most of those captains meet the team leaders of their biggest rival as they do in any other game on the schedule—they run to the middle of the field for the coin toss, shake hands, and come out fighting. When Rose and Lange met at midfield in several months, they would find a friendly enemy, a foe worthy of such a rivalry.

For the Harvard-Yale battle isn't one of wanton bloodlust. (Not in this century, anyway.) This may be one of the main distinctions separating the Ivy feud from that of other schools. Sure, each squad wants to soundly slaughter the other, but for the most part they complete said slaughtering with the utmost sportsmanship. College football enthusiasts who dismiss Ivy League football as second-rate and scoff at the title "The Game" perhaps mistake the cordiality for weakness, the manners for meekness. They don't comprehend the historical significance of the contest and how the teams are affected by tradition. The players respect the rivalry and the aura of reverence surrounding The Game, giving the contest a civilized face. The young men who play in it bask in the honor of being participants. That doesn't mean, however, that they don't plan to crush the other team and put their own stamp on the centuries-old clash. And perhaps no one looks forward to this opportunity as much as the captains.

Had it not been for a broken leg sustained while playing pickup basketball during summer break in 1999, Neil Rose would have finished his four years of eligibility in 2001 and spent the 2002 season at his first job. But the Ivy League, which prides itself on high standards and commitment to the student athlete, grants red shirts only for medical conditions. Luckily for the Crimson, Rose's injuries fit the bill, giving him a fifth year of eligibility.

If Rose had decided not to apply for a medical hardship waiver and skip his last year of eligibility, he would have left with nothing to prove. He would have graduated instead of just walking with his fellow classmates in the spring of 2002, holding both a degree from one of the nation's premier colleges and a litany of passing records. The fall of 2002 would have found Rose working under his mentor at Cadinha & Company, an asset-management company in Hawaii— not gearing up for another football season in Cambridge and enduring one more semester of school and another New England winter. Rose wouldn't have it any other way, though. He wasn't willing to pass up a year of playing football with some of the best friends he'd ever made. The real world could wait.

The inclusion of Rose's name on the Harvard roster for the 2002 season thrilled Crimson followers. He held twelve school passing records after Harvard's 2001 season and earned first team All-Ivy and All–New England honors for his record-breaking efforts. Rose's teammates were also thankful for his presence. Both the coaching staff and players knew that one of their greatest projected assets for the 2002 season was Neil Rose under center. At the 2001 football banquet Rose was announced as captain, the first Hawaiian to earn the distinction and the first quarterback to hold the honor since Carroll Lowenstein in 1951. Coach Tim Murphy did not seem surprised by his squad's selection.

"Neil was a leader for us throughout last season, and it is fitting that his teammates have recognized his contributions to Harvard football and acknowledged the leadership role he plays for our team," Murphy said.

Contrary to Rose, Yale defensive lineman Jason Lange didn't have to decide whether or not to continue playing football. He knew that the 2002 season, his senior year, would be the last of his formal football career. Lange simply wanted to build on the incremental success he had so far achieved in his first three seasons as a Yale Bulldog. When his teammates elected him captain at the conclusion of his All-Ivy 2001 season, Lange already considered his senior year his finest. Nothing he could do on the field could possibly bring him as much satisfaction as having his peers bestow such an honor. Some of Lange's biggest role models during his first three years were the respective captains, and he hoped to uphold the precedents set by them.

Lange represented the archetypal Ivy League player. He arrived in New Haven a true Renaissance man in the making, excelling in athletics, academics, and the arts while growing up in Hoffman Estates, Illinois. If Lange's affable and outgoing demeanor off the field didn't contradict the fierce nature of his nose tackle role, then one of his other passions did. A talented vocalist, Lange earned a spot on another Yale team, The Baker's Dozen a cappella group. But Lange had the tools to succeed at football as well.

At 6'3" and 285 pounds, Lange's size belied his exceptional quickness. Several Division I-A football programs recruited him, including Northwestern, Indiana, and Northern Illinois, but Lange thought he wouldn't see playing time at those schools until his red shirt junior or senior year. That might have been worth it if Lange planned to play in the pros, but he couldn't imagine making an NFL roster. He decided that he should get the best education available, and that meant the Ivy League.

When Lange told his parents that he planned on declining football scholarships to play in the Ivies—a league that doesn't offer athletic scholarships—the Langes tried to sweeten the pot with game show tactics reminiscent of Monty Hall. "I passed up a brand new car that my parents would have gotten me had I taken a full ride," Lange said, more proud than wistful.

The high school senior looked into the Big Three of Harvard, Yale, and Princeton, and in the end he found Yale the perfect match. The school's academic reputation spoke for itself. The football players were both driven and laid-back at the same time. But the most influential factor in Lange's decision was his discussion with Yale defensive line coach Duane Brooks. The coach's approach complemented Lange's unconventional style of play. Brooks didn't care how the guys lined up or what techniques they used. He only wanted his linemen to make plays. Yale made perfect sense to Lange. He could play football the way he liked, with players he liked, at a school that he liked. Lange had no regrets, especially after being voted captain.

The two leaders were directed to the gridiron within historic Harvard Stadium, the oldest poured-concrete stadium in the country and the first major permanent structure devoted to the playing of a sport. With no such edifice in the United States at the time of its construction in 1903, the stadium's builders drew inspiration from the Roman circus and a Greek stadium, a fitting design for the epic battles that have taken place in its confines.

As the two modern-day gladiators approached the field, a group of youngsters decked out in Harvard Crimson and Yale Bulldog regalia swarmed them. Living props procured by Harvard's media relations department from one of the many sports camps held at Harvard each summer, the kids peppered the players with questions. Veteran Harvard photographer Tim Morse took over, placing the captains on the concrete benches that form the stadium's horseshoe shape and directing the kids to surround the players. The kids needed no further directions. They shook pom-poms, screamed into megaphones, and cheered wildly for their designated team in a game that wouldn't take place for months—bringing genuine exuberance to allegiances assigned moments prior.

Morse moved to the stands to size up his shot. He had started taking the captains' photo for the Harvard-Yale game program cover in 1980, and the more cover photos that Morse took, the harder it became to come up with new ideas. Morse has shot the Harvard and Yale captains along the Charles River, in different spots at the stadium, and in front of Massachusetts Hall with then Harvard president Neil Rudenstine. During one photo cover shoot in Harvard Yard, a pack of nearly two hundred foreign tourists mistook the captains for professional football players. Unable to communicate with the non-English-speaking group, the captains just smiled, signed autographs, and posed for pictures.

As then, smiling broadly was the task at hand in Harvard Stadium. Lange and Rose beamed and the kids cheered as Morse clicked through several rolls of film, determined to shoot a masterpiece. Before long, the experienced Morse knew that he'd have the shot he was looking for when he developed the film. Finally, Rose and Lange shook hands, signaling the beginning of the 2002 season.

With the photo shoot completed, the focus in Cambridge turned to preparations for the first game of the year. While the Yale game loomed at the end of the schedule, there was still the pesky matter of nine other opponents who hoped to end the Crimson winning streak. On August 30 the Harvard coaching staff welcomed 110 players, including 35 freshmen, to begin formal practice in preparation for their Ivy League title defense. Head coach Tim Murphy's message to the team was simple and direct. Last year's season was a tremendous accomplishment, but repeating it would be a tremendous challenge. The Ivy League championship team doesn't relinquish the trophy until the next champion is crowned, but Murphy didn't want the team thinking about last season's glory. He removed the Pennsylvania Cup from the trophy case before the season began—as he has done both times Harvard has won the Ivy League under his command.

At the end of the first week's workouts on September 6, Harvard held a football media day at Dillon Field House. John Veneziano, Harvard's assistant director for sports information, worked the room like a politician, shaking that reporter's hand and clapping this one's shoulder, thrilled at the turnout. Twenty people attended, half of them from the media. The number pleased Veneziano, but paled in comparison to the media attention Harvard football received in past decades. Veneziano's task of promoting Harvard athletics was forever an uphill battle. With space in Boston's two major newspapers, the *Boston Globe* and the *Boston Herald,* always at a premium, "Johnny V" campaigned tirelessly for coveted column inches for Harvard's football program, as well as for the school's fleet of forty other men's and women's intercollegiate sports. In a city where all the major sports are represented, including Boston College's Big East Division I-A football team and Division I basketball team, Harvard sports don't steal many headlines.

Dealing with the media has been a feast or famine affair at Harvard. Veneziano's predecessors juggled much larger throngs of media at every turn. As late as 1940 there were seven daily newspapers in Boston, and Harvard football was literally the only game in town. By the time the American League's Red Sox made its appearance in 1901, the Harvard-Yale rivalry had celebrated its silver anniversary. The NHL's Bruins didn't play until 1924, the NBA's Boston Celtics didn't take to the parquet until 1946, and professional football didn't catch on for good in Boston until the Patriots arrived to stay in 1960. Only the National League baseball franchise Boston Braves, who started playing in 1876, shared the sports stage, and then not even in the same season.

Veneziano had no such luxuries, and getting Harvard sports information into the *Globe* or *Herald* wasn't his only challenge. He needed to get the Harvard campus excited about its sports teams.

The Crimson community supports its players, but it also realizes that Harvard's football team will never play for a national championship again. The stands aren't filled to capacity on bitter-cold game days, and you're not likely to see a row of crazed shirtless supporters with crimson *H*'s painted on their chests. When Harvard played its last home game against Penn during the 2001 perfect season, only 14,818 fans turned out for the game. By contrast, 30,898 fans turned out to see the 2000 Harvard-Yale game featuring two non-contenders. Although the week of the Harvard-Yale game is Veneziano's busiest week of the year, it is his easiest in terms of getting crowd support and media attention for Harvard's football team. And a good deal of that media attention centers on the coaches.

Coaches Murphy and Siedlecki were well aware of the Harvard-Yale rivalry prior to winning their respective positions. They knew that it was intense, hard fought, and critical to the annual schedule. Murphy and Siedlecki also knew that the rivals were respectful and, for the most part, friendly. This suited the two men perfectly—they had become friends in 1981 while beginning their coaching careers together at Lafayette. Murphy coached the defensive line and, fittingly, Siedlecki coached the offensive line. Their friendship bloomed in an effort to save some cash.

Earning just eleven thousand dollars apiece, the two decided to cut down on rent by moving into a one-bedroom third-floor apartment, accessible only by fire escape. Siedlecki got the bedroom while Murphy slept in the living room. They stretched the food budget by eating at the training table during the season and took advantage of special offers at local restaurants. "I don't think either one of us ever cooked a meal," Siedlecki said. "We didn't miss many Pizza D'Oro all-you-can-eat pasta specials."

Even though the pair shared nearly identical schedules, the strains of living and working together didn't have any negative impact on their friendship. Siedlecki, however, admitted that he played Oscar Madison to the meticulous Murphy's Felix Unger. Murphy concurred, noting that "Jack smoked these awful, cheap cigars and my clothes were proof of it."

Although Murphy slept on the couch, he never had to clean up his "room" for visitors. Siedlecki and Murphy spent little time at home. "A typical day for us consisted of sixteen hours of work followed by eight hours of sleep," Murphy said. The pair roomed together in one house or another until Murphy left for his new coaching job at Boston University in 1982, but it took another year for Siedlecki to realize just how busy he and the other coaches had been. Siedlecki received a phone call the spring after Murphy's departure, telling him that his lawn needed to be mowed. *Mowed?* As far as Siedlecki knew, he had been living in a row house that had no lawn. It turned out that no one had ever bothered to look out the back windows, never mind venture behind the house. Upon further inspection, Siedlecki discovered a backyard. It looked like a hayfield.

Siedlecki soon married, and he and his wife lived in the house for five years. When his wife met the eighty-year-old next-door neighbor, the woman was relieved. She was so glad to have a nice young married couple next door. It was much better than the two college coaches who hadn't even introduced themselves to her. Those guys never lifted a finger around the house. Siedlecki's wife didn't have the heart to tell the woman that one of those two coaches was her new husband.

Murphy and Siedlecki forged a lasting friendship at Lafayette. Even in the face of the Harvard-Yale rivalry, their loyalty to each other is never forgotten. Murphy met Siedlecki at midfield before the 2001 Harvard-Yale game, the game that Murphy needed to win to bring Harvard its first perfect season since 1913 and one of the most important games in his coaching career. Murphy turned to Siedlecki and asked, "How's Kevin?"—referring to Siedlecki's son who had been severely ill since June. "Even in that atmosphere," said Siedlecki, "family came first."

The two head coaches became friends long before their involvement with the Harvard-Yale game, but others have become friends because of it.

Ninety-three-year-old Jim DeAngelis grew up in New Haven, Connecticut. Big Three football was the pinnacle of the sport in the late teens and twenties, and DeAngelis and his friends worshipped Yale's football teams. They tried to sneak into games at the bowl and steal footballs from the field as mementos. Though DeAngelis loved the Bulldogs, he figured his dreams of playing on the team were purely schoolyard fantasies. "My family had limited means," DeAngelis said, remembering the circumstances more than seven decades later. "Never did I believe that one day I would be a student at Yale, let alone a member of the football team."

He was wrong. By 1931, Jim DeAngelis had become a guard on the Bulldogs freshman squad.

DeAngelis's future gridiron enemy Herman Gundlach grew up in Big Ten country, Michigan's Upper Peninsula. Gundlach, now ninety, didn't see his first Harvard game until 1929, a thriller that ended 14–12 in favor of Michigan. He watched the Crimson again the following year as a student at Worcester Academy in Worcester,

Massachusetts. "Our Worcester Academy team was bused to Cambridge for the game," Gundlach recalled. "In that win over Yale, Barry Wood was fantastic." From then on he was hooked on Harvard football.

The two met for the first time during the 1931 freshman Harvard-Yale game. Instead of a proper hello, Gundlach greeted DeAngelis with a vicious leg tackle. The Yale guard's leg was nearly broken, and DeAngelis spent the following two weeks on crutches.

Gundlach's intensity was grounded in his Harvard education—he learned the rivalry's importance straight from the head of the university. One morning Gundlach encountered Harvard's then-president A. Lawrence Lowell in Harvard Yard, near two of the newer houses, Lionel and Mower. The impeccably dressed Lowell removed a pair of work gloves from his coat, put them on, and began to inspect and rearrange the ivy growing on the new residences.

Gundlach was thrilled at the opportunity to talk to the president. "Good morning, President Lowell," Gundlach said. Lowell looked up and asked, "What is your name?" "Herman Gundlach," the boy replied. Lowell then said, "And you live in this building so you are a freshman. Good morning, Student Gundlach. You see, that sounds strange, don't you agree? You are Mr. Gundlach and I am Mr. Lowell. You must be on the football team, as I noted your early arrival this fall before the other freshmen," he said. The two discussed football and engineering before parting. Whenever they met on campus afterwards, they'd greet each other. "Believe me," Gundlach recalled, "it was always *Mister* Lowell."

One morning Lowell stopped Gundlach after saying hello. "Well, Friday you play Yale," he said. "Are you and your teammates determined to win? Do your best?" Gundlach assured him that they were. Lowell then took a piece of paper out of his vest pocket and handed it to the freshman.

"Tell your coach to try this formation on any kicks," instructed Lowell. Gundlach took the paper and thanked Lowell. He unfolded it as the president walked away.

"It was a diagram of the old flying wedge, similar to the short on-side kick still used today," Gundlach said. Harvard had successfully exploited Yale's weaknesses with the wedge years before, and Lowell thought it was worth another try, despite the fact that the wedge had been outlawed in 1894 due to the sheer violence it triggered. Anything to defeat those Elis.

Gundlach and DeAngelis battled each other for four years (each winning twice), but the only knowledge they had of each other was what they knew from the field. After graduation the men went their separate ways without so much as a friendly hello muttered between them.

Fifty years later, far removed from their playing days, the pair's passion for the Harvard-Yale game hadn't waned. During an alumni luncheon prior to the 1985 game their paths crossed. One of Gundlach's teammates, Bob Brookings, spotted friends from the Yale team that he and Gundlach had played against. Brookings introduced his former teammates to the Bulldogs and Gundlach ended up speaking with DeAngelis. "From that point on we were fast friends," Gundlach said. "We finally buried all the old animosities."

Gundlach and DeAngelis discovered that they had much in common, including wintering in Florida. They've gotten together in the Sunshine State nearly every year since and talk from time to time throughout the year including, of course, during The Game. They usually attend the Friday luncheon before The Game and watch the junior varsity match together on the sidelines. On Saturday morning, however, things are different. The two men have never and will never sit together during The Game. As elder statesmen and the two oldest living former captains of their respective schools, DeAngelis and Gundlach have earned rightful seating priority at the bowl and stadium, and take their seats accordingly. The men who fought so gallantly against each other nearly seventy years ago forgo watching the game side-by-side for another reason, much more important than good seats. If they sat together, their friendship might not last through the fourth quarter.

Rarely does the Harvard-Yale game produce friendships like that of DeAngelis and Gundlach. In fact, the game's hallmark of mutual respect between the opposing players and coaches took some time to develop. It didn't begin in 1875. Actually, during the earliest years, the participants in the Harvard-Yale game often stepped outside the bounds of what had been described as "gentlemanly" play. You could even call it wanton bloodlust.

* * *

The game that best illustrated the rivalry's bitterness and the sport's unmistakable brutality, the one where no friends were made, was a game dubbed "The Bloodbath in Hampden Park," also known as "The Springfield Massacre." The field in Springfield, Massachusetts, offered the ideal neutral territory for two schools that lacked a stadium. A logical halfway point between New York City and Boston, Springfield allowed fans to travel to the contest by public transportation. The city also didn't mind the one-day twenty-five-thousand-person rise in population—it provided a nice economic boost for business owners.

Yale captain Frank Hinkey called a meeting the night before the 1894 Harvard-Yale game, nineteen years after the two first played. The team had traveled to Springfield to spend the night before the game at the Springfield YMCA. Yale alumnus and future coaching legend Amos Alonzo Stagg, who went on to be known as the Grand Old Man of the Midway and coached for forty-one years at the University of Chicago, had arranged the lodging for the Bulldogs. Hinkey liked the idea of his team not traveling on the day of the game. His men would wake up fresh and fully rested, a condition that would help them follow through on Hinkey's game plan. (In the early days of college football, the captain served as almost a player/coach. Yale technically had a field coach, but Hinkey wielded more power. The players would more readily listen to the man who would be taking hits next to them than the sideline boss.)

Hinkey likely didn't need to hold a meeting. His teammates knew what he would ask of them. Unleash fire and brimstone upon the Crimson. Leave nothing on the field but the scattered bodies of the opponent. Hurt them. According to Tim Cohane's *Yale Football Story*, Hinkey's instructions were anything but vague. If there was any doubt of his intentions for the unfortunate Crimson, they were removed when he told his players what to do in the event of a fair catch by a Harvard player. "Tackle them anyway and take the penalty," Hinkey commanded. After four years, his status as Harvard public enemy number one was secure. Hinkey wouldn't have it any other way. He thrived on doling out punishment, particularly to Harvard players.

Before Hinkey arrived at Yale, an annual drubbing of the Crimson was routine. Harvard may have won the first game between the two schools, but Yale took over as top dog starting with the second game. After losing the inaugural battle they trained ferociously, mastering tackling and blocking techniques, vowing to perfect the game Harvard had taught them. The training paid off, and the Yale winning streak grew. And grew. And grew. The "little brother" syndrome subsided somewhat. Yale simply couldn't lose to Harvard in football, and the Blue faithful swelled with pride. But finally, in 1890, the inevitable happened. After a fifteen-year drought, Harvard finally beat Yale. Making the loss all the more painful was the fact that Yale should have won. They had Pudge Heffelfinger on the roster.

Heffelfinger earned All-American status three times at Yale. *The Week's Sport* announced the first All-American team in late 1889 or early 1890, just in time for Heffelfinger. The idea for individual recognition belonged to either Yale captain Walter Camp or Caspar Whitney, the newspaper's managing editor and the reigning sportswriter of his day. Regardless of who fathered the All-American concept, Yale had plenty of them and even in football's early days the title held weight. In order to snap Yale's string of victories, the Crimson had to neutralize Heffelfinger. Harvard managed the improbable task with sustained double-team blocks. But Heffelfinger didn't go down without a fight. Harvard wore down the powerful guard to the point that he had to be carried off the field at the game's end. Harvard won its first national championship with the 12–6 win, capping an 11–0–0 season. (The team didn't find out about the title, however, until half a century later. The Helms Athletic Foundation began awarding national championships in 1941, fifty-one years after Harvard's second victory over its archrival. In order to link the national championship to the origins of the sport, the Helms Athletic Foundation awarded the titles retroactively for all years between 1883 and 1941.)

The 1890 Harvard victory seemed to have disrupted the football universe. Yale was supposed to win, or at least tie, when the two schools met on the playing field. This is how it had been since the second meeting. Harvard's win angered the Yale football gods. They delivered to the Yale squad a Fury. He would mete out punishment and restore Yale's position as the nation's supreme football power. His name was Frank Hinkey.

Twenty-year-old Hinkey arrived at Yale as a 5′9″, 145-pound freshman. The scrappy boy had a lung problem that doctors told him would curtail his life span, and he was encouraged to live an easy, healthy lifestyle. That meant not playing football. Hinkey would have none of it. No way would his body rule his life. Hinkey played football with reckless abandon, hurling his body into oncoming opponents with utter disregard for the physical consequences. Off the field he stayed up late and drank the worst brands of whiskey. Just to spite his weak lungs, he smoked cigars by the box, the cheaper the better.

As a freshman Hinkey became a starter, through the only means possible at the time. Players then didn't relinquish or share their positions. Without an injury to a starter, substitutions just didn't happen. Backups normally earned a starting spot when a starter accepted his diploma at graduation. Luckily for Yale, a fortuitous midseason injury to the man ahead of him on the depth chart gave Hinkey his shot.

Walter Camp, the team's captain, marveled at the young man's abilities. Camp, a militant when it came to physical conditioning, couldn't figure out how a small man of ill health, one who treated his body so poorly, could perform as Hinkey did. He referred to Hinkey as "the disembodied spirit" for the freshman's effortless drifting through opposing interference to get to the ball carrier. When the unfortunate carriers met up with Hinkey, they typically found themselves suddenly and viciously hurled to the ground. No one tackled like Hinkey. The tightly wound ball of hate compensated for his size with unequaled speed and violence. As sportswriters said of Hinkey, "when he tackled 'em, they stayed tackled" and "when he hit 'em on his blocking assignment, they stayed hit."

Hinkey's teammates also knew him by another nickname: "Silent Frank." The boy kept to himself and let his playing do the talking. Part of that tactic may have been temperament—Hinkey's bottled-up anger and short fuse didn't mix well with forming friendships. One night teammate George Foster Sanford heard a scuffle in the adjacent room. Sanford investigated only to find Hinkey whaling away at a much larger man cowering on the floor. The two hundred-pound Sanford grabbed Hinkey by the shirt and, lifting him clear off his feet, hurled Hinkey into the wall. Panting, Hinkey stared wild-eyed at him and said, "Sanford, that was the greatest sensation I've ever experienced—try it again!" It turned out the larger man had picked a fight with Hinkey. Though volatile and completely willing to defend himself, Hinkey wasn't an instigator off the field.

Thankfully for his teammates, Hinkey saved his rage for their opponents. He eagerly awaited his first Harvard encounter in 1891. He itched to tackle the Crimson. Somebody had to exact revenge for Pudge Heffelfinger. The two teams both held perfect records, putting the national title on the line as well.

Hinkey shone under such pressure, and it didn't take long for him to make an immediate impact on The Game. With Yale holding a slight 4–0 lead, Harvard halfback Tom Corbett attempted to sweep Hinkey's end. Unfortunately for Corbett, Hinkey hated being thought of as the weak point. He made an example of the Harvard halfback, exploding into Corbett and popping the ball out of his hands. As a flattened Corbett lay on the ground watching helplessly, Yale halfback Laurie Bliss streaked twenty-five yards into the end zone for the clinching touchdown. Harvard's quest for a repeat undefeated season came to an abrupt end. The win also resulted in Yale regaining the national crown with a perfect record of 13–0–0. Hinkey had restored order.

The following year, 10–0 Harvard and 11–0 Yale again entered their annual contest with perfect records. Hinkey had continued his assault on opponents throughout the season, and Harvard was well aware of the danger Hinkey posed. The Crimson devised an ingenious plan to counter the formidable end. Lorin Deland, a Harvard graduate and Boston businessman, formulated a mass-attack formation based on decidedly warlike precepts. The idea was to exact the opponent's point of greatest weakness with your greatest strength, a concept that Deland, a chess expert, delighted in. He called the play "The Flying Wedge."

The Crimson debuted the play in The Game. Harvard lined up with two groups behind the line of scrimmage. Quarterback Bernie Trafford then signaled by waving his arms, causing the groups to race forward and converge, forming a *V* in front of Trafford. The Harvard quarterback handed the ball off to fullback Charlie Brewer. The entire Crimson team surged forward with Brewer engulfed by his teammates. The play gained thirty yards before Yale's captain Vance McCormick and the irrepressible Hinkey could finally combine to make the defensive stop.

The frustrating new formation incensed Hinkey. After Yale took over offensively on a Harvard fumble, Hinkey cleared a path for running back Bliss by obliterating Harvard end Slugger Manson and tackle Jim Shea. Bliss followed Hinkey's block again on the next play and scored the game's only touchdown.

Tensions rose and tempers flared as a result of Harvard's Flying Wedge and Hinkey's patented ferocity. In the stands, Yale alum Pudge Heffelfinger, the recently graduated three-time All-American, became so aroused by the game's building fervor that he jumped a fence along the field's perimeter. It took three members of the local police force to finally restrain and subdue him.

The Flying Wedge not only incited Yale players and fans. It also raised eyebrows on the rules committee, which wasn't happy about the mass-attack formation's enhancement of the game's brutish reputation. Tactically, the Flying Wedge succeeded. Defending against the formation was nearly impossible. The man with the ball had to be tackled to end the play, and the Flying Wedge protected the ball carrier with nearly the entire team surrounding him. The defense needed to put several players in the wedge's path to slow it down and get to the ball. When the defense finally managed to trip up the ball carrier or get to him through the protective wall of bodies, the play always ended in a huge gang tackle. Hundreds of pounds of body weight collapsed in a heap, the players' arms and legs intricately tangled. Unprotected heads cracked against one another or collided with elbows and knees. In the Flying Wedge a player could just as easily be hurt by his own players as by the opposing ones. The committee struck back before the 1894 season, outlawing such formations and eliminating the practice of players wearing special belts with handles that teammates clutched to form the interlocking wall. (The Flying Wedge formation was later monumentalized in a life-size sculpture in the NCAA Hall of Champions in Indianapolis, Indiana.) Harvard would have to find another way to shield its ball carriers from Hinkey and the rest of the Bulldogs.

Not a problem. This was Harvard. Solving intractable problems was second nature.

The idea for the Crimson's next trick was sparked during the 1893 game against Cornell, a game played in miserable rainy conditions. When the traditional uniforms of moleskin trousers and canvas jackets became saturated with water, each player carried an additional thirty pounds. The inevitable slowdown was unacceptable. After exploring alternate fabrics for uniforms, Harvard found that a high-grade thin-layer leather resulted in only one additional pound of water weight in rain. The fact that the slippery leather made tackling difficult was merely a coincidental side benefit.

To the amazement of the Yale team and twenty-five thousand spectators at Hampden Park in Springfield, Harvard jogged onto the field in 1893 in shiny leather uniforms designed by a trendy Boston tailor. Harvard wanted to experience the winning feeling of 1890 again whatever the cost—and that cost was a princely $125 per uniform. Hinkey immediately launched into a tirade over the leather uniforms and argued with Harvard captain Bert Waters and the officials over the legality of the fabric. Hinkey lost. Nothing in the rule book addressed fashion requirements.

Hinkey, of course, knew the rules. He had spent the previous night telling his teammates which of them to break. But the argument served as a stall tactic to allow time for someone to track down some resin. The resin provided the necessary additional traction for the Yale players to grab hold of the gimmicky Harvard innovation. Again, Harvard's unconventional tactic proved futile. Yale won the game on Frank Butterworth's one-yard touchdown run, the only score in the game.

In 1894, the sport of football came under attack by Harvard administrators. Harvard president Charles Eliot's contemporary diatribe decried "The Evils of Football," saying that:

> The American game of football, as now played, is unfit for colleges and schools . . . the public has been kept ignorant regarding the number and gravity of injuries . . . violation of the rules by coaches, players, and trainers are highly profitable, and are constantly perpetrated by all parties . . . as a spectacle football is more brutalizing than prize fighting, cock fighting, or bull fighting . . . football sets up the wrong kind of a hero—the man who uses his strength brutally, with a reckless disregard both of the injuries he may suffer and of the injuries he may inflict on others. That is not the best kind of courage or the best kind of hero.

Despite Eliot's position, the Crimson football program continued.

Harvard and Yale met at Hampden Park for what turned out to be the final time in 1894. Nothing about the pregame festivities hinted at the violence to come. At half past one in the afternoon with the temperature in the low forties, the players began to arrive amid elaborate pomp and ceremony. The appearance of each school, first Yale, followed by Harvard, jumpstarted demonstrations that featured waving banners, horse-drawn coaches, and cheering supporters festively decked out in the respective colors of blue and crimson. One hundred Boston police officers, who traveled by train to assist the Springfield police in keeping the huge influx of rabid fans in order, stood sentry around the field's perimeter. The grand entrance parade harkened back to the Colosseum of ancient Rome. Hinkey, the sport's most ferocious gladiator, was ready for his farewell performance.

Entering the game a slight favorite, Harvard quickly gave up a touchdown. Then the innovative streak kicked in, and Harvard revealed the reverse play. Quarterback Robert Wrenn handed off to halfback Edgar Wrightington for what appeared to be a run around the right end. Fullback John Fairchild had lined up at left end as a harmless decoy until Wrightington reversed the play to Fairchild. Hinkey, pursuing the original ball carrier, wheeled around and somehow tracked down Fairchild. Fairchild paid dearly. Hinkey unloaded on the Harvard player with a ground-shaking tackle, driving him into the turf in what was described as one of Hinkey's most vicious tackles. Hinkey did not like to be fooled.

With a first down at the Yale four-yard line after the play netted sixteen yards, the Crimson were stopped twice for no gain at the middle of the Eli line. On the next play, Harvard halfback Johnny Hayes did the impossible. Courtesy of a devastating double-team block on Hinkey, Hayes circled around left end and scored. It was the first Crimson score against Yale since the 1890 victory, four long years earlier. It was also the first, last, and only time that any player succeeded in an attempt to get around Hinkey's end.

The game became increasingly more violent. Harvard's Charlie Brewer suffered a broken leg, yet played on until he could bear the pain no longer. The Crimson frustration reached a boiling point and Yale made it clear that the Bulldogs had no intention of backing down. The blatant injury attempts began when Harvard's Bert Waters jabbed a finger into Frank Butterworth's eye. Harvard's Wrightington bore the brunt of Yale's anger at Butterworth's injury. After Wrightington called for a fair catch and rolled to the ground, his collarbone was snapped by a pair of Hinkey knees. Harvard fans called for Frank's head, but it may not have been the elder Hinkey who caused the injury. Some contended that sophomore Louis Hinkey was at fault and that Frank took the blame to protect his sibling. Frank knew that Harvard would seek to take him out at the first opportunity anyway—if they could indeed hurt him.

The assaults continued. During an official's conference, Yale's tackle Fred Murphy backhanded Harvard's Bob Hallowell, crushing his nose into a crooked, bloody mess. Murphy also poked Hallowell's eye, drawing blood before the Crimson caught up to him. They were not happy. They left Murphy crumpled in a heap on the field. Murphy, who was already woozy from an earlier blow to the head (his teammates had to point him toward the Yale goal before each play) was carried by stretcher from the field and unceremoniously dumped onto a pile of blankets so the medical personnel attending him could quickly return to the game.

Yale's Al Jerrems was the last player to leave the game by injury— yet another blow to the head—but he was not the last to be removed overall. Harvard's Hayes and Yale's Richard Armstrong slugged their way to ejections. In all, the teams needed a combined nine substitutes during the game. This was remarkable—during football's early days, the starting eleven played the entire game, both on offense and defense. The term "two-way player" applied to everyone. The substitutes were supposed to remain on the sidelines, not actually play in the game.

The following day rumors swirled that Yale's Fred Murphy had died from his injuries. Not true—he merely stayed in a coma for several hours before waking. Newspapers treated the game like a crisis, listing the injured players in the same format as dead or wounded disaster victims. Reporters wrote that a mob mentality had prevailed despite the aggregation of Boston policemen. The violence on the field spilled over to the postgame, as rival student fans fought in the streets while returning to the train station.

The public outcry following the game was swift and far reaching. It had been by far the roughest, most blatantly violent "big game" yet played. The sport was now under fire from every corner of society. Members of the clergy and law enforcement officials issued denouncements that only fanned the smoldering flames between the two schools. The press vilified Hinkey in particular, making him the poster boy for the antifootball movement.

The notorious Hinkey was indeed one of the more violently aggressive players, but he was also one of the best. In fact, Hinkey was hailed by coaching legend Pop Warner as "the greatest football player of all time" for his ability to combine the attributes of "determination and fighting spirit." He has remained one of only five players to ever be named a four-time All-American during his collegiate playing days. Hinkey suffered defeat only once in his career, versus Princeton (6–0) in 1893 in a game where he was forced to the sidelines with a head wound. Of course, Hinkey returned to the game, his head swathed in blood-soaked bandages. All told, the Elis were 52–1 with forty-eight shutouts in a row when "the disembodied spirit" was at left end.

Yale's captain-elect Brinck Thome was upset about Harvard's silence regarding the press treatment of Hinkey, and the Bulldogs refused to respond to Harvard's demand for an apology for the violence until the Crimson supported the game in print. But by the time that Harvard captain-elect Brewer finally issued a statement to exonerate Hinkey publicly in the spring of 1895, it was too late. With support from the school presidents, the Harvard and Yale administrations suspended all athletic competition between the two schools for one year and football for two seasons. The Bloodbath in Hampden Park almost ended the sport entirely.

But thanks mostly to the efforts of one man, the game of football survived.

The unlikely savior arrived in the form of Bill Reid, a former Harvard player. By the early 1900s Yale's Walter Camp had instituted the concept of professional coaching, and prior to the 1905 season Reid took over Crimson fortunes. Football stood at a most precarious crossroads. The antifootball crusaders of the 1890s had gathered strength, and they had plenty of ammunition. The previous season had resulted in a long list of casualties. A 1904 *Chicago Tribune* study noted 18 football related deaths and 137 serious injuries nationwide at all levels, and the Harvard administration seriously considered abolishing the game.

In October 1905, President Theodore Roosevelt (an 1880 Harvard grad, former member of the Harvard boxing team, and an avid football fan) summoned representatives of the Big Three to Washington, D.C., to discuss the state of the game: Yale's Walter Camp, the Intercollegiate Football Association rules committee's most influential member; Reid, the Harvard coach; and Princeton's John Fine. The three recognized themselves as the sport's dominant triumvirate, and they pledged to set a good example during the 1905 campaign through good sportsmanship and fair play.

The game's problems dated back to the Camp-approved rule change in 1888 that allowed tackling below the waist. As a result, defenses increasingly jammed the line, forcing the offense to advance the ball behind a mass of blockers. During the intervening years the rules committee had made several attempts to open up the game including allowing the quarterback to run with the ball. Defenses, however, adjusted quickly, able to both crowd the line and still cover the flanks.

The Big Three presidential promise didn't curb the game's roughness in 1905. The Harvard-Penn game in November at Franklin Field stood out in its brutality. Early in the game, Harvard center Bartol Parker punched his counterpart from Pennsylvania, resulting in Parker's ejection. Later, a Penn player deliberately kneeled on the face of a Harvard player, resulting in another ejection. In all, officials assessed 210 yards in penalties.

The annual marquee game of the season between Harvard and Yale did nothing to dissuade the supporters of football abolition. A Harvard Stadium record crowd of forty-three thousand witnessed by far the roughest contest between the two since the 1894 massacre at Springfield. A vicious high/low tackle by Yale's Jim Quail and Tom Shevlin on Harvard's guard and kicker Francis "Hooks" Burr created the biggest stir. The Crimson insisted that Burr had signaled for a fair catch and should not have been subject to the hit at all. Referee Paul Dashiell claimed he didn't see Burr's signal. (Dashiell's missed call resulted in the well-known official never working another Harvard-Yale game in his career.) The play infuriated Harvard fans and prompted Major Henry L. Higginson, a member of the Harvard Board of Overseers and the man who donated Soldiers Field to Harvard, to send a message to Coach Reid. He wanted Reid to pull the Crimson off the field. Reid decided to play on, and Yale prevailed 6–0, its fourth straight victory over the Crimson.

The cloud over the sport mushroomed. Columbia, Northwestern, and Union announced that they were dropping football. On the West Coast, Stanford and California decided to switch from football to rugby.

The overall demeanor of the 1905 season alarmed President Roosevelt. His son played on the Harvard freshmen team and had reportedly been singled out for a severe pounding in the Yale game, his nose badly broken. A stern Roosevelt requested a postseason meeting in Washington, D.C., with Coach Reid, alone, to discuss the state of the game.

Reid recounted his solo visit years later to Harvard graduate Dave Mittell. Upon his arrival at the White House, Reid enjoyed a sumptuous lunch in the company of the president, Mrs. Roosevelt, and the German ambassador. After dining, the president excused himself and went out to the patio with Reid.

"You gave me your word," the president began, "that no Harvard man would be caught up in this unsportsmanlike brutality. What happened to that young man in the Pennsylvania game?"

Reid looked Roosevelt in the eye and replied, "Mr. President, there were extenuating circumstances. Mr. Parker, our center, was kicked in the balls."

Roosevelt nodded and answered, "I cannot dignify the incident with a response in words, but nevertheless, we must clean up this game or it will die."

Individuals from all segments of society began decrying the game's brutality. The man who held the greatest of all individual athletic crowns in the most barbaric of sports was, unimaginably, on the side of the growing antifootball legions. Legendary heavyweight boxing champion John L. Sullivan told prominent football official and rules committee member Paul Dashiell: "Football! There's murder in that game. Sparring! It doesn't compare in roughness or danger with football. In sparring you know what you are doing. You know what your opponent is trying to do and he's right there in front of you, and there's only one. But in football, say there's twenty-one people trying to do to you."

At Harvard it appeared that President Charles Eliot's prayers were answered. On January 10, 1906, the Harvard Board of Overseers voted to permit no further football games at Harvard until the board reviewed and acted on changes in the rules.

The death of a Union College player in a game versus New York University caused NYU chancellor Harry McCracken to request a meeting that led to the formation of the NCAA as a governing body for college sports. This was a huge step, but the most significant event for the immediate development of modern football was the opportunity for newer rules committee members to step out of Camp's shadow.

Despite the barely concealed bitterness on the part of Reid toward Camp after their last gridiron encounter—on the field following the infamous 1905 playing of The Game—Reid cozied up to the Yale legend to insist that he was the proper choice to rewrite the rules section of Camp's annual guide, the manual that laid out the official parameters of the college game. Camp's first guide appeared in 1894 and since then he'd done nearly all of the writing. Reid wanted to eliminate the existing confusion regarding the current rules and their interpretation and to put in place a system of changes that he knew he had to have in order to gain the approval of Harvard's Board of Overseers. Amazingly, Camp agreed to let the Crimson coach try.

Reid worked in conjunction with the Harvard Graduates Athletic Association, a seven-member committee that included five former coaches. The nineteen rules that Reid proposed included extending the distance for a first down from five to ten yards, outlawing the interlocking of arms while blocking at the line of scrimmage, and establishing a neutral zone between offensive and defensive fronts, a concept Camp had been seeking to implement for well over a decade.

Reid issued a warning with his presentation to the rules committee: "Either these nineteen rules go through or there will be no football at Harvard; and if Harvard throws out the game, many other colleges will follow Harvard's lead." No one disputed Reid's statement. Harvard's influence was vital to football's survival. The rules committee approved the reforms on March 31, 1906, and two days later Reid received the news he had anxiously awaited. The Harvard Board of Overseers, by a narrow margin, decided to go against President Eliot's wishes and sanction football for the 1906 season. Reid had both a reformed game and a place to coach.

Reid's heroic efforts went a long way toward preserving the sport of football and the Harvard-Yale game. His belief in the utter importance of the rivalry—and a civil game free of mayhem—is the same blend of passion and respect that gets inculcated in all players and coaches who give their best to The Game, who attempt their own heroics on the field. Invariably, however, some life-changing event puts The Game, and the concept of heroism, into perspective.

"I recall Coach Eddie Casey, whom I admired and respected,

assuring us in the locker room of the Yale Bowl in 1934 that what we did in the next hour would be the most important hour of our lives," Herman Gundlach remembered. Harvard lost the game, and Gundlach agonized over the result for ten years.

"Then, in March 1945 crossing the Rhine in Germany, I smiled and said to myself, 'No, Eddie, *this* is the most important hour of my life,'" Gundlach said.

"I was suddenly relieved of that loss."

4

Duty, Honor, Football

TIM MURPHY DIDN'T HAVE to cross the Rhine to run full force into his own understanding of heroism. During his team's landmark undefeated season in 2001, he merely watched the events of September 11 unfold.

That morning, a member of the defensive coaching staff burst into the offensive staff meeting and flicked on the television. The coaches watched in confusion as smoke billowed from the top floors of One World Trade Center in New York City. The puzzlement turned to horror as a second plane flew into view, smashing into the second tower in a fiery ball and removing all question of intent. Murphy and his staff stayed glued to the television for the rest of the meeting. They watched incredulously as the attack continued with another commercial plane slamming into the Pentagon and a fourth plane crashing in a field in Pennsylvania. Suddenly football didn't seem so important.

By afternoon Harvard and Holy Cross hadn't yet canceled their game for that weekend, so the Crimson continued preparing for the season opener. During practice Murphy talked with his players about the tragedy and then held a moment of silence for the victims. The league decided to cancel the games later that week.

A year later, more than ten thousand people gathered at the Tercentenary Theater in Harvard Yard to commemorate the first anniversary of the terrorist attacks on America. Harvard President Lawrence H. Summers addressed the crowd, campus religious leaders offered words of comfort, and musicians celebrated the victims, especially the several members of the Harvard community killed in the assault. That night, the Lars Anderson and Harvard bridges spanning the Charles River glowed during a public candlelight vigil.

Yale also held a day of hope and remembrance on September 11, 2002. The library staff provided a quiet refuge for students, faculty, and staff in Sterling Memorial Lecture Hall. Staff members submitted inspirational messages and every eleven minutes volunteers read a different one. Music groups performed at various locations around campus throughout the day, and Yale's observances ended with a candlelight vigil on Cross Campus.

Coaches Murphy and Siedlecki didn't dwell on the day's events in practice, both feeling that the players likely welcomed the thought of concentrating on something other than the somber anniversary. Both squads still had to prepare for the opening games now just ten days away. Former coach Carm Cozza, however, had plenty of time to prepare for his first radio broadcast of the 2002 season, which gave him the liberty of pausing to reflect.

Cozza's thoughts turned to Kristen Engelke Lee and her son Zachary. The terrorists claimed the life of her husband, Richard Lee—one of Cozza's former players—shortly before Zachary's second birthday. Lee worked for Cantor Fitzgerald, the bond-trading firm whose offices were on the floors struck by the first hijacked plane.

Cozza remembered hearing about Lee. "It was devastating. We had thirty-five former players working in the towers," Cozza said. "We were fortunate to lose only one. Richard was such a conscientious young man that the result of him being at work earlier than he had to be made him a victim."

Lee's teammates from the class of 1991 rallied around his memory. They established a fund to pay for his son's education, in some small way hoping to repay the generous, unselfish nature Lee showed them.

Lee's Yale football career, like his life, ended prematurely. At 6'4" and 265 pounds, Lee played defensive tackle as a sophomore and junior. In the 1988 Harvard-Yale game, he hurt his shoulder and had to leave the game. Lee cried over the injury, but not because of the pain. He could tolerate the pain. Lee just wanted to play on against his Crimson rivals. The injury caused him to miss his senior season, but Lee loved the game enough to remain on campus after his classmates graduated so he'd have one more season to play. Unfortunately, another injury cut his last year short and ended Lee's career for good.

"He was a good player. Not a great player. But he always worked hard despite some assorted injuries," Cozza said. "His teammates loved him. Everyone wanted to be his friend. He was a happy-go-lucky, fun-loving guy. He brought the coaches chocolate-covered macadamia nuts when he returned from his home in Hawaii. A thoughtful kid."

The injury-ridden career disappointed Lee, but it didn't devastate him. An ambitious and intense individual, Lee's pursuits extended beyond the gridiron. He played bass and sang for Skunkhead, a campus band that played fraternities and local bars. He founded and operated the Berkeley Bagel Bar, a popular campus coffee and bagel shop that students frequented. Lee's humorous comic strip *The Drunk Kids* ran in the Yale *Herald*. The political science major concentrated on Soviet politics and learned to speak Russian. Lee simply excelled in all that he did.

The terrorists who murdered thousands of civilians on September 11 attacked the World Trade Center to strike at a symbol of American strength and power. Many heroes emerged on that day, from the responding emergency personnel to the men and women who simply went to their jobs on that fateful morning. Richard Lee died a hero, especially to those who knew him. But Lee was just one of a number of Harvard and Yale players who went on from The Game to perform valiantly later in their lives.

Yale's John Downey capped his college football career with a 14–6 win over Harvard in 1950. Downey, also a wrestling standout, didn't know at the time that it was the last Harvard-Yale contest he'd see for many years. While working at his first job he became embroiled in such a dangerous ordeal that he thought he might not survive.

Downey joined the CIA after graduating from Yale in 1951. The following November he flew with a group of operatives into Manchuria, China, to rendezvous with and extract an agent who'd been dropped into enemy territory earlier. The unmarked C-47 dropped to an altitude of fifty feet over a snowy landscape when all hell broke loose. Two white tarps hid an enemy ambush. Behind the camouflage sat two .50-caliber antiaircraft guns. The guns erupted, decimating the cockpit at point-blank range. The two pilots, Robert Snoddy and Norman Schwartz, never knew what hit them. The plane crashed into a bank of trees, spilling two bruised but otherwise unharmed operatives into the snow.

The Chinese had captured the agent scheduled to meet up with the rendezvous party, and the agent had talked. Some Chinese soldiers raced to the crash site and trained their weapons on Downey and Dick Fecteau, the other surviving agent. One of them spoke English. "You are very luck to survive a crash like this," he said, "but your future is very dark."

Downey spent five months in solitary confinement in Manchuria before being moved to Green Basket Prison in Beijing—a dank, notorious dungeon with no heat or running water. The captors separated Downey and Fecteau, and the two men endured two years of mental torture before seeing each other again at their espionage trial in Beijing. The court-appointed defense lawyer didn't dispute the charges against Downey and Fecteau. He just begged for a merciful sentence. Because the two remained tight-lipped during captivity, the Chinese didn't know much about them. The judge did know that Downey graduated from Yale and that Fecteau graduated from Boston University. The judge had never heard of Boston University but he did know Yale, and Downey's alma mater earned him a stiffer sentence. The judge reasoned that Downey must have been ranked higher than Fecteau if he attended Yale. Fecteau got twenty years. The judge sentenced Downey to life.

Downey had little to look forward to during his time in prison. The Chinese interrogated him on a regular basis, asking the same questions over and over. They never tried to beat the answers out of him, torturing him mentally instead. The guards told him to stare at a spot on the wall and think about his crime. They gave him decent meals and then without explanation switched back to the regular menu: a bowl of gruel in the morning and a bowl of soup and two pieces of bread for lunch and dinner. They also left him alone in his cell for days at a time, with nothing to do and no one to talk to. Fighting boredom turned out to be one of the most trying aspects of his imprisonment. The Chinese did allow Downey to receive mail starting in 1953 or 1954, and the correspondence from friends and family comforted him. The letters and news clippings about one of his passions in particular helped him pass the time: Yale football.

Downey's love affair with Yale football began at an early age. His father, a Yale Law School graduate, took a seven- or eight-year-old Downey to his first game during the Bulldogs' Heisman heyday, and the boy watched football idols Larry Kelley and Clint Frank star in the Yale Bowl. Later, when he attended prep school in Wallingford, Connecticut, Downey and his Choate football teammates cleared tables in the dining hall whenever Choate boarded Harvard and Princeton teams before games at the bowl. In exchange the players earned complimentary tickets to the games. He saw his first Harvard-Yale game in 1945 and played in two of them as a Yale student.

"I don't remember much about the first Yale-Harvard game that I played in," Downey said. "I just remember that we won. I vividly remember taking the field for the 1950 game, though. It was my last game and I remember thinking how fortunate I was to be a part of the Yale-Harvard rivalry. We won that day, too. I'm proud of the fact that Yale beat Harvard both times I played in the game."

Former Yale sports information director Charlie Loftus sent an imprisoned Downey detailed Bulldogs football packages that included newsletters with game accounts and diagrams of all the plays from the game. "I certainly had a lot of time to study them and looked forward to their arrival with great anticipation," Downey recalled. "It was a very pleasant thing."

Other people keeping a vigil for Downey knew how much Yale football meant to him and they sent him game stories as well, help-ing Downey face an uncertain future as the weeks slid into years and then, unimaginably, into decades. But a postcard he received from his mother's friend ended up inflicting its own brand of torture. In early December 1968 a postcard arrived with uplifting news: "Jack: Yale undefeated, champions 29–13!" Downey's sports magazines lagged behind the other mail, arriving just in time for Christmas Eve. He eagerly flipped through the pages to read about Yale's big victory, the 29–13 League championship-clinching win. Instead, he found the tale of fourth-quarter Harvard heroics that led to a 29–29 tie and a shared title.

"There was a howl of agony," Downey recalled. "I was probably the last guy on earth who really cared about the game to learn the score. In a way, that was my most memorable Harvard game." Finding out about the 29–29 1968 tie may have been one of Downey's more memorable moments during an otherwise bland prison routine, but undoubtedly his best moment came on March 12, 1973.

Fifteen months after the Chinese nonchalantly released fellow prisoner Fecteau by directing him over a footbridge that took him into Hong Kong territory, they released Downey in a much more official manner. The Red Cross talked with the Chinese captors for a few hours and then escorted Downey into Hong Kong. "When I got across the border, people from the U.S. consulate, state department, CIA, and a British army doctor met me," said Downey. "It was quite different from my understanding of Dick Fecteau's release."

Twenty years. Twenty years of missed holidays and time with his family and friends. Twenty years of not knowing if he'd ever go home. Twenty years that Downey considered boring and wasted. Downey could have recouped something from his ordeal, could have reaped financial rewards from his capture and imprisonment. He had many lucrative offers to tell his story. But he turned them all down. "I wasn't going to make a living as the CIA agent who was imprisoned in China for twenty years," Downey said.

Instead, Downey went to law school. Harvard Law School. The former Bulldog didn't stay in Cambridge, though. Remaining true to Yale, he took his Harvard Law degree back to New Haven and opened a private practice.

*   *   *

Harvard's 1968 team, the one that had caused Downey's anguish half a world away, included a player who could relate to Downey's plight. Harvard's Pat Conway patrolled the field at safety on the 1968 team. A year earlier he patrolled a different field, reciting Hail Marys instead of defending against them, constantly aware of what could happen to him in the event of his capture.

Conway entered Harvard in the fall of 1963. He played football his freshman year and as a sophomore made varsity at fullback. Conway's success on the football field didn't follow him into the classroom, however. "I left Harvard because I was on probation. I wasn't allowed to play football and I lost my academic scholarship. All because I wasn't doing well in school," Conway said. "I left because I badly needed to change my environment in order to reassess and redirect my life."

With war raging in Vietnam, Conway thought he'd have to go into the military eventually. He figured he'd get it over with sooner rather than later. He didn't think much about the gung ho fighting aspect—the physical challenge interested him more. "I joined the Marines for one simple reason. I thought they were the roughest, toughest fighting outfit I could join and I wanted to test myself," Conway said. "I figured I might end up in Vietnam, though the idea of shooting at people—and someone shooting back at me—wasn't a big concern at the time. Later I was to find out it was my biggest concern."

With one month to go in his six-month fighting hitch in Vietnam, Conway landed under live fire at Khe Sanh in February 1968. "There were times at Khe Sanh when I was sure I was going to die. There were days when we didn't have any food or water," he said. "They bombed us all night just to keep us from sleeping." During his time at Khe Sanh a bomb exploded near Conway, rendering him temporarily deaf and burying him in dirt. Even though flying shrapnel had struck him in the head at Hill 674 in Hue, this was his closest call. But Conway recovered and flew home, and the U.S. Marines discharged him in March of 1968.

Conway's experience in Vietnam challenged him, just as he'd hoped. He couldn't wait to re-enroll at Harvard in the fall, but not until after a nice, long vacation. Conway traveled to Puerto Rico to spend a summer teaching scuba diving and to put the dark images of combat behind him. While in Puerto Rico, Harvard head football coach John Yovicsin sent him a letter. "He wrote that I had one year of eligibility left and wanted to know if I wanted to play football again," Conway recalled. "The idea intrigued me. I figured I would get to meet some of my new classmates—most of my prior friends had graduated, and I didn't know a soul. Plus, I would get a little exercise even if I didn't make the team."

Conway accepted Yovicsin's offer.

The Crimson welcomed him with open arms, no matter what their particular views of the war might have been. They supported Conway for what he'd been through, totally in awe of his combat experience. "I'm sure it created quite a stir among my new teammates when this 'old man' showed up," Conway said, "but I never felt any resentment." Conway's teammates focused on helping the veteran learn how to play defensive back, his new position, rather than dwelling on the war. Other students on campus forced Conway to think about his time in Vietnam, however, and not in a positive way.

Everywhere Conway went on campus he encountered war protests. He saw flyers advertising antiwar rallies, watched crowds listening to speakers assail the government's involvement in Vietnam, and observed picket lines snaking in front of administrative buildings. And it angered him. He'd been there. He'd seen friends die in combat. Conway staged a one-man protest in response.

"I made it a regular habit of wearing my olive green USMC utility jacket," Conway said. "I'd find classrooms that were being picketed and walk right through the picket lines. Whenever a 'Cliffie' or other student stepped in my way, protesting that I had to stand in unity with them, I told them to move or *be moved*. As I made my way through the lines I entered the building to a lot of jeering."

The booing and hissing didn't upset Conway.

"Little did they know, I would then exit the rear of the building in search of another picket line at another building in order to do it all over again," Conway said. "At night I would tell my roommate how many different classes I had attended that day. I got a lot of pleasure out of it."

Conway enjoyed disrupting the picket lines, but it didn't have much effect on the overall antiwar sentiment around campus. It was just his little way of expressing his views as someone with firsthand knowledge of what the war was like. He got greater satisfaction out of disrupting passes on the football field. Conway's transition to defensive back suited him, and his decision to play one more year helped the 1968 team exponentially. Despite a few painful injuries Conway factored prominently as one of the Harvard defense's "Boston Stranglers" in the Crimson's famous 29–29 "victory" over Yale.

"The '68 game was overwhelming. All during the season both teams were winning and the talk of a showdown in November was constantly mentioned as each team continued to win," Conway recalled. "During the week leading up to the game I wasn't participating in contact drills. I received a concussion in the Brown game the week before, and I was still recovering from a couple broken ribs that I received earlier in the season. Those ribs really bothered me. They hurt all the time."

Luckily for Harvard the team doctor cleared Conway to play against the Bulldogs. Conway forced Yale's star running back Calvin Hill to fumble the ball three times, and one of those turnovers led to Harvard's first touchdown of the game. Conway then watched the offense deliver the miracle comeback.

"When Varney caught that final pass, bedlam broke loose. People were jumping, dancing, and hugging. If you had a uniform on you could kiss any girl at the stadium. A crush of people swarmed the field—it took me forty-five minutes just to get to the locker room," Conway said. "I remember Calvin Hill came into our locker room to congratulate us. It was a nice gesture. I don't know if I personally would have been up to it myself if I had been in his place."

Conway received a bevy of awards for his final season. The Associated Press, United Press International, and league coaches all made him an All-Ivy selection. The Associated Press also named Conway to the All-East team. Combined with the collective success of the team, Conway couldn't have been happier. But all the honors he received on the field didn't compare to his proudest moment of the year at the end-of-season football dinner.

"Nathan Pusey, the college president, left a group of dignified alumni, took me aside, and shook my hand. He told me that he was impressed by a statement I'd made to a reporter at the beginning of the season," Conway said. Before the first game of the year, which coincided exactly with the anniversary of Conway's arrival at Khe Sanh one year earlier, the reporter asked Conway if he was scared to play his first football game in three years.

" 'Scared'?" Conway had replied. " 'Scared' was experiencing mortar fire at Khe Sanh. 'Scared' was a helicopter landing in a hot zone. 'Scared' was being in a firefight. Being in a football game is exciting and fun . . . not 'scary.' "

Conway couldn't believe that Pusey even knew who he was, let alone remembered his comments from three months before, but the president complimented Conway on his words and wished the senior continued success. Conway knew he'd come full circle. From a confused sophomore with a dismal academic record to a soldier on the front lines in Vietnam to a Harvard football hero with exemplary grades, Conway had taken a dangerous, circuitous route to find himself.

Many other Harvard and Yale football players took a similar path. Not all of them survived.

*   *   *

Alexander Dickson Wilson had the misfortune of playing for Yale during legendary coach Percy Haughton's reign at Harvard. The teams on which Wilson played lost three in a row to Harvard—not even as the team captain in 1916 could the Binghamton, New York, native lead his team to victory over the Crimson. Wilson may not have been able to triumph over Harvard, but it didn't affect his leadership abilities. When he graduated from Yale in 1917 he took his skills to a different squad and a battlefield far away.

In August 1917, after completing the first Officer's Training Camp at Madison Barracks in Sacketts Harbor, New York, Wilson received a commission as a second lieutenant of infantry. He was stationed at Camp Zachary Taylor in Kentucky and worked his way up to first lieutenant of infantry by October. In May 1918, Wilson went to France with the Eighth Brigade of United States Regulars, and beginning in August he served as commanding officer of Company A, 59th Infantry. The men under his command proudly followed Wilson's orders. They respected his democratic leadership techniques. Though he led them, Wilson treated them as equals.

A sergeant in Wilson's company remembered a speech Wilson gave to the troops one night. "Wilson said that while he had never been under shell fire he would try and be a man and make the best of it, and if he should show a yellow streak no one ever need salute him and he wouldn't say a word," wrote the sergeant in a letter published in *Yale in the World War*, Volume II. "In turn, if any man under his command was yellow he need not salute for he, Captain Wilson, would not return that salute but would have the man up before a general court. And true he was a man of men, one who would always use the best judgment about all things and one who would take his mess kit and eat what his men did and take only the same portions they did."

Wilson's men felt that their commanding officer always showed the best judgment, but one night he couldn't resist the thrill of a foolhardy challenge. Wilson learned that the company sergeant had crawled about 150 yards to some apple trees the previous evening—apple trees positioned between their company and the enemy. Wilson went down the line and found the sergeant. "Well, sergeant, have you an apple for me?" Wilson asked. The sergeant told him that he didn't, so Wilson decided that they'd go get some more apples together.

When they reached the apple trees, Wilson could see a trench about 200 yards beyond. He whispered to the sergeant that he didn't think the enemy occupied the trench. The sergeant, who had received machine-gun fire from that very trench while on patrol, knew that it held enemy soldiers. But he bit his tongue, not wanting Wilson to think he was afraid, and the two crept deeper and closer to danger. Suddenly, star shells lit the night sky bright as day, machine guns erupted, and bullets whizzed overhead. Wilson and the sergeant dove for cover in a hole. It was three o'clock in the morning. The enemy kept the apple-seekers pinned in the hole until dark the following night. To make matters worse, it rained the entire day. But Wilson and the sergeant managed to crawl back unharmed, and the company took the enemy trench system soon after.

Wilson's luck ran out at the end of September. During the Argonne offensive, at daybreak on September 29, he received orders to move his men forward. Wilson knew that artillery support was too far back to help his company. But orders were orders. Company A began pushing ahead over open ground. Without warning, artillery fire pounded the ground around them and machine guns pelted the troops with bullets. Wilson called out to the sergeant. "Let's you and I see if we can locate the gun that is cutting our men to pieces," he said.

The two men pressed on, crawling on all fours until they reached a high spot. Wilson got hit in the arm near his shoulder. A bullet tore through the sergeant's forearm, breaking both bones. They scrambled for a shallow trench. Wilson made it, but the sergeant was hit again, this time in the hip. He lay fifty feet from the trench. Wilson crawled out of the trench and back in the line of fire to help the sergeant the rest of the way. Another soldier wrapped a bandolier string around the sergeant's arm to stem the bleeding. "Gee, I'd like to locate those dogs," Wilson said. His last words. A bullet suddenly ripped through his helmet and entered his skull through his eyebrow. He died instantly.

"His loss was mourned by all," the sergeant wrote in his eyewitness account of Wilson's courageous leadership. "But the ways of battle—the brave and the best seem always to get killed. Thus passed the most popular officer or man who ever donned a uniform."

Those who knew Wilson weren't surprised by the heroic stories that poured in from the front after he died. He used his rank to inspire his charges, not to make them fear him. He viewed his company as teammates and set an example for them to follow. Wilson employed the same type of leadership on the battlefield that he had learned on the football field, his turn at directing the Yale eleven honing his ability to command.

Coincidentally, Yale's former football captain earned that title again, this time as a captain in the army. Wilson's official commission as captain was dated September 28—one day before he died in action.

🏈   🏈   🏈

Not all of the men who went from the bowl and the stadium into legendary combat theaters of another sort were loud, rile 'em up, lead-the-charge types. Others were obedient role players. Frederick

Greeley Crocker wasn't one of the bigger men on the 1933 Harvard varsity team, but what he lacked in size he made up for with heart. An aggressive but average player, Crocker played consistently and quietly. When his team needed him the most, however, Crocker answered the call.

With the ball on Harvard's forty-four-yard line and the Crimson clinging to a 6–0 lead over a Yale team that had won the last two meetings, quarterback Danny Wells faded back and launched a long pass to the right side of the field. Crocker, the substitute end, raced past Yale's safety and captain Bob Lassiter at the Yale fifteen-yard line. Crocker reined in the pass, hustling over the goal line for a fifty-six-yard touchdown reception. The second-quarter score helped seal Harvard's 19–6 victory.

Crocker graduated in 1934 and remained at Harvard as a student in the business school. He worked for Hayden, Stone & Company for three years after earning his MBA before joining A.E. Staley Manufacturing Company in Boston as a salesman. In 1941, he went on active duty with the navy as an ensign. The navy assigned him to a destroyer on convoy in the North Atlantic, the USS *Ingraham*.

Aboard the *Ingraham,* Crocker and the rest of the crew served as the convoy escort for ships traveling between the United States, Iceland, and the United Kingdom. The convoy ships brought much-needed supplies to the Allies fighting off Hitler's advance. Like Crocker's assignment as a substitute end on the Crimson football team, the *Ingraham*'s unheralded duty in a supporting role didn't provide many chances at glory. The Germans understood the importance of the *Ingraham*'s escort duties, though. As long as ships continued to bring the Allied troops the necessary supplies, it would be harder for Hitler to accomplish his master plan. The *Ingraham* sailed under the constant threat of German U-boats, always one torpedo strike away from interruption of the Allied supply lines.

On the night of August 22, 1942, thick fog blanketed the North Atlantic. Visibility didn't exist. The *Ingraham* received notice that another destroyer, the *Buck,* had collided with a merchant ship off the coast of Nova Scotia. Navy officials dispatched the *Ingraham* to investigate the accident and to assist the crew of the *Buck*. En route, the *Ingraham* suffered a similar fate. The destroyer rammed the *Chemung*, an Allied tanker. The weaponry aboard the *Ingraham*, the very arsenal meant to protect the convoys that the ship escorted, proved to be its undoing.

Crocker and the rest of the *Ingraham*'s crew didn't stand a chance. The depth charges located at the ship's stern exploded on impact, dooming the destroyer. The ship sank almost immediately, plummeting to the ocean floor and leaving a single survivor, Ensign Roy Owen.

Crocker left a widow and three sons behind when he perished. All of his sons attended Harvard. In recognition of Crocker's ultimate sacrifice, in 1949 a group of former Harvard football players established an award in his name. The Frederick Greeley Crocker Award is given annually to the Harvard football player who in the opinion of his teammates possesses the initiative, perseverance, courage, and selflessness which were demonstrated by Ted Crocker. In recent years it has carried a "Most Valuable Player" connotation. Harvard football players recognize that greatness off the field transcends greatness on it.

🏈 🏈 🏈

Harvard's Frederick Greeley Crocker Award isn't the first to be named for a war hero. Honoring the memory of a fallen soldier by recognizing an individual who demonstrates similar character traits is common. It is more common, however, for organizations at both the college and professional levels to name athletic awards after former players who excelled in a particular sport or individuals who dedicated their lives to a sport. When Yale needed a namesake for an award to be given to the school's top male athlete, one man in particular offered the opportunity to name it for both a war hero and star athlete: William Neely Mallory. The William Neely Mallory Award is given to "the senior man who on the field of playing and in life at Yale best represents the highest ideals of American sportsmanship and Yale tradition."

Bill Mallory captained Yale's undefeated 1923 team as an All-American fullback. The 1923 team defeated Army, Georgia, North Carolina, and Maryland on its way to a perfect record. More important, Mallory's team beat Harvard 13–0 to close out the season. It was Mallory's only win over the Crimson, and Mallory's dedication to his teammates directly led to Yale's victory.

Before the 1923 season began, Yale didn't have a placekicker. Mallory had no experience kicking but took it upon himself to learn. Anything to help the team. Mallory had every reason to think he could fill the void. When he attended Pomfret School in Connecticut as a high school student, the hockey team needed players. Though he'd never skated, Mallory laced 'em up. He ended up captaining the hockey team as a senior. Booting field goals on grass would be a breeze for Mallory, but he didn't take his athleticism for granted.

Mallory built goalposts behind his family's thirty-room estate in Memphis and spent his summer practicing. He kicked footballs through the makeshift uprights until he knew his team could count on him when it mattered. Mallory's first opportunity to showcase his new skills came when Yale played Army midway through the season. Army took an early lead, but two Mallory field goals proved the difference and Yale remained undefeated. True to form, Mallory accomplished his greatest feat versus Yale's primary enemy, Harvard.

Yale traveled to Harvard Stadium in 1923 for one of the rivalry's most memorable games. The Bulldogs hadn't scored a touchdown in Cambridge for sixteen years, but Mallory had no intention of graduating winless versus Harvard. He would have an uphill battle. The stadium could have served as the venue for the Harvard-Yale crew race on game day. Torrential rains formed two-inch-deep puddles on the muddy turf. Players lost their footing easily, slipping and sliding all over the field. The officials carried towels so players could wipe mud from their eyes between plays, and the pigskin may as well have been slathered with grease. Mallory didn't care. He kicked field goals from the twenty-four and twenty-nine-yard lines, and he provided critical blocks on teammate Ducky Pond's seventy-four-yard touchdown romp, the touchdown that ended Yale's long end zone drought at Cambridge. Mallory also kicked the extra point in the stadium slop.

The former Yale captain and Skull and Bones member entered the College Football Hall of Fame in 1964 along with Army coaching legend Earl "Red" Blaik and SMU all-time great Kyle Rote (later a New York Giants quarterback). Nonetheless, none of Mallory's All-American and Hall of Fame football exploits compared to his contributions to the Allied cause in World War II.

In May 1942, at the age of forty, Mallory entered the military as a captain. Well beyond drafting age, Mallory joined the cause simply because he wanted to. As a member of the Army Air Corps, Mallory was serving as an intelligence officer with the Tactical Air Force in Italy in 1944 when he conceived a brilliant plan to choke the German lines of communication. He called it "Operation Mallory Major."

The captain displayed a tremendous aptitude for selecting appropriate bombing targets that would hamper German military movement and disrupt their supply lines. After success in impeding German progress in central Italy, Mallory studied maps and gathered information about targets along the Po River. Mallory believed that the Allies could sever German communications with a steady bombing campaign on bridges spanning the Po at intervals along an eighty-five-mile stretch of the river.

Mallory examined the targets and compiled detailed information about each of them. He factored in the terrain and logistics of bombing the bridges, and he contemplated the impact his plot would have on the enemy. After exhaustive research and careful planning, Mallory delivered his plan to his superiors. They agreed with Mallory's plan and, under Mallory's close supervision, made preparations to carry it out.

On July 12, 1944, Operation Mallory began. For seventy hours Allied planes set their sights on twenty-four bridges the Germans used to cross the Po River. Over the course of three days bombs rained on the targets Mallory had selected. When the dust settled, twenty-two of the twenty-four bridges had either been completely destroyed or rendered unusable. The flawless execution of Operation Mallory produced exactly the results Mallory envisioned. With enemy communication severed and transportation paralyzed, the Allies were able to progress steadily toward Rome. Mallory, by then a major, earned the military's Legion of Merit for his ingenuity.

According to the executive order that established the award, the Legion of Merit "is awarded at the direction of the President to members of the United States armed forces . . . who have distinguished themselves by exceptionally meritorious conduct in the performance of outstanding service." Mallory undoubtedly deserved it.

On February 19, 1945, Mallory boarded a plane in Italy for a flight home. If he had his choice, Mallory likely would have remained an intelligence officer in the military, but army regulations required for him to be discharged. At forty-two, Mallory was deemed too old. A hero's welcome awaited him in Memphis, but Mallory never made it. The plane crashed on takeoff, killing Mallory and nine others.

Memphis lost one of its favorite sons, a local boy who made good and who never forgot from where he came. The town would always remember him as a savvy businessman and a generous civic leader. Soldiers grieved for a brilliant military strategist and selfless officer. Yale reflected on one of its all-time football greats, a consummate leader and fearless football player who Walter Camp once called "the greatest defensive fullback in the history of the game." Mallory's family lost a devoted husband and proud father. No matter which part of Mallory a person knew, the man clearly affected many lives.

Testaments to Mallory today stand in several places around the country. In August 1945, the Tennessee State Department of the Veterans of Foreign Wars established the William Neely Mallory Post 2120. In August 1949, the air force renamed the 830th Air Force Specialized Depot in Memphis in Mallory's honor. Rhodes College (formerly called Southwestern) in Memphis dedicated the Mallory

Gymnasium on December 10, 1954. Eight years later Pomfret School in Pomfret, Connecticut, dedicated Mallory Field, an athletic field big enough for two gridirons. Despite all the places named after Mallory his son, William Neely Mallory Jr., discovered just how prominent his father was at Yale nearly thirty years after Mallory last suited up for the Bulldogs.

"Unpacking my luggage in my room on Yale's Old Campus in September 1951, I discovered I had brought no handkerchiefs from Memphis," Mallory recalled. "I walked out of the south end of the Old Campus and saw across the street a men's clothing store named White's. I entered and asked a salesman to see the handkerchiefs." Mallory quickly picked out a half dozen. The salesman asked him how he'd like to pay for them. Since Mallory had always charged his clothing to a family account in Memphis, he responded, "Please charge it." But this wasn't Memphis.

"Do you have an account?" the salesman asked.

Before Mallory could answer, a man in his mid-fifties appeared from the store's back room and approached the student and the salesman. "I know who you are. Aren't you from Memphis?" he asked.

"Yes," said Mallory.

"You look so much like your father I would know you anywhere. You're Neely Mallory, Junior. My name is White," said the store owner, extending his hand. "I knew your dad and saw him play many times. The 1923 team was the best in history and Mal was the best defensive back to play for Yale."

White opened Mallory's charge account on the spot.

"On and on he went about the exploits of the 1923 team and my father," Mallory recalled. "I was simply amazed to hear Mr. White talk in such glowing terms about him. I knew he was captain of the 1923 team and an All-American, but thirty years later? This visit with Mr. White was the first real inkling I had of how great a player my father was and the lasting impact he had on the Yale fans that saw him play."

Heroes tend to rise during times of utmost adversity, and few situations are more adverse than the daily life-and-death struggle that accompanies war. Mallory, like many other former Harvard and Yale players who went on to fight for their country, earned the label of "hero" while battling enemies on foreign soil. In 1947, Harvard player Chet Pierce battled a domestic foe and took a step toward defeating it by simply setting foot on a football field.

🏈   🏈   🏈

Pierce entered Harvard in 1944. At 6'4" and 230 pounds, the seventeen-year-old freshman commanded attention when he trotted onto the stadium turf for his first varsity football game. People didn't notice Pierce because of his size, strength, or speed. They noticed that he was black. The only black player on the team. Pierce heard a single racial slur when he debuted, the only time he remembered an openly racist remark at Harvard. For the four years Pierce started at tackle he remained the only black player on the Crimson football team.

A quiet, studious man, Pierce shunned the spotlight. He didn't want to be held up as an example or viewed as an oddity because of his skin color. He couldn't ignore the fact that he'd be treated differently, but for the most part he just wanted to be left alone to study. He came to Harvard to fulfill his dream of one day becoming a doctor, not to break ground in the fight for racial equality. In the spring of 1947, when a classmate told Pierce about the serving policies of a Cambridge bar, however, Pierce took a stand.

"Well, there was somebody I knew who worked for the *Crimson,* and he was seeing a waitress at a bar which no longer exists," Pierce recalled. "This place, she mentioned to him casually one night that they didn't serve Negroes. He got irate and called me and asked me what I was going to do about it."

Pierce rounded up a group of friends and headed to Club 100 just off Harvard Square. Pierce's party included one other black student, Hallowell Bowser. The white students entered without incident, but when Pierce and Bowser reached the door the club's owner, John Jarvis, intercepted them. Jarvis asked for their membership cards.

"The deal was, you were supposed to be a member to get in. You had to have a membership card," Pierce said. "But, of course, that was just a pretense."

Bowser remarked that none of the other students had cards. Jarvis replied, "I'm not worried about them. It's you two I'm talking to." Two white students in Pierce's group argued with Jarvis, but the club owner wouldn't yield. Pierce and Bowser left without incident. This time. They weren't through with Jarvis and Club 100.

Pierce and Bowser complained to Harvard's student council about the business's practices. But Club 100 wasn't a Harvard entity, so the student government didn't have any power over its policies. That didn't mean they couldn't do anything, though. Based on Pierce's account of the incident, the students knew that Jarvis couldn't be swayed with arguments in favor of racial equality and harmony. They hit the club owner where it would hurt him most—in the wallet.

Jarvis's Club 100 thrived on steady income from thirsty Harvard students looking to blow off a little steam. A bar within walking distance of a college was a cash cow for the stubborn owner. The student council organized an immediate and boisterous boycott. If Jarvis didn't want Harvard's minority students in his place, he'd have to get along without the rest of them. The news of the boycott spread like wildfire and soon landed in Boston's newspapers. National wire services picked up the story soon after.

Jarvis didn't bend under the pressure of the negative press, thinking he'd weather the storm until it blew over. The students leaned harder on him, organizing picket lines and leaflet campaigns. The Cambridge Civic Unity Association spoke in support of the boycott. Not a single student wanted Harvard's spring break to arrive sooner than Jarvis did. With the students away for a while, he thought he would resume his business undeterred. To Jarvis's dismay, though, many students skipped vacation and stayed in Cambridge to continue protesting Club 100. With no classes scheduled, the students had plenty of time on their hands, and they devoted much of it to vocal protests of Jarvis's business.

Three weeks after Pierce gathered his friends to bring Club 100's prejudices to light, Jarvis finally conceded. He signed a statement agreeing to admit patrons regardless of race, creed, or color. The Club 100 boycott, started by Pierce's unwillingness to accept a bar owner's intolerant admittance policy, ended as one of the first Harvard demonstrations protesting racial inequality. Pierce's actions meant that he, Bowser, and any other minority could belly up to Club 100's bar without a fictional membership card. Pierce wasn't interested, though. He didn't drink anyway.

Pierce may have started the whole affair by forcing Jarvis to enforce his unwritten patronage policy, but he stayed in the background as the protest grew. The next time Pierce stared down racism, in the fall of 1947, he couldn't avoid the spotlight.

Harvard had scheduled the University of Virginia for a game during the 1947 football season. The venue was Charlottesville, which posed a problem. University of Virginia officials contacted Harvard athletic director Bill Bingham, attempting to diffuse a potentially volatile situation. While they welcomed the opportunity to face one of the nation's great football schools, Virginia officials preferred that Harvard leave Pierce in Cambridge. The request infuriated Bingham. Not only would Harvard bring Pierce, Bingham planned on joining the team for the trip. If things got ugly, Bingham wanted to be there. Pierce's presence as a black player squaring off against an all-white team at an all-white college in the segregationist South could turn a crowd ugly at the least, riotous at the worst.

While college officials from Virginia and Harvard argued about Pierce making the trip below the Mason-Dixon line, the football players had already discussed the matter. During the summer before the 1947 season began, some of the older Harvard players had written to Virginia's captain, Larry Baumann. They told him that Pierce would be lining up against Virginia. Harvard wouldn't play without him. The Virginia players voted and decided that the fame their team would gain by playing and possibly beating Harvard, then one of college football's premier teams, outweighed the consequences of allowing a black player on their home field. The vote was unanimous. Bring on Pierce.

Virginia officials finally relented and agreed with their team.

The Crimson band played boisterously and a crowd of well-wishers cheered the Harvard players when the team boarded a train destined for Virginia. The reception upon the team's arrival was significantly frostier.

Virginia officials acquiesced in letting Pierce take the field, but they weren't about to let one Harvard football player completely overturn the manner in which blacks were treated in the South. The hosts made thinly veiled attempts to provide Pierce with separate-but-equal accommodations that kept him out of all-white premises. "The Virginia people were going to put the team at a Charlottesville hotel. All except me. They were going to give me a whole mansion behind the hotel so nobody could say I didn't have a nice place to stay," Pierce said.

Harvard coach Dick Harlow didn't accept such treatment. "Fine," the coach said, "we'll put our first twenty-two players in there." When the team went to dinner they found that Virginia had arranged a private dining room for the visitors. Pierce could eat with the rest of the team, but he had to enter through a rear door and meet the team in the dining room. "We'll all use the same door that Chester uses," Harlow said.

"And we did. Together. As a team," Pierce recalled. Harlow worked hard to put Pierce at ease, and so did the rest of the team.

While Pierce studied in his room, teammate Wally Flynn went out for a while. He returned with the game program for the next day. Flynn wanted to show Pierce the player profiles. "Not to worry, Chester," Flynn said. "Look at those guys. They're all from Pennsylvania and won't care what color you are." Flynn had also spoken with Baumann, Virginia's captain. Baumann and Flynn had served together in the navy, and Baumann assured him that there wouldn't be any trouble on the field.

The coaches and players did all they could to assure Pierce that he needn't be nervous, but nothing could have prepared the players for what they saw when the team buses pulled into the parking lot at Virginia's stadium. Men on horseback circled the buses waving Confederate flags and whooping rebel yells. The hostile crowd shouted racial slurs at the "damn Yankees" as the Harvard team made its way to the locker room. The crowd concerned Harlow. These people would be in the stands shortly.

Harlow addressed Pierce specifically during his pregame speech and amplified the magnitude of the historic event. Before the team took the field Harlow pulled Pierce aside. " 'You're going on the field with me,' " Pierce recalled Harlow saying. "He got on my inside, closest to the stands. I assumed it was in case any bottles or whatever were thrown at me. A very nice gesture by the coach."

No one in the crowd of twenty-two thousand threw anything at Pierce, but they let him know what they thought about him playing on their home turf. A steady stream of racist remarks poured from the stands. Spectators waved Confederate flags proudly—shops in Charlottesville sold out of the flags a week before the game as Virginia fans readied for Harvard's invasion. As the players promised, though, they treated Pierce like any other Harvard player on the field. Of course, that still wasn't necessarily a good thing for Pierce.

Virginia destroyed the Crimson. They pushed Harvard all over the field and scored at will. Virginia fans gradually turned their attention away from Pierce and from what his presence on Virginia's field meant. The Cavaliers' 47–0 win demonstrated that the school deserved to play against the nation's best teams, and that turned a sour crowd into a joyous one. When Pierce left with an injury late in the game, the fans actually cheered for him. Pierce's historic presence in Charlottesville became a footnote to a game Virginia won convincingly.

Pierce put the game behind him, shrugging off the racial comments and forgetting about the way he was treated. Pierce played against Virginia because he loved playing football and because Harvard scheduled the game. The fact that his appearance made inroads to racial equality on the football field mattered to Pierce, but he certainly didn't want people to remember his football career for the Harvard-Virginia game. A 47–0 loss wasn't a worthy legacy.

The 1946 Harvard-Yale game in which he played, however, was.

*   *   *

The return of the greatest generation prompted a football resurgence at both Harvard and Yale. The Allied forces had won and Americans reaped the benefits in a far more affluent postwar country. To the victors belonged the spoils. A sense of entitlement emerged in the average citizen. The opportunity to own cars, homes, and televisions didn't belong solely to the wealthy members of American society anymore. The prosperous environment also affected another area previously reserved for the privileged, as the GI Bill opened doors at campuses nationwide, including those of Harvard and Yale.

For the first time admissions became an issue. The demand for enrollment suddenly exceeded the number of students that each institution normally accommodated. Students from Choate, Andover, and Groton couldn't count on a guaranteed trip down the well-worn path from prep schools to the Ivies. Under the GI Bill's new guidelines the admissions departments at Ivy League campuses rushed to adjust entrance factors and requirements amid a flood of applications from the brightest public school graduates across the nation. More families could afford college tuition in the wake of World War II than ever before, and that led to a more diverse student body.

The 1946 Harvard team featured the most eclectic cast of characters that had ever put on the Crimson jersey, many of them heroes from the war. Tackle Vince Moravec saved a dozen of his fellow crew members after the ship on which he served had been torpedoed. Moravec earned the Congressional Medal of Honor for his feat, but he refused it. In his mind he'd simply done his duty. To honor him more than any other soldier wouldn't be fair. There was end Bob Drennan, a member of Patton's Third Army during its triumphant sweep across France. He was one of the first Americans at the liberation of Auschwitz, one of the most notorious Nazi concentration camps. Before back Tom "Chip" Gannon starred in three different sports at Harvard he earned recognition from the Army Air Corps as a decorated B-17 pilot. Back Kenny O'Donnell navigated a B-17 that was shot down over Germany. O'Donnell, who somehow miraculously made it back to Allied lines, later gained greater fame as the White House chief of staff to JFK, whose brother Robert tenaciously played end in the 1946 Yale game.

Along with the many battle-hardened World War II veterans, the team included a few holdovers from the informal Harvard teams that played during the war in 1943 and 1944, and some college youngsters fresh out of private and public high schools. The odd mix of players created a complicated situation for Harvard coach Dick Harlow to manage.

Coach Harlow had served his country in both world wars. As a young man of twenty-eight, he had been a first lieutenant in the infantry during the Great War. At age fifty-three in 1942, Harlow fought as a commissioned lieutenant commander in the navy. He became seriously ill at Midway Island, losing fifty pounds and spending several months confined to the infirmary. The Dick Harlow who returned to coach at postwar Harvard at age fifty-six was a shell of the man that the Crimson had hired a decade earlier to awaken them from the malaise of the 1932–1934 seasons, the first non-Harvard man to guide the program and the man who had snubbed seventeen other college coaching offers to take the Harvard job.

Harlow could not draw on his wartime experience as a means to impress and inspire his team in 1946. Many of his new players had seen and been through worse than he had. In addition, Harlow's postwar charges consisted of many GIs that had learned football before the war at other schools. The old-college-spirit approach to teaching the game, the one Harlow was always most comfortable with, didn't suit them. Despite these negative factors, the older, physically stronger, well-conditioned squad possessed perhaps more pure talent than any Harvard team before or since.

Harlow's health and communication problems couldn't prevent the talented Harvard eleven from their most successful campaign since Barry Wood's final season fifteen years earlier. A 13–12 win at Princeton highlighted the Crimson's 7–1 record. In the first game with the Tigers since 1942, freshman halfback Gannon dashed sixty-six yards for a touchdown that keyed a dramatic victory. Going into the Yale game, Harvard had one blemish: its loss to Rutgers.

The postwar influx of veterans didn't hurt Yale's team either.

Yale boasted a particularly formidable team. A number of veterans who attended Yale prior to the war included tackle John Prchlik, a gunnery officer; center Swede Larson, a former Marine; tackle Cotty Davison of the Army Air Force; end Dick Jenkins, a heavily decorated infantryman; end Vincent Lynch, an honored Navy pilot from the Pacific; and John Ferguson, an Army lieutenant involved with the investigation of Japanese war atrocities.

Two other players arrived at Yale via strangely coincidental routes. Fritz Barzilauskas, a guard at Holy Cross College, transferred to Yale after the war. A B-26 pilot and Army Air Force lieutentant, Barzilauskas survived a German POW camp after being shot down—valiant war story, but one shared by one of his new teammates. Tackle Bill Schuler transferred to Yale from Auburn. Also a B-26 pilot, he lived through a plane crash brought on by enemy fire. Like Barzilauskas, Schuler endured a German POW camp as well. (To top it all off, both men went on to play in the NFL, Barzilauskas with the Boston Yanks and Schuler with the New York Giants.)

In addition to those familiar with Yale football, several outstanding war veterans new to the Eli program arrived in New Haven. Three of these players in particular defined Yale's offense. Robert "Tex" Furse, who had spent the three previous years in the Army Air Corps, gave the Bulldogs a T-formation quarterback with excellent passing accuracy. Ferd Nadherny at fullback had the combination of power to run inside and the speed to run outside and catch the ball out of the backfield. The third addition was the most significant of all, from a social as well as an athletic standpoint. Levi Jackson became the first black player in Yale football history.

A New Haven native like Walter Camp, Jackson had attended Hillhouse High School. An outstanding all-around prep athlete, he turned down several scholarship offers and a professional football contract offer from the New York Giants. He instead opted for the service. At Camp Lee in Virginia, Jackson had won the acceptance of a base made up almost entirely of white southerners. He had been carried off the field after leading his Lee team to a victory over a rival base, a significant accomplishment for a third-generation descendant of slaves. His admittance to Yale was momentous. Jackson was one of only three blacks in a school population of 850 students.

The 1946 Yale team stumbled only once leading up to the Harvard game, a 28–20 loss to Cornell in a game that featured an electrifying eighty-four-yard kickoff run by Jackson. Nicknamed the Ebony Express, Jackson drew comparisons to his boyhood idol Clint Frank, the second of Yale's two Heisman Trophy winners.

The 1946 teams at both Harvard and Yale hummed along like two powerful locomotives on parallel tracks that eventually merged for one fateful clash that recaptured the imagination of the postwar sporting public. The matchup between two sensational freshmen backs, Yale's Jackson and Harvard's Gannon, provided just one of the subplots to the epic story set to unfold at the stadium.

The success of the two squads rekindled the football spirit at both Cambridge and New Haven. The Eli band serenaded the team and a large gathering of students cheered for the players at Yale's final practice before embarking on a Boston-bound train for the game. At a Harvard pregame rally flames from bonfires illuminated the night sky, an all-too-real wartime reminder for some, as the band rang out some familiar marches. Harvard hadn't sold out the stadium for nearly a decade, since fifty-seven thousand people came to watch Heisman Trophy winner Clint Frank in 1937. But the 1946 crowd would be even larger. The Harvard ticket office returned nearly a hundred thousand dollars received for ticket requests that they couldn't fill.

Game day dawned bright but bitterly cold, with a nearly gale force wind whipping from the south. Undeterred fans hit up scalpers for tickets. The scalpers happily obliged, getting as much as eighty dollars for a pair of tickets valued at eight.

Harvard won the toss and took advantage of the situation at the outset. With the first-quarter wind at their backs, the Crimson promptly marched fifty-five yards, Chip Gannon carrying the final two yards into the end zone for the game's first touchdown. Emil Drvaric booted the conversion. Harvard, the ten-point underdog, led 7–0.

The Crimson's first quarter onslaught had just begun. Gannon, a southpaw slinger, then took to the air. From the Harvard forty-three-yard line Gannon began the next drive with a forty-seven-yard completion to end Johnny Fiorentino. From the Yale ten-yard line Gannon tossed to his other end, Wally Flynn. Flynn made the catch at the six and eluded Jackson, a safety on Yale's defense, and crossed the goal line. Drvaric again converted the extra point. Harvard 14, Yale 0. The Harvard fans screamed and danced in the stands while the Yale side sat still in stunned silence.

The ever-innovative Harlow had devised a new formation especially for the Yale game that he called "Triple Wing." It totally befuddled the Yale defense. The strong winds knocked out Yale's telephone connection in the press box, complicating matters for the Bulldogs. The Yale coaching staff had no way to relay adjustment instructions from its perch high above the stadium. The period was almost over before a courier with the press-box spotter's counterplan could provide Coach Howard Odell with any updated intelligence.

Yale enjoyed the wind at their backs after the second quarter swap of goals. The Elis' first possession began with Jackson catching a Harvard punt one-handed. His eleven-yard return from midfield set the Bulldogs first and ten at the Harvard thirty-nine-yard line. The Eli line—massive for its time, averaging 206 pounds per man—took control as consecutive totes by Art Fitzgerald, Ferd Nadherny, and Jackson positioned the ball at the seventeen-yard line. Not to be outdone by Gannon, his brilliant freshman counterpart on the Harvard side, Jackson exhibited his double-threat prowess by faking an end run, stopping, and heaving a pass to Fitzgerald, alone in the end zone. A botched snap on the conversion attempt kept the score at 14–6.

Quarterback Tex Furse led Yale's next scoring drive, a fifty-yard march to the end zone. Two passes to end Jack Roderick quickly moved the Bulldogs halfway to the Harvard goal line. Respectful of the pass, Harlow's defensive alignment became more susceptible to the run. Yale took advantage as two Jackson carries set up a line smash by Nadherny, who crashed in from nine yards out for the second Yale touchdown. A successful point after cut the Harvard lead to 14–13 at halftime.

As the second half began, the wind, and with it all the momentum, remained at the backs of the Eli team. Moments after the third quarter started, Furse and Roderick hooked up for a thirty-seven-yard touchdown pass. Roderick made the catch at the twenty-eight and hugged the sideline all the way to the end zone to give Yale its first lead of the day, 20–14 after a successful extra point kick. Yale wasn't through.

The Bulldogs again demonstrated their offensive versatility as Nadherny busted a twenty-yard run to set up his second touchdown jaunt, this time from the five-yard line. The point after set the score at Yale 27, Harvard 14. Not even the wind helped Harvard in the fourth quarter. Though Yale didn't score again, neither did the Crimson. Yale dominated the rest of the game and won 27–14. For the first time in sixty-three Harvard-Yale contests, the team that scored the first touchdown lost.

*   *   *

Fifty-six years later, Coach Siedlecki dreamed of his Bulldogs pulling off such a victory. It wasn't impossible—the very existence of so many classic contests in the annals of The Game revealed how the powerful urge to best an ancient rival and uphold a mighty legacy could permeate even the shakiest of teams and inspire an outrageous win. His players certainly had plenty of predecessors to emulate.

And November was two long months away. A lot could happen during the Ivy League season.

The Father and His Sons

THE ANCIENT EIGHT. The very name suggests timeworn majesty, classical exclusivity, and a disdainful indifference toward change of any kind. It should come as no surprise, then, that the Ancient Eight of the Ivy League have held fast to the ideals of their founders, even in regard to the football schedule. The schedule has remained a model of consistency since the Ivy League began in 1956: it starts on the third Saturday in September and ends on the Saturday before Thanksgiving, with the Ivy League teams playing one another in the same order each year. Each team plays three nonleague opponents each year, usually during the first four weeks of the schedule, and none of those nonleague games have any bearing on the Ivy League championship.

Such a short season would seem to leave precious little room for error, but it actually provides a key safety valve. Most Division I-A schools begin angling for a bowl game from the season-opening kickoff, and every win is critical. But Ivy League teams don't compete for bowl bids, only for the Ivy championship. So all those nonleague games truly are tune-up sessions. Murphy and Siedlecki would get the chance to closely evaluate their team's game readiness and tweak problems before facing the meat of the Ivy League.

There is a slight drawback to this plan—one Tim Murphy felt acutely heading into the season opener on September 21, 2002.

Every other college football conference in the nation abandoned the one-time customary start to which the Ivy League had upheld, and by this point in September nearly every team had two games under its belt. This included the College of the Holy Cross in nearby Worcester, Massachusetts, Harvard's first opponent of 2002. Ranked twenty-third nationally in Division I-AA and with two games—both wins—to its credit, Holy Cross could snap Harvard's eleven-game winning streak and kill the Crimson momentum before the Ivy League title defense even started.

Murphy knew the danger Holy Cross represented, especially its star wide receiver, Ari Confesor. In the Crusaders' season opener versus Army, Confesor racked up an incredible 321 all-purpose yards, including a 95-yard kickoff return for a touchdown. Georgetown somehow managed to hold Confesor to 173 overall yards in the Crusaders' rout of the Bulldogs the following week. Quite simply, Murphy's defense needed to contain Confesor in order to win.

The offense would help matters somewhat. In Carl Morris, the Crimson had its own dominant wide receiver, and Murphy hoped that Morris would be working extra hard. After the star's epic performance during the Penn game in 2001, the speculation on his NFL potential took on a life of its own, heating up as the 2001 Ivy League Player of the Year opened his senior season against the Crusaders. "I did feel the added pressure of the high billings and expectations that were placed on me going into my senior year, but I still felt very confident because of the amount of work that I had put into improving myself and my team," Morris said. "I spent the summer working out with our strength coaches, Coach Hayes and Coach Nash, and I felt they got me and my teammates in the best shape we'd ever been in." The pro scouts were watching. Morris knew it, Murphy knew it, and Holy Cross wished that Morris would crack under the pressure.

Wish denied.

The receiver picked up right where he left off, thrilling the Harvard Stadium crowd and demolishing the Crusaders. More than ten thousand witnesses saw Morris catch eleven passes for 210 yards, the third-highest single-game total in school history. He converted two passes into touchdowns, one of them his fifth touchdown catch over 60 yards in his career. On a critical third down situation late in the game, he lined up in the backfield and took a direct snap. He scampered 9 yards for a first down and kept Confesor and Holy Cross from staging a comeback. Not simply a receiving machine, Morris gave the NFL scouts a taste of his toughness and versatility when he unleashed a devastating block on a Holy Cross linebacker, leaving the unfortunate defender pancaked on the field to the cheers of the Harvard faithful.

Not to be outdone by his favorite target, Neil Rose had an outstanding day at quarterback. Nineteen of his twenty-two pass attempts found their mark, three resulting in touchdowns and only one in an interception. Despite the turnover, Rose otherwise smoothly controlled the offense to a 28–10 lead by the third quarter. The Morris-Rose combination, still potent after several dormant months, was packing its usual one-two punch. Murphy exploited Holy Cross's wariness of the dynamic duo with a 34-yard halfback option pass from Rodney Byrnes to a wide-open Morris on Morris's second touchdown of the day. Rose and Morris were on the verge of running the field all day, but a high hit from Holy Cross's Andy Ackermann knocked the quarterback out of the game in the third quarter. Fearing that his starter had a concussion, Murphy sent sophomore backup Ryan Fitzpatrick in to close out the contest.

Fitzpatrick, a slightly shy, clean-cut player, looked young enough to still be a student at Highland Park High School in Mesa, Arizona. Like some of the other players on his prep team, during his junior and senior years there he'd received recruiting letters from PAC 10 schools. None of them followed up with any serious scholarship offers, though, so Fitzpatrick looked deeper into the mail pile, where he found letters from some Ivies. It was a good thing the Ivy League sought out the rangy 6'3" sophomore because he never would have looked to play football there. "I didn't even know they played football at Ivy League schools until I started getting letters," Fitzpatrick confessed.

Curious, he began to follow the Ivy League games in the newspaper box scores. As a quarterback, Fitzpatrick was impressed by the high-scoring offenses. Ivy quarterbacks seemed to throw a lot of touchdown passes. Perhaps it was time to make his first trip to the East Coast.

Fitzpatrick visited Yale and Dartmouth unofficially with his father the summer between his junior and senior years in high school. After having researched the background of Ivy League football, the Yale Bowl amazed him. "It was an awesome sight. So rich in tradition and history," he said.

Fitzpatrick and his parents also visited Boston, designating Harvard as one of his official recruiting trips. They went in December, and the kid from the desert got a taste of New England winters. Big, white drifts piling up in Harvard Stadium, sleet sliding under the rental car. The snow not only introduced him to a new climate, it also helped ease his worries about what kind of people went to Harvard. The kind that started big snowball fights with passing tour groups. Maybe these people weren't so stiff after all.

"I had a lot of questions. Would I fit in? Would I be able to talk to these guys?" Fitzpatrick said. "It's *Harvard!*" Meeting the players and coaches erased any doubt that he would enjoy four years in Cambridge. Harvard player and fellow Arizonan Ryan Dickerson made the senior even more comfortable. "He calmed my fears about the weather and my ability to adjust to it on the field," Fitzpatrick said.

And there was that Ivy emphasis on offense that had piqued his curiosity. During the visit Harvard's offensive coach Jay Mills reviewed the complex, impressive schemes, thrilling Fitzpatrick. The Crimson depended on its quarterback to make a lot of decisions, a component that Fitzpatrick thrived on. He was hooked.

Fitzpatrick also made an official visit to Princeton with his father and a friend from a rival high school, but it didn't feel as right. "Something was missing. Harvard seemed to have it all," he said.

Harvard it was.

Fitzpatrick made an immediate impact when he arrived in Cambridge for his first season in 2001. He worked his way up to the number two quarterback spot as a freshman, playing behind Neil Rose, and when Rose got injured he started his first game against Dartmouth. Fitzpatrick wasted no time getting his name into the record books.

Dartmouth led 21–0 at the half and it looked like Harvard's shot at an undefeated season was over. Unwilling to leave his first start as the losing quarterback, Fitzpatrick went to work. In the second half, the freshman methodically erased the deficit and brought Harvard all the way to a 31–21 victory. Fitzpatrick had engineered the biggest come-from-behind win in the 1,149 game history of Harvard football. Not a bad way to prove yourself to the coach.

Murphy needed Fitzpatrick again versus Holy Cross, this time to preserve a win. Not a big deal for Fitzpatrick after what he did against the Big Green in 2001. After all, the Crimson had an eighteen-point lead.

In the fourth quarter, Confesor capitalized on a chink in the Crimson armor. Rose and Murphy watched on the sidelines as the Crusader hauled in a twenty-four-yard touchdown pass from Brian Hall to cut the lead to 28–17. Four minutes later, Harvard needed to punt on fourth down.

"As God is my word," said Harvard coach Tim Murphy at the press conference after the game, "I told our punter, 'Do not kick the ball to [Confesor]. Do not even think about it.'"

The punter did not obey.

Confesor took the ball the distance, tying a Holy Cross record with the eighty-five-yard return. The score remained 28–23 after a failed two-point conversion, but the momentum heavily favored Holy Cross.

The Crusader defense smelled blood, but Fitzpatrick and the Harvard offense fought them off and converted three third-down situations into first and ten. With no timeouts remaining and under two minutes on the clock, Fitzpatrick calmly iced the victory with a nine-yard sprint to Holy Cross's seven-yard line. His first down allowed Harvard to keep possession and run out the clock on the last four plays.

Minus the punting gaffe, Murphy couldn't have been more pleased. The Crimson defeated an unbeaten team that was in mid-season form, and not with a one-trick-pony offense, either. Though Rose and Morris provided the bulk of the firepower, Nick Palazzo and Rodney Thomas chipped in on the ground with over sixty yards rushing apiece. Rodney Byrnes collected six passes for forty-three yards and a touchdown in addition to his wobbly pass to Morris for a score. Fitzpatrick completed only two passes on two attempts, but he could run—and not like a typical quarterback. He tucked the ball deep, clamping it fiercely into the crook of his arm. He followed blocks and juked defenders with quick cutbacks and sidesteps. Most important, though, Fitzpatrick showed Murphy that he could rely on him as another offensive element.

* * *

While the Crimson fought the invading Crusaders in Cambridge, the battle of the bulls unfolded in the Yale Bowl. The University of San Diego Toreros trekked across the country to take on Siedlecki's Yale Bulldogs for the second time in history. San Diego hoped to avenge a 17–6 home loss to Yale in 1999. While most Ivy League schools choose Patriot League foes for the first game of the season, Yale keeps things fresh by playing more obscure schools. Siedlecki tries to pick an opponent that will give the team a chance to travel outside the normal realm of the Northeast, enabling Yale to promote its program to a different audience. Unless a recruit in California travels to Ivy League country, he probably won't see the Bulldogs in action. Splitting a two-game series with teams like San Diego lets Siedlecki showcase Yale's talented players. Many of them could play football at the national Division I-A level, but choose to go for the best education possible over playing on the best football team possible.

Exposing the Bulldogs to like-minded prep talent is key to reloading the team for next year.

San Diego arrived with a 1–1 record, each game with decidedly lopsided results. The Toreros lost to Azusa Pacific in the opening game 41–25, and turned the tables on the University of Laverne with a 39–8 victory in which quarterback Eric Rasmussen completed nine of eleven pass attempts for 299 yards and four touchdowns.

Despite the brief history between the teams, Siedlecki believed he knew what his team would face. San Diego had a 250-pound battering ram of a fullback who forced a respect for the running game, and the team also threw the ball very well with a wide-open offensive style. With the weekly challenges upcoming in the pass-oriented Ivy League, San Diego appeared to be a good test for a Yale secondary hit hard by preseason injuries. A pair of Yale's experienced cornerbacks, Steve Ehikian and William Jacobs, were starting the season on the bench, riding out their injuries. Along with the experienced Barton Simmons, the relatively untested tandem of junior Greg Owens and sophomore James Beck rounded out Rick Flanders's pass defense for Yale's opener.

Yale quarterback Alvin Cowan remained the key question on offense. Cowan celebrated his twenty-first birthday the day before the Bulldogs' season opener, secure in the knowledge that in his third season on the Yale campus, his moment had arrived. Siedlecki had named him the Eli starting quarterback over sophomore Jeff Mroz. While scrimmaging against Union College in early September, Cowan impressed Siedlecki by completing twelve of eighteen passes for 192 yards and two touchdowns and by exhibiting a flair for leading the team. Siedlecki knew the Bulldogs needed to believe in their quarterback in order to finish higher than Yale's predicted sixth-place slot. The belief might be there, but the experience wasn't— Cowan had only taken a few snaps at the varsity level.

Cowan, however, didn't have a shred of anxiety or doubt, satisfied with his sure-handed receivers, an experienced and talented offensive line anchored by senior center David Farrell, and running back

Robert Carr in the backfield. The self-assured junior believed all along that this offense was his, even in the midst of preseason competition with sophomore Jeff Mroz. "I'm pretty confident in what I can do and what the guys around me can do," Cowan said with just a hint of Texas drawl.

This proved to be quite an understatement.

In only its second game against the Bulldogs, the San Diego Toreros landed in Yale's record books. Unfortunately for the visitors, they became a footnote forever linked with the most miraculous quarterback debut in school history. During the 49–14 trouncing Cowan decimated the San Diego defense. He shredded them in the air with eighteen of twenty-two passes completed for 283 yards and three touchdowns. He chewed up a league-high 114 yards of turf and crossed the goal line on foot three times. Six touchdowns, a new Yale record. "When you consider he had never taken a varsity snap, I cannot recall anyone having a better performance in a first game," Carm Cozza noted in his color commentary.

Siedlecki had chosen wisely. The Ivy League took notice—Cowan earned Player of the Week honors for his record-breaking performance. The Bulldogs might be a legitimate threat, and not just because of Cowan. Tight end Nate Lawrie caught eight passes for 155 yards and a score. Robert Carr rushed for 104 yards. The Ivy League chose running back David Knox as its Rookie of the Week for his 62 yards on eight carries.

Cowan's accolades didn't stop at Ivy League headquarters. In the next week's issue of *Sports Illustrated,* Cowan appeared in the "Faces in the Crowd" feature. The Yale quarterback beamed at the sight. Many athletes dreamed of it, but few saw their image in the world's most widely read sports magazine. Though thrilled by the results of his first game, Cowan remained humble. "You really can't take credit for something like that," Cowan said. "The guys that were surrounding me were making plays as well. Obviously, as the quarterback you get all the credit but it's not all that hard to find receivers when the guys on the offensive line were giving me all the time in the world to make these passes."

Meanwhile, the Yale defense submitted a dominant performance of its own, notching four sacks, ten tackles for a loss, two forced fumbles, and keeping the beleaguered Toreros to 255 yards of total offense. Jason Lange and company held San Diego's fullback to a scant 79 yards rushing on twenty-four carries, stuffing the running game, and Flanders's charges also showed promise against the pass.

"Obviously, I've never started another game against another Ivy League team but if we come together, I think it's realistic for us to win the Ivy championship," Cowan said, exuding confidence in the surprising Bulldogs, now an outside contender. The fortunes of the 2002 Yale team suddenly seemed as big as Texas.

Siedlecki had gotten the unimaginable out of the players he had, but such feats were simply expected at Yale. Siedlecki's ability to convert sound coaching decisions into wins played a major part in his receiving the coveted head coaching position at the school that pioneered football.

Siedlecki had some sizable shoes to fill and a substantial legacy to live up to when he became the thirty-second coach in the storied annals of Yale football on December 19, 1996. Not only was he succeeding Carm Cozza—the winningest coach in Ivy League football history, a coach who remained on the Yale campus—he was stepping onto a downhill slope. The Bulldogs had slumped to a 13–27 record during the previous four seasons, including two straight losses to Harvard. Both old Blue and young were in agreement when Cozza left: whoever took over would be well advised to turn around Eli fortunes quickly. And, if he planned on staying, beat Harvard, *immediately*. Yale fans might be a little patient for an Ivy League title, but the constant crowing from the Cambridge set got under the skin. In regard to the Crimson and The Game, Siedlecki was on the clock the second he arrived.

If he coached the way he looked, the Bulldogs would certainly be well disciplined. Siedlecki's chiseled features and dark crown of stubble gave him a tough, hard appearance, not unlike that of a marine drill sergeant. But as an Ivy League outsider, Siedlecki's selection as Yale's new head coach created some trepidation among members of the Yale community, and members of the media reiterated the skepticism. Brian Dohn, a columnist for the *New Haven Register*, wrote at the time of Siedlecki's hiring: "Enthusiasm and energy count. But so does knowledge of the Ivy League and the Academic Index and the idiosyncrasies and traditions of Yale and Yale football. That is why Siedlecki wasn't given a ghost of a chance when this process started. That is why it is perplexing that he was hired."

In addition, rumors ran rampant that former star Bulldog running back Dick Jauron, the then-defensive coordinator of the Jacksonville Jaguars who went on to be head coach of the Chicago Bears, had been the number one choice for the position. Siedlecki immediately handled the stigma of being second choice, tackling the issue with extreme candor at his first press conference.

"Whenever jobs like this open, very good people get involved. I feel tremendously fortunate to be standing here today. Maybe I'm the last guy standing. I don't care. I'm the new head coach at Yale," he said, demonstrating what the press would come to see as his characteristic control over the situation.

Had the Bulldog faithful taken a hard look at the man's track record, they might have breathed a little easier.

Siedlecki was far from unfamiliar with succeeding a coaching icon. In his previous position at Amherst, Siedlecki replaced Jim Ostendarp, another coach who had occupied the same position for thirty-two years. Siedlecki also boasted firsthand knowledge of ancient college football rivalries, having served as an assistant at Lafayette from 1981–1987, coaching in the annual war with Lehigh, the most-played series of all time.

Amherst College was Siedlecki's second head coaching opportunity. In 1992 he inherited a program that had gone a dismal 1–14–1 over the previous two seasons. By his second year the Lord Jeffs were on the winning track. By Siedlecki's fourth year they were 7–1 and New England Small College Athletic Conference champions. For his estimable efforts, Siedlecki was named the 1996 American Football Coaches Association Kodak District I Coach of the Year (his second time earning the title).

The progress at Amherst bore a striking resemblance to Siedlecki's first head coaching job at Worcester Polytechnic Institute (WPI), where he coached from 1988 to 1992. At WPI he started a renaissance that resulted in a 36–11–1 overall record, including a 33–7–1 mark through the last four campaigns. His 1990 squad went 8–0–1, the only undefeated team in school history. Similar to his achievement in his last year at Amherst, Siedlecki's last WPI team finished 9–2 and qualified for the NCAA Division III playoffs. Siedlecki garnered his first AFCA Kodak District I Coach of the Year award.

The man with a well-earned reputation for successfully directing gridiron reclamation projects seemed to grasp the significance and emphasis of his latest challenge. When it came to student athletes, Siedlecki fully believed that the former always came first.

"I'm very excited about the opportunity to coach at a place that is so rich in tradition," Siedlecki said. "The goals of the program are clear to me . . . beat Harvard and win the Ivy title. I spent my entire career trying to get this job. I wanted to be with the best student athletes because it's fun to coach guys who have that kind of intellect."

Siedlecki's first season in his dream job, 1997, was an absolute nightmare. With no experienced varsity quarterbacks on his roster, Siedlecki's first Bulldog team finished 1–9. But Yale played competitively in all but two Ivy contests while posting the deceptive record, including a 17–7 loss to the first Harvard team to finish undefeated in Ivy League play.

Siedlecki's third head coaching position proved equally as charmed as his first two. His second Yale team completed the biggest turnaround in the history of Eli football. Siedlecki implemented more of his wide-open offensive theory, and the Bulldogs shattered fifteen offensive records as a result. Selected to finish eighth in the Ancient Eight in 1998, Siedlecki's team compiled a 6–4 overall record, placed second in the Ivy League race, and captured the Big Three crown. The exclamation point on the season was a grinding, defensive-dominated, old-time-football 9–7 victory over Harvard at sold-out Harvard Stadium. The Yale community did not have to wait long for an encore.

The 1999 edition of the Blue lost a heartbreaker on opening day to Brown by a single point. They did not lose again, including a scintillating final minute comeback victory over Harvard before 52,484 screaming fans at the Yale Bowl. The two-year turnaround now depicted a complete reversal of fortune from 1–9 to 9–1. Thirteen Yale players received All-Ivy recognition and the team rewrote fifty-three school records. For the third time, at the third stop in his head coaching career, league officials recognized Jack Siedlecki as Coach of the Year, this time as the most outstanding coach in New England.

The 2000 campaign ended with a 7–3 finish as Yale became the first school to reach the eight-hundred-win plateau in NCAA history, and they also defeated Harvard, 34–24. Three straight winning seasons, three straight trouncings of the Crimson.

The 2001 season soured Siedlecki's streak. After an auspicious 3–1 start, a loss to a formidable Penn eleven began a downward spiral that the Bulldogs could not turn around. An uncharacteristic string of five straight losses followed. Though a win over Harvard might have provided some solace, a gallant effort by an injury-ravaged Yale team was not enough to thwart a Harvard team intent on making history. Harvard completed its first perfect season since 1913 in a 35–23 Crimson victory at the Yale Bowl in front of a crowd of over fifty thousand. Now, with the 2002 season-opening victory over San Diego, Yale fortunes were looking up. The man with a reputation for rejuvenation seemed poised to revive his team yet again.

Not doing so would mean letting down Carm Cozza, the Bulldog faithful, the Eli heritage, and the most important individual the sport of football has ever known—the man guarding the Yale Bowl with a gate that bears his name: Walter Camp.

* * *

Perhaps college football icon John Heisman said it best, "What Washington was to his country, Camp was to American football—the friend, the founder, and the father." Walter Camp stood at the start of college football, where he watched the inaugural Harvard-Yale game from the stands. A New Haven resident and a senior at the Hopkins School, the seventeen-year-old talented all-around athlete excelled on the baseball diamond as a pitcher. The new game of football appealed to Camp, always one for new challenges. Whenever he wasn't on the mound, Camp practiced his kicking skills with his Hopkins classmates. In the fall of 1876 Camp continued his education at nearby Yale and joined the football team.

The Yale team elected Gene Baker as captain of the 1876 squad, a veteran who had played and lost to Harvard in the first match. Baker and his teammates agreed that Yale should pursue the Crimson's rugby-style game and abandon the more soccer-oriented game that Yale had been playing since the Columbia match in 1872. When the two schools returned to Hamilton Park in 1876 for the rematch, Baker's Bulldogs felt that this would be their year. Baker did everything he could to ease the way toward victory. He honed his team's running and tackling techniques, and the players practiced with a rugby ball that Harvard sent in the spirit of good sportsmanship. Baker capitalized on the Crimson goodwill in order to minimize Yale's inexperience at the rugby-style contest, demanding a few changes in the rules that had governed the first game in 1875, especially the number of players. The teams would field eleven players to a side, instead of fifteen. Harvard also concurred that touchdowns still would not count in the scoring, the same format as in English rugby. A team could score points on a touchdown only by kicking a goal after advancing the ball over the goal line. Pregame oddsmakers made Harvard as much as a 5–1 favorite, but Baker still felt confident.

Under these concessionary rules, Yale managed to stem the tide of the Harvard offense's first-half advances. Camp, well ahead of his time in his dedication to off-season and supplemental training, played a prominent role in the overall Eli defensive stand. The 157-pound halfback made an immediate impact when he corralled a much bigger man with a wrist grab and flung him to the turf, fearlessly demonstrating Yale's fierce desire to prove who was really number one in the college football pecking order.

For seventy-five minutes the game remained scoreless, until Yale's Oliver Thompson drop-kicked the ball over the crossbar of the Harvard goal from thirty-five yards away. An ensuing end zone celebration by the Bulldogs delayed the game for twenty minutes. Despite crossing the Yale goal line three times during the rest of the contest, Harvard failed to convert any of its kicks. Yale engineered a major upset (1–0), evened the series at a game apiece, and took back its pride.

Indeed, a role reversal of sorts reverberated on a grander scale. Yale had originally suggested a series of games between the two schools after losing to Harvard in 1875. Harvard rejected the idea. It was now the Crimson, in the aftermath of this second meeting, suggesting a series of games. Perhaps losing didn't suit the Crimson constitutions. This time Yale, the new top dog, sniffed and said no. Yale was through accommodating Harvard. It could wait a year for a shot at redemption, just as Yale did. Yale, however, declined on a more diplomatic basis than spite—even though spite alone would have been good enough for most Elis.

Yale cited the number of players on the field as its major sticking point. Harvard wanted to increase the number, while Yale held steadfast on the eleven-man game. Harvard's own stubbornness forced it to further delay a chance at redemption—with no subsequent resolution, Yale and Harvard did not meet in 1877. Both teams played a four-game season nonetheless: Yale went 3–0–1 in its four matches, while Harvard matched the number of wins but posted one loss.

In 1878 Walter Camp succeeded Baker as Yale's captain. Harvard and Yale resumed play that year after finally reaching an agreement on the rules: Yale conceded on the number of players, but won out on the issue of counting only goals kicked, not touchdowns, in the scoring. Again a drop-kick goal by Oliver Thompson accounted for the game's only score in a 1–0 Yale triumph, this time away from New

Haven at Boston's South End Grounds. In 1879 the game returned to Hamilton Park in New Haven. A perfect forty-five-yard drop-kick by Camp cleared the crossbar late in the first half, but the referees called the score back because of a holding infraction. The two squads played to a scoreless tie, resulting in a series tally of two wins for Yale, one for Harvard, and one tie after four meetings.

With no eligibility requirements at the time, Walter Camp's playing career spanned five full seasons (1877–1881) and part of a sixth before a knee injury ended his playing career in 1882. Finishing as an undergraduate with a Bachelor of Arts degree in 1880, the football legend returned to play while attending Yale medical school and became the only three-time captain in Yale history. During Camp's reign, college football's first and most singularly dominant dynasty had begun. Camp's Yale teams compiled an overall record of 25–1–6, with a record of 4–0–1 versus Harvard. The only loss was a 1–0 defeat to Princeton in 1878. Princeton's single score was the only point that Yale allowed from 1876 until the Princeton game in 1882. When the knee injury ended his playing days that same year, Camp saw no need to stay at the Yale medical school (the aspiring doctor had just discovered that he could not stand the sight of blood). His impact on football, however, was just beginning.

In 1883 Camp got a job as a salesman for the Manhattan Watch Company of New York. The following year he moved over to the New Haven Clock Company. From 1883–1887 he served as an unpaid coach, or overseer, of the Yale team, functioning in an all-encompassing advisory capacity directly to the team captain. Yale's record over this period followed the fortunes of Camp's tenure as a player: an overall record of 41–1–2, the only loss to Princeton (6–5) in 1885, and four more victories over Harvard, by an aggregate score of 121–14. (The Harvard faculty banned football from Cambridge in the 1885 season, concerned about the excessively brutal direction of the game, thus Yale only played Harvard four times over the five-year period.)

By 1888 Camp's position with the watch company changed, and

he no longer traveled extensively for business. Camp filled his new-found free time with football, forming Yale's graduate coaching system. (Prior to 1888 college football teams were guided by their captains, players like Frank Hinkey, who doubled as on-field coaches.) With Camp's plan, the team's playing captain from the previous season, now an alumnus, became the head field coach under Camp's direction. A core group of other players who had recently completed their eligibility returned as assistant coaches, working with the current players at their former positions. Camp had created the current unit-by-unit coaching system that proliferates in the modern game.

Camp's graduate coaching system succeeded with assistance from an unusual ally. The same year Camp started the coaching system, he married. Alice Graham Sumner, the sister of a prominent Yale sociology professor, had no background in athletics whatsoever, let alone in the intricacies of football. Nevertheless, Alice Camp dedicated herself to learning the game. By attending and outlining the events of each practice, Alice became the vital link that allowed her husband both to work at the clock company and to meet each week-day evening to analyze the day's practice with his captain, head field coach, and other players. The Camps' dinner hour became a daily football review session for the newlyweds, sandwiched between his day job and night meetings. The quirky system worked with the precision of one of the fine clocks that surrounded Walter by day.

Camp's implementation of Yale's graduate coaching system made Yale the original training ground for American football coaches. Camp's understudies in New Haven included Amos Alonzo Stagg, who coached a remarkable fifty-four years—forty-one of them at the University of Chicago, an early football power and member of the original Big Ten conference—and Howard Jones, the man who fashioned the first football powerhouse of the West Coast at Southern California from 1915–1940 and led the Trojans to five Rose Bowls.

Walter Camp's record for the five-year period that he officially coached Yale (1888–1892) sparkled at a gaudy 67–2. Only the 1889

Princeton squad and 1890 Harvard team managed to defeat Camp's Bulldogs. Harvard won on a dramatic saving tackle by Bernie Trafford on Yale fullback Ben Morrison in the game's waning moments. The Crimson had neutralized the fiery Pudge Heffel-finger and preserved Harvard's first victory over Yale since the inaugural match—ending a fifteen-year drought.

The loss was but a blip on the radar screen. The week following the Harvard game, Yale bounced back with an impressive showing, humbling Princeton 32–0 at Eastern Park in Brooklyn. The victory was especially notable for another reason. A crowd of thirty thousand attended the game, and Yale pocketed $11,185 for the afternoon, its share of the gate receipts. Over the course of the season, Camp's Elis netted $18,392 for Yale's coffers, enough to fund Yale's entire athletic program with a surplus of over $1,500. Thanks to Camp, Yale's football team became big business for the school.

Prior to the 1892 season Camp received a letter—one of hundreds he'd gotten since Yale's rise—seeking his renowned coaching skills. The letter asked for advice "on the best way to develop a good football team," and came from James H. Kivlan, a machine-shop instructor at a small school in Indiana called Notre Dame. Notre Dame had played five games from 1887–1890, but had recently suspended its program. Camp answered Kivlan, just as he had all the others who solicited his advice. Over the next sixty-three years Notre Dame posted a single losing season.

Winning and Camp went hand in hand. It seemed nearly impossible to defeat him, and to do it consistently was unimaginable. During Camp's last year as head coach in 1892 he produced his finest work, one of Yale's best squads of all time. It was if he was testing the limits of his power, pushing the football gods. They smiled benevolently. His undefeated, untied, and unscored-upon team defeated thirteen opponents by a combined score of 435–0.

Camp also became, by far, the game's most recognizable figure. Above and beyond his mentoring of the Yale program, he wrote extensively about football and other sports, training and exercise, and bridge. Camp also officiated at college football games, and he held the supreme position of authority on the Intercollegiate Football Association's rules-making committee. His success in conditioning his players proved his fitness wisdom—Yale's gridiron dominance gave him clout with the American public. If Camp said exercise was good for you, then it must be true. Camp proposed the idea of tax-funded playgrounds for children and he used his physical fitness expertise to create "Camp's Daily Dozen," a series of morning calisthenics for adults. He recorded his Daily Dozen on a five-album set that included a wall chart with illustrations of the proper technique for each exercise, which retailed for ten dollars. It has been said that Camp was, more than any other individual, responsible for getting the average person to exercise with his Daily Dozen routine.

Despite his accomplishments on the field as a player and off the field as a coach, Camp's biggest contributions to the sport of American football came from his participation on rules-making committees. The regulations under which Harvard and Yale played their second game (1876) became the foundation that Camp built upon to create the game of American football. Those rules stipulated eleven players per side with six forming a rush line the width of the field, two halfbacks behind the rush line, and three other players spaced across a wide area behind the halfbacks. The field size was 140 yards by 70 yards. A form of a kick—punt, place, or drop—put the ball into play. A rugby-like scrum, in which the two rush lines attempted to gain possession by kicking the ball, followed a tackle. Finally, at the point of being tackled a player could either lateral the ball to a teammate or drop-kick the ball in an attempt to retain possession for his team.

Following the game, a historic rules committee convention in 1876 at the Massasoit House in Springfield brought together representatives from Harvard, Yale, Columbia, and Princeton—half of the eight schools that would later form the Ivy League. The schools formed the Intercollegiate Football Association at the convention, and adopted, for the most part, the English Rugby Union Code of rules established in 1872. There was one glaring difference. Rugby scoring was based only on goals (kicks through goalposts), but the Springfield representatives, clearly influenced by the McGill-Harvard matches of 1874 and 1875, decided that touchdowns would also be counted in the scoring. The controversial new rule stated, "A match shall be decided by a majority of touchdowns; a goal shall be equal to four touchdowns; but in case of a tie a goal kicked from a touchdown shall take precedence over four touchdowns." Yale balked at the scoring change and at another rule restoring fifteen men to a side, and refused to join the association. The Elis were furious. Yale already had played Harvard's game by (mostly) Harvard's rules. They also beat Harvard in the second meeting. Now Harvard had infiltrated Yale's original association and sought to take it over completely. Maybe Princeton and Columbia didn't mind falling in line behind Harvard once again, but Yale wasn't having it.

Eventually, cooler heads prevailed and Yale decided to join Harvard and the other schools in 1879. Like it or not, Yale still needed Harvard. The school wasn't giving up on its ideas, though. Yale would acquiesce—and then mold the association from the inside. They needed someone strong and firm to represent the Bulldogs, someone who knew how to get what he wanted. They sent Walter Camp.

Camp made his first appearance at an Intercollegiate Football Association rules meeting in 1879, when he was still a player. (In football's early days, the players were the authorities on the game. There were no veterans to consult. The players had to make it up as they went along.) No meek wallflower, Camp's persuasive arguments gained some ground for the Elis. The association members agreed to change the number of players back to eleven and reduced the dimensions of the field to 110 yards by 53 yards. Camp's third suggested change, however, affected the game to the greatest extent.

Camp strongly believed that the team that held possession of the ball should be allowed to maintain possession. The rugby scrum that took place immediately after an offensive player was downed oftentimes caused possession to change after a single tackle. Camp disagreed with this idea and devised a more democratic plan. He proposed a system where a separation occurred between the downing of a ball carrier and the beginning of the next sequence. The break in the action allowed each team to position themselves on offense and defense respectively. It would then be the responsibility of the center on the offensive team to heel the ball to a teammate (the forerunner of the center snap). This groundbreaking idea vaulted football away from rugby and sent it rocketing on a new trajectory, one that would evolve and establish the distinctive new game of American football.

Although unquestionably an epochal innovation, the transition from scrum to scrimmage produced one glaring flaw. The new system had no method to exchange or relinquish possession from one team to another, except after the team in possession of the ball scored. No requirement, incentive, or penalty regarding advancement existed. Players could run forwards, sideways, or right out of their own end zone and still keep the ball on offense. The most extreme example of Camp's imperfect new rule occurred in the 1881 Harvard-Princeton game. Princeton kept the ball the entire first half and never scored. Harvard received the second half kickoff and also maintained possession for the entire half without scoring. The game ended in a scoreless tie. Something needed to be done. Walter Camp, of course, had a solution.

At the 1882 rules committee convention Camp outlined the concept of downs, saying that if in three tries a "team shall not have advanced the ball five yards or lost ten, they must give up the ball to the other side. . . ." The other convention delegates immediately questioned how yardage would be determined, and again Camp had the answer. The field would be marked with horizontal chalked lines every five yards, forming the appearance of a gridiron.

With a fixed point of reference on the field, the committee could now name the positions of the players on the field more accurately. The players at the outside of the rush line at scrimmage became the ends. Inside the ends were the tackles, their labels reflecting a major part of their function. Next came the guards, who provided protection for the center, the player responsible for initiating each down. The committee then assigned the names of the backing positions: quarter, half, and full, based on their positioning behind the line of scrimmage. All of the back position names were direct descendants of rugby-named designations.

Camp continued to dominate the rules committee with his innovations—up next, in 1883, was a new scoring system. The committee adopted his suggested point values as follows: touchdown (four), goal after touchdown (two), field goal (five), and safety (two). In 1885, Camp successfully submitted the first penalties involving loss of yardage (five yards) for infractions such as delay of game and offsides. In 1887 Camp and the rules committee legalized the technique of blocking or running interference for a ball carrier, though the practice had existed in different variations for almost a decade.

Camp's devotion to football never ended. Appropriately enough, the man suffered a heart attack at a rules committee convention in 1925. He never recovered and died peacefully in his sleep the following day. The world of football lost its father, and sportswriter Grantland Rice best captured the sentiments of Camp's brethren in his nationally syndicated *New York Herald Tribune* newspaper column.

How often must have come to Walter Camp the memory of old football battles in rain and snow, in sun and shadow— the flying tackle and the savage line thrust—the forward wall braced for the shock—the graceful spiral careening against a sky of blue and gray—the long run down the field—the goal line stand—the forward pass—the singing and cheering of great crowds—young and old America gathered together on a golden afternoon, with bands playing and banners flying—It may have been in the midst of such a dream that the call to quarters came, and taps was sounded as the Great Knight came down the field.

Walter Camp had almost single-handedly formed modern football, his critical genius giving Americans a sport of their own. His legacy forever linked the New Haven college to the origin of the game, and all those who followed him as Yale head coach knew that it was their duty to uphold Camp's legend.

Those who took the position as Harvard's head coach vowed to topple it.

* * *

On December 6, 1993, Tim Murphy became the thirtieth head coach of Harvard football. Tall and lean, with angular features, the new coach looked as if he could suit up and take the field if necessary. But there was no mistaking who was in charge. His serious manner, firm handshake, and commanding voice exuded authority.

In order to accept officially, Murphy made a clean break from the Division I-A ranks, rejecting a five-year contract extension from Cincinnati and withdrawing his name from the second interview process at Duke. Murphy informed his Bearcat staff that he took the Harvard coaching job because it was "one of the best positions in the country." Crimson fans pondered what might happen if the new coach was drawn back to Division I-A, but Murphy's comments at his coming-out party put the old Varsity Clubbers at ease. "When I was single and coaching at Maine, I was on that other track. I could see myself at Miami or Notre Dame some day," Murphy said. "Now I'm married with small children and I look at things differently. This could be a really good situation for our family." For Murphy, a self-confessed "Boston guy," the desire to come home and be closer to his family made the prestige and security of the Harvard head coaching position extremely appealing.

Athletic director Bill Cleary, one of the most ardent spokesmen on behalf of the preservation of college sports ethics and the ideal of amateurism, could barely contain his enthusiasm on Murphy's hiring. "We had a wonderful group of candidates, and Tim believes in the Harvard philosophy. We are delighted he's opted to choose Harvard."

At Cincinnati Murphy had received a base salary of $110,000, a car, a $3,000 personal expense budget, a $25,000 salary for hosting radio and television shows, a country club membership, and free use of the college's facilities for a summer camp. His coaching staff consisted of eight full-time assistants, a part-timer, and two graduate assistants.

At Harvard, Murphy traded it all in for a 40 percent base pay cut and virtually no match for the additional perks. His Harvard coaching staff consisted of just six full-time assistants and a part-time freshman coach. The downgrade, a rare act in the increasingly money-driven world of sports, seemed natural to Murphy.

"Whether they're Ivy League, scholarship, or Division III, kids play because they love the game," he said. "When I made eight hundred bucks (as Brown freshman coach) and worked in a factory I enjoyed coaching as much as when I made a six-figure income. Money's great; it's not why I got into coaching."

A thirty-year-old Murphy began his head coaching career in 1987 at Maine as the youngest head football coach in the country, and he promptly led the Black Bears to an 8–4 record, a share of the Yankee Conference title, and the school's first-ever trip to the NCAA Division I-AA playoffs. Murphy received the first of his three Division I-AA New England Coach of the Year awards for his first-year efforts as head coach.

In 1989 Murphy left Maine and inherited a moribund Cincinnati football program that resided annually at the very depths of Division I-A. The beleaguered Bearcats' last winning season had been some seven years earlier. The rebuilding process by the transplanted New England native took a little time. The Bearcats were 2–19–1 in Murphy's first two seasons playing one of the nation's most difficult schedules, but by the third and fourth seasons Cincinnati had become competitive.

Then, in 1993, Murphy elevated the Bearcats program to heights it had never known. The 8–3 finish was the school's best overall mark in seventeen years and resulted in a twenty-seventh-place ranking in the *USA Today*/CNN national poll at the end of its season, the highest finish in the program's history. During this, his final campaign in the Queen City, Murphy solidified his reputation for a multiple, pro-style offense, which had earned him notice during his first head coaching assignment at Division I-AA Maine. The Bearcats' 302 points were the most in forty years and the team established all-time records for offensive plays, first downs, and fewest turnovers. In addition, Cincinnati captured the Independent Football Alliance championship.

Cincinnati's accolades attracted attention, but interviewers at both Harvard and Duke sought him out for reasons beyond his coaching skills. Murphy brought the Bearcat program to NCAA compliance, restored the scholarship numbers, and put a totally despondent renegade football organization back on track to achieve success at the Division I-A major college level. The College Football Association recognized Murphy's Cincinnati program as one of only twenty Division I schools that had graduated a minimum of 70 percent of its most recent recruiting class. The fact that the thirty-six-year-old Murphy had achieved all this while beginning with a condemned stadium and no practice facilities was unbelievable. Most career coaches would have used the Cincinnati experience as a springboard to a more prominent Division I-A program.

Murphy, however, became Joe Restic's successor. Restic, a former coach in the wide-open Canadian Football League, completed a twenty-three-year run as Harvard head coach in 1993, a run that had been characterized by consistent contender status for the Ivy League title and a signature offense known as the multiflex that, win or lose, was always entertaining. Under Restic the Crimson captured five Ivy League titles as he coolly directed Harvard fortunes in his annual head-to-head competition with Yale's Carm Cozza. Similar to Cozza's final years, Restic endured a difficult stretch over his last three seasons. The Crimson were a disappointing 10–19–1, and Restic's final game before his retirement was a heartbreaking 33–31 loss at the Yale Bowl.

Murphy fared no better in his first experience of The Game. After a 3–2 start in 1994, the Crimson dropped four of their last five and Yale easily handled Harvard, 32–13, in front of the home crowd at Harvard Stadium.

The following year magnified what the Harvard-Yale game and its relation to a successful season is all about. On a cold rain-swept day at the Yale Bowl, a 1–8 Harvard team, led by the brilliant running of Eion Hu, rallied to defeat a 3–6 Yale team, 22–21, on a dramatic three-yard touchdown run by Hu with twenty-nine seconds remaining. Despite Harvard's overall disappointing record, Murphy found himself up close and personal with a legion of jubilant supporters glad to have a victory over Yale to carry them through the long Boston winter.

Murphy and the Crimson made significant improvements in 1996. A 4–6 overall record did not accurately measure the program's progress. The team may have lost six times, but four of the team's losses were by no more than seven points. The most important margin, however, was a five-point victory over Yale in Carm Cozza's final game as head coach.

Then, in 1997 it all came together for Murphy and the Crimson. Harvard attained its first-ever perfect Ivy League season (7–0) and a 9–1 record overall, the magic capped off by a third straight victory over Yale in New Haven.

The Crimson developed a penchant for heartbreak the next three years. The 14–16 combined record did not begin to tell the story of a team that almost every week entered the fourth quarter leading or tied, only to see victory slip away. The Harvard-Yale game became an illustrative microcosm of each of the three seasons. From 1998 to 2000 the Crimson led in the second half of all three games, only to watch helplessly a come-from-behind Eli victory celebration.

In 2001, Murphy completed a stunning reversal. The Crimson fashioned its first undefeated, untied campaign since 1913 and finished the season ranked nineteenth nationally in Division I-AA. Eight players made the All-Ivy League first team. Coach Murphy captured the Division I-AA New England Coach of the Year award for the second time while coaching Harvard, and for the third time overall. He also was named the AFCA Kodak District I Coach of the Year. Murphy's coaching efforts also earned him another important honor. His name became linked to the coach that led Harvard's 1913 team to a perfect record. Being mentioned in the same breath as the legendary Percy Haughton was an honor no one in Harvard football circles took lightly.

* * *

By 1907 the Harvard gridiron inferiority complex had sunk to new lows. Yale reigned as the undisputed preeminent football program of the game's infancy. Camp's genius had built a powerful machine, and the Yale teams included the likes of All-American standouts such as guard Pudge Heffelfinger, end Frank Hinkey, end/guard Gordon Brown, tackle James Hogan, and fullback Ted Coy, each among the all-time best at his position. All attained multiple All-American recognition and later entered the National Football Foundation/College Hall of Fame. Between the first meeting of the two ancient rivals in 1875 and 1907, a victory over Yale had become a maddeningly rare occurrence. Only the undefeated 1890, 1898, and 1901 Harvard teams claimed that distinction.

Percy Haughton was a rock-solid 180-pound blocking tackle and adept kicking specialist on the 1898 squad that defeated Yale 17–0. His punting played a prominent role in the Crimson's uncharacteristic success. Immediately following graduation Haughton briefly worked for his father for a meager weekly wage. It was a job, but not what Haughton had in mind. When an opportunity to succeed the legendary Pop Warner as head coach at Cornell presented itself, a paying coaching job, Haughton jumped at the chance. In two seasons guiding the Big Red, Haughton compiled an impressive 17–5 record. Despite his coaching success in Ithaca, Haughton returned to Boston to pursue a career in finance as a bond salesman.

His return in 1908 allowed him to keep his hand in the game of football as a volunteer assistant coach at Harvard, and the timing couldn't have been more fortunate. Bill Reid quit his post as Harvard's coach in 1906 after two seasons. Despite a two-season record of 18–3–1, Reid considered his time at Harvard a failure because he'd lost twice to Yale. Joshua Crane, Reid's successor, fared no better and lasted a single season. Crane's 1907 Harvard team finished the season with three straight losses, the last one another shutout defeat at the hands of Yale. Six straight shutout losses to Yale and the growing Bulldog dynasty grated on the nerves of the Crimson, particularly the older, upper-crust, elite alumni. The fact that the Elis had taken Harvard's original game and ascended to become the most recognizable football power in the nation angered anyone with ties to the nation's oldest college.

The coaching system in Cambridge allowed the captain to appoint an unpaid head coach, and Harvard captain-elect Francis "Hooks" Burr insisted upon Haughton. The frustrated alumni smelled salvation in this move, and the deep-pocketed men offered to chip in a salary. The impatient Crimson backers wholeheartedly hoped that Haughton could take the Elis down a peg. The Yale athletics superiority complex bordered on smugness, as exemplified by the comments of former Yale player and coach Pa Corbin. Speaking at a Princeton alumni club banquet held in Boston in November 1907, Corbin commented, "I hope that Harvard will get a system and method that will make her really formidable in football, but until she does we must count Princeton as our dearest foe."

The hiring of Percy Haughton has been referred to as the single most significant event in Harvard football annals. Indeed, the Haughton Era (1908–1917) has been unsurpassed in Crimson history. The man brought continuity and a singular commitment to build a successful program, beginning with overhauled offensive and defensive systems. Haughton relied on two key elements in his attack—deception and power. Multiple fakes and motion among the backs and ends created confusion among opponents. Haughton pioneered the use of the "mousetrap play," an early version of trapping defensive linemen that he had employed as a Groton schoolboy before attending Harvard, and he frequently used unbalanced lines and backfield formations to reshuffle the standard T-formation. Haughton also instituted the breakthrough concept of "roving center," a predecessor of the modern middle linebacker, who called defensive signals to counter offensive formations.

As all great coaches since, Haughton was a true student of the game. He combined elements of several successful programs of the day and translated it into his own at Harvard. Haughton attributed the element of deception to Pop Warner. The discipline came from the Army teams. The power from Pennsylvania. A dedicated commitment to fundamentals and prowess on the lines from Yale and Walter Camp. Haughton thrived by, above all, keeping his mind open to new techniques.

This included seeking assistance from the Oval Office.

Haughton wanted to hire a lieutenant, Ernest Graves, to round out his dream coaching staff. Graves had attained great fame as the line coach at West Point. His familiarity with the Yale technique of line play, along with subsequent strategies he developed during his playing and coaching career at Army, placed Graves technically well ahead of his coaching time. Graves, however, served in the engineering corps, and the army assigned Graves to the Washington, D.C., barracks. In addition, the army policy at the time did not allow the detachment officers to coach at civilian colleges. The newly appointed Harvard coach decided to play on the Crimson loyalty of President Theodore Roosevelt, Harvard Class of '95. Haughton sent a message to the White House requesting the transfer of Lieutenant Graves to Cambridge.

Upon receiving the request, President Roosevelt handed the Harvard emissary a note to deliver to the Secretary of War—and future president—William Howard Taft, a Yale graduate. The note read: "I was a Harvard man before I was a politician. Please do what these gentlemen want." Secretary Taft had no alternative but to comply with the president's wishes. Lieutenant Graves arrived in Cambridge in time for the second half of the season. He played a prominent role in Harvard's four-game winning streak through the stretch run of the 1908 campaign en route to a 9–0–1 record culminating in a 4–0 victory over Yale at New Haven.

Haughton indelibly left his mark on the game in that contest, his first encounter with the Elis as head coach. Both teams entered the game undefeated and once tied. A crowd of thirty-five thousand at Yale Field witnessed a clever substitution by Haughton that resulted in the game's decisive play and provided a classic example of the coach's deceptive skills. Haughton inserted reserve fullback Vic Kennard to attempt a goal from the Yale twenty-five-yard line. Kennard drop-kicked the ball—with his left foot. The Yale team did not realize that the unknown Kennard was left-footed, and its attempt at a block attacked the right side of Kennard's body as the ball was already spiraling toward the crossbar. Sportswriters lauded the "wrong side" kick as having made the difference in a contest dominated by the respective defenses, and Haughton ended the Crimson's long six-year nightmare.

Haughton's coaching at the 1908 Harvard-Yale game became better known for another reason. The fiery coach reportedly strangled a live bulldog in the presence of his team to inspire his charges. While the legend has been disproved from a literal standpoint (he throttled a fake bulldog), Haughton's tenure as head coach of the Crimson did kill the Eli momentum.

Yale's dominance of football in another area also ended during Haughton's tenure. A vocal member of the rules committee like Walter Camp, Haughton objected to the rules concerning the forward pass. Under the existing regulations the ball had to be thrown five yards right or five yards left and five yards behind the place the ball was put into play. An incomplete pass resulted in a fifteen-yard penalty.

Camp and his constituents wanted the forward pass eliminated, feeling that changes to promote end runs would open up the game. Haughton disagreed with Camp's theory. After some experiments of his own with defensive adjustments, the Harvard mentor concluded that teams could easily neutralize end runs. The only way to open up the game in Haughton's eyes was to modify the forward pass. The Harvard coach gathered rules committee supporters of his own and committed an act of football heresy: he challenged Camp's authority. Haughton argued in favor of loosening the current restriction to make the forward pass a more viable weapon. Amazingly, Haughton and his group won the battle over Camp and his loyalists. The committee eliminated the rigid restrictions on the forward pass, and added new rules protecting a pass receiver before and during the ball's flight.

Beyond this important victory in the rules committee, Haughton pushed the game forward as he sought to make it a more cerebral exercise. Although no one questioned the toughness of Haughton's players, his teams were at the forefront of making the game a less brutal endeavor. They relied on exemplary conditioning, mental discipline, and military-like precision to separate themselves from their gridiron opponents. The consummate motivator also explored the psychological side of his profession, maximizing his players' performance as no one had before. Haughton knew which buttons to push in order to have his team in position to win each Saturday, and he did so without apology. If it meant berating them all week in order to achieve this goal, so be it. Haughton demanded respect from his players. He aspired to results, not popularity. As George Frazier wrote in a 1960 *Esquire* article titled "Harvard vs. Yale: The Best of Everything," even Haughton's praise was coarse. After a 36–0 win over Yale in 1914, Haughton said to his team: "Well, boys, I said a lot of mean, cutting things to you this season, didn't I?" He paused briefly before yelling, "Well, God damn it, I meant every damn one of them!"

Haughton used featured All-American players such as Charlie Brickley and Eddie Mahan to lead the Crimson juggernaut to a thirty-three-game unbeaten streak from 1911 to 1915, and Harvard continued to manhandle Yale. The highlights under Haughton included a Harvard victory that spoiled the opening of the Yale Bowl

Harvard's record-setting quarterback and captain Neil Rose led the Crimson to a perfect season in 2001.
(Courtesy of the Harvard Sports Information Department/CW Pack Sports)

Opponents found Yale captain and defensive lineman Jason Lange an imposing sight in the trenches.
(Courtesy of the Yale Athletic Department Archives)

A familiar sight: Harvard's all-time receiving leader and NFL prospect Carl Morris breaks loose for a long reception.
(Courtesy of Rich Lange, Illustrating What Matters Most)

Yale head coach Jack Siedlecki didn't let pre-season poll results faze him and kept his team in contention for the title in 2002. (Courtesy of the Yale Athletic Department Archives)

Above: Yale defensive coordinator Rick Flanders faced big challenges in 2002 with a young corps of defensive backs and a number of star wide receivers on opposing Ivy teams. (Courtesy of the Yale Athletic Department Archives)

Right: Harvard head coach Tim Murphy had a tough act to follow in 2002 after ending the previous season unbeaten. (Courtesy of the Harvard Sports Information Department)

Yale junior quarterback Alvin Cowan's record-breaking first start landed him in *Sports Illustrated*.
(Courtesy of the Yale Athletic Department Archives/Sabby Frinzi)

Yale sophomore quarterback Jeff Mroz competed with Cowan for the starter's role before the 2002 season.
(Courtesy of the Yale Athletic Department Archives/Sabby Frinzi)

Harvard sophomore quarterback Ryan Fitzpatrick gave Coach Murphy plenty of options at the pivotal position.
(Courtesy of the Harvard Sports Information Department)

Above: Harvard coach Percy Haughton, who became the first professional football coach when he took over the Crimson in 1908. (Courtesy of the Harvard Sports Information Department)

Above: Yale's Walter Camp (1880). Legendary coach John Heisman said of Camp: "What Washington was to his country, Camp was to American football—the friend, the founder, and the father." (Courtesy of the Yale Athletic Department Archives)

Right: Harvard coach Bill Reid, who saved football from extinction when several college administrators wanted to ban the sport in 1905 due to injuries and escalating violence. (Shown here in his playing days.) (Courtesy of the Harvard Sports Information Department)

Yale guard Pudge Heffelfinger (1891), the first professional football player. (Courtesy of the Yale Athletic Department Archives)

Yale end Frank Hinkey (1895). One of only eleven four-time All-Americans in college football history, Hinkey remains one of the sport's most formidable players of all time. (Courtesy of the Yale Athletic Department Archives)

Yale's Albie Booth (*above,* 1932) and Harvard's Barry Wood (*right,* 1932). Their epic gridiron battles from 1929 to 1931 thrilled national audiences. (*Above*: Courtesy of the Yale Athletic Department Archives; *right*: Courtesy of the Harvard Sports Information Department)

The 1968 Harvard-Yale game scoreboard tells the story. Fans mobbed the field after Harvard's 29–29 "win" in the most famous of all The Games.
(Courtesy of the Harvard Sports Information Department)

Yale coach Carm Cozza. He patrolled the Blue sidelines for thirty-two years and was inducted into the College Football Hall of Fame in 2002.
(Courtesy of the Yale Athletic Department Archives)

Yale's Chuck Mercein, number 30 (1965). He went on to play for the Green Bay Packers and accounted for more than half the yardage in the Packers' game-winning drive in the 1968 Ice Bowl, one of the most famous contests in sports history.
(Courtesy of the Yale Athletic Department Archives)

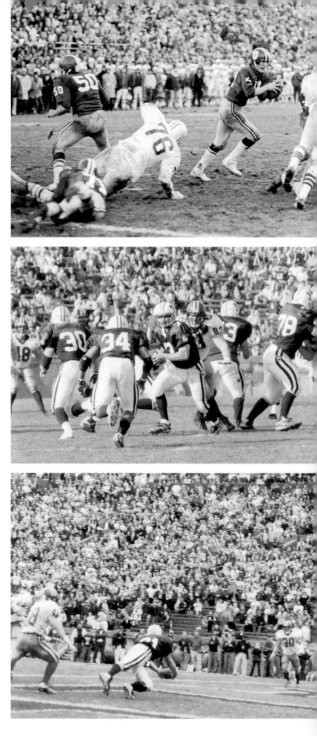

Harvard quarterback Milt Holt (with ball). He led the Crimson in the 1974 Harvard-Yale game, the best ever played by the rivals. (Courtesy of the Harvard Sports Information Department)

Yale's southpaw quarterback Joe Walland, the most prolific offensive player in Yale football history. He saved his best game for last in his improbable 1999 performance versus Harvard. (Courtesy of the Yale Athletic Department Archives/Stephen Fritzer)

Yale wide receiver Eric Johnson, the Bulldog's all-time leading receiver, was an All-Rookie tight end in 2001 with the NFL's San Francisco 49ers. Johnson's key reception from the 1999 Harvard-Yale game is known as "The Catch." (Courtesy of the Yale Athletic Department Archives/Jim Mendillo)

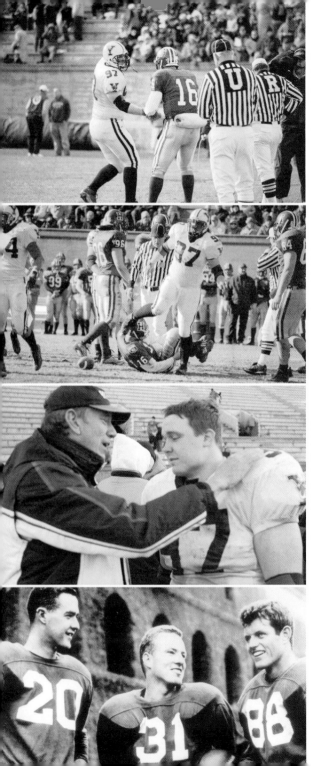

Yale captain Jason Lange and Harvard captain Neil Rose shake hands a final time after the coin toss.
(Courtesy of Rich Lange, Illustrating What Matters Most)

Lange steps over a fallen Neil Rose after an early first quarter sack.
(Courtesy of Rich Lange, Illustrating What Matters Most)

New York governor George Pataki brings his exuberant support for his alma mater down to the sidelines. He's seen here with Jason Lange following the 2002 Harvard-Yale game.
(Courtesy of Rich Lange, Illustrating What Matters Most)

Before he battled on the Senate floor, Senator Edward Kennedy suited up for the Crimson. He's shown here with teammates Phil Haughey (*left*) and Leo Dudley (*center*). Kennedy scored the only touchdown in Harvard's 1955 loss to Yale.
(Courtesy of the JFK Library)

in 1914; and a 41–0 shellacking of the Bulldogs in 1915, the worst in the forty-four-year history of Yale football, that prompted the following in a *Boston Globe* game summary: "Never before in a big game has the winning team played the better football in every department of the game or the loser been so hapless to stave off an overwhelming defeat."

The most storied of all sportswriters, Grantland Rice, recounted in his syndicated newspaper column a discussion at midcentury regarding Haughton, one of the greatest college football coaches of all time. Jesse Harper, Knute Rockne's coach at Notre Dame, contributed the following observation to the discussion.

> Here was a great coach—not merely a good one. He was colder than an iceberg, harder than granite. But he was brilliant—a natural leader. He was to football what General George Patton was to our armies. Haughton never had the amazing personality of Rockne. But he knew more football than anyone else except Pop Warner. He gave the game more. He worked day and night. He hated football writers, so they hated him. He hated practically everybody except his own Harvard team. He could hate them too. He was ruthless. But don't let anyone tell you that Percy Haughton wasn't one of the greatest coaches of all time. I couldn't place a coach above him.

Rice offered the following summation: "Cold, hard, austere, he was one of the greatest."

Coach Tim Murphy was walking in the shadow of Harvard football's patron saint.

6

The Ancient Eight

I N THE EARLY GOING OF 2002, keeping up with the likes of Percy Haughton came as easily to Coach Murphy as good jobs come to Harvard alumni. The Crimson's solid defeat of Holy Cross kept the winning streak intact, proved that 2001 wasn't a fluke, and tantalized Murphy with thoughts of another perfect season. Rose threw pinpoint passes. Morris rapidly accumulated yardage with catch after catch. Balestracci menaced the opposing offense. It seemed like old times, and the Crimson coach had no complaints.

Murphy wasn't the only coach smiling after his team's debut. In New Haven, things were looking up for Coach Siedlecki. Sure, he wasn't building on a double-digit win streak, but his Bulldogs gave Siedlecki reason to believe that big things lay ahead. Yale's offense had a fiery leader in Alvin Cowan, and the kid's six-touchdown performance had proven that he was absolutely the right choice at quarterback. Captain Jason Lange steadfastly led the defense, handily putting away San Diego with few problems.

Despite their respective wins, Siedlecki and Murphy had to keep the victories in perspective. A win is a win, but beating San Diego and Holy Cross didn't count for anything in the grand scheme of the Ivy League championship. The only way to secure that crown is to beat league opponents in what is essentially a season-long round-robin tournament. With Harvard and Yale facing off in the final week of

the season, the outcome of The Game frequently has title implications. Preseason polls be damned, if Harvard and Yale played as they
both had on opening day, it looked as if the fight for the championship might again play out during The Game.

Harvard opened Ivy League play in Providence on September 28,
facing a vengeful Brown squad. Brown coach Phil Estes and his Bears
had a major score to settle with the Cambridge men. In addition to
losing to the Crimson on a fourth-quarter touchdown pass from
Rose to Morris in their 2001 meeting, Brown still held a grudge with
the Crimson. Brown head coach Phil Estes publicly blamed Harvard
for reporting the Bears in 1999 for NCAA rules violations. The investigation tarnished Brown's 1999 Ivy League crown and led NCAA
officials to disqualify Brown from Ivy League contention in 2000,
eliminating the possibility of the Bears shooting for back-to-back
championships. Brown also wanted to put to rest another argument:
which team had Division I-AA's premier wide receiver.

Brown's 6'5", 230-pound Chas Gessner ranked second on *The
Sporting News*'s list of top receivers in Division I-AA—right behind
Harvard's Carl Morris. Both Gessner and Morris earned preseason
All-American status. The 1999 Ivy League Rookie of the Year and
2001 Payton Award finalist, Gessner had turned the heads of NFL
scouts just as his counterpart at Harvard had.

This final matchup with Gessner motivated Morris. He wanted to
convince the fans in Providence that *The Sporting News* ranked the
two heavyweight Ivy receivers correctly. But in Morris's mind, even
the one-on-one showdown and the presence of pro scouts eager to
watch the battle took a backseat to notching another win. If the
Crimson could capitalize on momentum from the Holy Cross victory
and pummel Brown, Harvard would take the first baby steps toward
a repeat Ivy title. Back-to-back champions. Morris liked the sound of
that. If he could show up Gessner now, all the better, but he'd have
the chance to individually battle the Brown standout later at pro
scouting camp.

Clear skies, low winds, and the strong arms of Harvard's Rose and

Brown's Kyle Slager (a transfer from Division I-A University of Arizona) forecast a day filled with pass attempts. More than thirteen thousand fans turned out, celebrating Brown's homecoming festivities and eager to see the antics of Morris and Gessner. Neither player, however, became the talk of the game.

The two did turn in solid performances, with Gessner out-dueling Morris. Slager threw for 300 yards on the day, 159 yards attributed to Gessner, who also scored two touchdowns. Morris hauled in nine passes for 103 yards and posted one score, but he faced an extenuating circumstance that factored into his performance. Neil Rose didn't finish the game.

Rose took a nap on the bus ride from Boston to Providence, and something inexplicable happened while he dozed in his seat. He woke to sharp pains shooting down his right leg. When the bus pulled into Brown, a panicky Rose limped to the field to test this strange injury. His heart sank. He couldn't even put weight on the leg without pain, never mind running, walking, or scrambling in the pocket. Agonized, Rose had no choice but to tell the coaches. He furiously wanted to play, but he couldn't let a bum leg jeopardize the chance for a win.

Harvard trainer Gary Geissler didn't think the situation was hopeless. He identified Rose's injury as a back problem, not a leg issue, and he worked with Rose during warm-ups. Suddenly, Rose's bulging disc popped back into place. The pain subsided immediately. Rose jumped up and tested his leg. He could put weight on it. He could walk. He jogged a little. Still no pain. Pushing the limit, Rose discovered he couldn't run at full speed, but that didn't matter. He damaged defenses from the pocket. As long as he could drop back, he would be fine.

Unless, of course, he got flattened—something all too familiar for Rose from his days as a high school quarterback. He'd once been sacked twenty-six times in a single game as University High School's signal caller.

Midway through the second quarter, Rose scrambled as the Brown defense covered his receivers. One of the corners dove at Rose's knees, sending him flipping through the air. He landed right on his tender back, his knees up near his facemask. Pain exploded through his back and leg. This time the agony was unlike anything he'd ever felt, and Rose was no stranger to the trainer's table. Blinded from the pain, Rose could barely see Murphy's next play call from the sidelines. Luckily, Murphy directed him to hand off to Palazzo from the shotgun. The play worked to perfection and Palazzo covered the twenty-five yards to the end zone.

With 7:38 remaining in the second quarter and the Crimson doling out celebratory helmet slaps to Palazzo, Rose hopped out of bounds on his good leg. Wincing, he collapsed on the sidelines and stayed on the ground for several minutes. The pain was unbearable. Geissler finally moved Rose to a table in the locker room, where the fallen quarterback again lay prone for several minutes. Rose shoved a towel into his mouth and bit down with each excruciating wave. He couldn't even take off his own equipment. Rose felt useless, fragile. Unreliable. He heard the home crowd's roar, wending its way into the depths of the visitor's locker room. Though he had no idea what was happening, he knew without question that it wasn't good for his team. Was his career over? *"How could it end like this?"* he asked himself over and over.

While Rose writhed in pain in the locker room, Murphy turned the offense over to understudy Ryan Fitzpatrick. With Fitzpatrick in, the game plan changed. The sophomore offered Murphy the darting and juking capabilities of a running back, opening up a new dimension of the Crimson attack. While Fitzpatrick didn't match Rose in terms of arm strength and total passing ability, he could throw accurately and effectively enough to make Brown aware this replacement was ready, willing, and able to get the ball to Morris. And if that didn't happen, he might just bowl the Bears over himself to get the first down.

Fitzpatrick entered the game with Harvard trailing 18–7 and under eight minutes to play before halftime. When the Bears and

Crimson retreated to their locker rooms for midpoint instruction, Harvard led 21–18. Fitzpatrick had cobbled together an amazingly quick set of scores. A touchdown pass from Fitzpatrick to Morris and a one-yard plunge into the end zone by Nick Palazzo vaulted Harvard ahead, giving the Crimson a huge mental advantage going into halftime.

The quick turnaround didn't surprise anyone on the Harvard side. Both Fitzpatrick and Rose made excellent decisions in what to do with the ball, so the offense had few problems adjusting to the quarterback change—a switch that for most teams dramatically affects the offense's ability to make plays. The offense also knew that Fitzpatrick had the skill and talent to direct such a feat. The first time Fitzpatrick stepped in for Rose during the Princeton game his freshman year, he led the Crimson on an eighty-yard touchdown march to win the game. When Murphy called on Fitzpatrick for fill-in duties against Dartmouth that same year, the freshman quarterback engineered the biggest come-from-behind win in Harvard football annals.

Fitzpatrick thwarted the Brown defense for the remainder of the game. He did it through the air, completing ten of sixteen passes for 113 yards. He did it on the ground, running for 131 yards. Eight of his rushing attempts went for more than 8 yards, and Fitzpatrick became the first Harvard quarterback in a decade to run for more than 100 yards. And not to be overlooked, he also outran the entire Brown team by 6 yards. Half of Fitzpatrick's runs came on passing plays, but Murphy didn't mind. He'd given Fitzpatrick curt, specific instruction when he sent the sophomore into the game: "Go out and do whatever you need to do." If nothing else, Fitzpatrick knew how to follow directions. The Crimson managed to eke out a 26–24 victory.

The Morris-Gessner matchup took top billing in the pregame coverage of the Harvard-Brown contest, but after the game it was all about Fitzpatrick. In Harvard's second game, and for the second time that year, the sophomore had handily finished what Rose started. For those Crimson fans wondering about life after Rose and

Morris, Fitzpatrick showed them that Harvard had a future, and he was it.

He showed Rose, too.

After a healthy dose of Advil and with the assistance of crutches, Rose managed to watch the end of the fourth quarter from the Harvard bench. He witnessed Fitzpatrick's come-from-behind effort to keep Harvard's winning streak intact with a mixture of pride and personal disappointment. Rose had to admit that the competitor in him wasn't ready to see his reign as the starter come to such an end. He vowed not to let a pesky back problem separate him from his job. As long as Rose remained healthy, Murphy backed him as the starter. The team still belonged to the hobbled Hawaiian captain. He would get healthy. The future would have to wait.

* * *

Fitzpatrick wasn't the only double-threat quarterback in the Ivy League ranks. Yale's Alvin Cowan looked to build on the amazing record-setting numbers from his first varsity start as the Bulldogs' quarterback. The Cornell Big Red, Yale's first Ivy opponent of the season, intended to stop the rising star. They didn't care about all the attention Cowan received from his six-touchdown game versus San Diego. The ECAC Player of the Week Award, the Coca-Cola Gold Helmet Award, and the mention in *Sports Illustrated*. . . . whatever. If Cowan wanted to make a difference as Yale's quarterback he'd have to prove himself versus the Ivy League on September 28.

Not only did the Cornell players stop Cowan's ascension, they brought him crashing back to earth.

Cornell promptly scored on its first offensive drive, a sixty-five-yard romp downfield that resulted in a 6–0 lead after a failed extra point attempt. Cowan entered the game with Yale behind for the first time in his short tenure as the starter. On the second play from scrimmage, Cowan took the snap and countered away from his two receivers to influence linebacker flow to the wrong direction. He then rolled left and looked downfield. The Big Red had swarmed

Ron Benigno, the primary receiver. Cowan instinctively went for the big play, a deep pass down the sidelines to secondary receiver P. J. Collins. In his fervor to stun the Cornell defense with a long pass right out of the gate, Cowan momentarily forgot that no one protected his back side on this play. Big Red cornerback Kyle Thomas leveled him as he released the ball.

Pain immediately radiated from Cowan's ankle. He shrugged it off, thinking it was a sprain. After he limped noticeably on the next two plays, Siedlecki called a timeout to assess the situation. The doctors poked and prodded, and only then did Cowan realize that the pain emanated from his leg, not his ankle. X-rays later showed a broken leg. Siedlecki sent in backup quarterback Jeff Mroz.

A slim, sinewy Mroz entered Yale's training camp in 2002 fully expecting to earn the starter's job. Of course, so did Cowan. Siedlecki let the two of them battle for the position, but at the time he had no idea how much the quarterback competition would help the team. Now, still early in the season, the memory of taking first-team snaps was fresh in Mroz's mind. He knew the offense. He could control the team. He wanted to prove that Siedlecki had picked the wrong starter.

Born into a family of quarterbacks, the dark-haired Mroz grew up in Greensburg, Pennsylvania, part of the western half of the state's fertile football breeding ground (home turf of Joe Montana, Joe Namath, and Dan Marino). He had been honing his technical skills for years. Siedlecki believed in Mroz's abilities to execute the plays, but the sophomore didn't have the same leadership qualities as Cowan. Mroz, who typically seemed calm and even a bit withdrawn, let his playing speak for him, quietly leading by example. Cowan wore his emotions on his sleeve. He'd readily castigate a teammate for dropping a soft pass but he'd also be the first to give a player a congratulatory slap on the helmet for making a good play. Losing Cowan's enthusiasm at the helm removed an intangible asset from the offense. Siedlecki could only hope that Mroz's playmaking ability could make up for it.

Mroz eagerly took the field. The switch was so smooth that Jason Lange, pacing the sidelines and focused on his defensive responsibilities, didn't even notice that Cowan had been replaced until after several plays had occurred. With the sudden change in quarterbacks, Siedlecki opted for the running game. He felt that softening the Big Red defensive front with 5'7", 185-pound fireplug Robert Carr offered the best chance to win. His instinct was right. The Bulldogs responded to Cornell's touchdown with one of their own, a four-yard scamper by Carr.

Then he ran away with the game.

Carr finished the afternoon with 235 yards on twenty-eight carries and four touchdowns, including a 45-yard run to the end zone. The junior tailback also rushed his way into Yale's record books, breaking Rich Diana's 1981 single-game rushing record of 222 yards. Yale demolished the host team, 50–23, but Carr's record and the offense's fifty-point output weren't the only stories of the game.

While the offense busily added to Yale's mounting total, Jason Lange and his crew rallied around Mroz as well. The Yale defense obliterated Cornell, holding them to a meager 78 yards of total offense over three and one-half quarters of play. Coach Flanders's defensive backs contained Keith Ferguson, Cornell's marquee receiver and a recognized threat throughout the league, allowing him only four catches and 29 receiving yards. The defense even helped with the scoring on a 21-yard fumble recovery by James Beck.

In a postgame interview, Coach Siedlecki exuded optimism.

"We faced a lot of adversity in the game and overcame it and we need to build from there," Siedlecki said. "I've got a real good feeling about this football team right now. They didn't blink. They didn't step back. They didn't feel sorry for themselves. They said, 'Hey, we've still got to go out there and play football.' With preseason injuries and now this, they've overcome more adversity than any team I've ever coached."

Siedlecki could picture a November upset at Harvard Stadium. He just didn't know which quarterback to envision.

Cowan didn't waste time feeling sorry for himself. It wouldn't help him or his team. "I broke the fibula on my right leg, right next to the calf muscle," Cowan recalled in 2003, his gregarious demeanor and broad smile only slightly dampened. "Doctors referred to that area as breaking it 'up high' because it didn't involve any of the ligaments, tendons, or bones in my ankle. That was a good thing as far as recovery time went." The driven quarterback set out to heal his leg. Fast.

*   *   *

With one win apiece in league competition, both achieved with a back-up quarterback at the helm, Harvard and Yale showed early resiliency and depth—two necessary components for finishing atop the Ivy heap. There wasn't much a coach could do in terms of resiliency. Siedlecki and Murphy couldn't force their teams to let losses roll off their backs and come out fighting the following week. They couldn't make their players rally around another teammate after a starter's injury. The coaches could only look for that quality in the young men they recruited.

And courting, charming, and luring such young men to campus is the only way to provide depth on the roster. The football fortunes of both schools rely heavily on the coaching staffs to bring in quality players. After all, not many high school All-Americans look past the colleges where football players are kings and administrations are their subjects, where the vast athletic complexes dwarf the libraries and coaches make more than professors, and where a player can major in recreation studies and concentrate on his future pro career.

Recruiting in the Ivy League is vastly different from the rest of college football, although it all begins identically. The Ivies are subject to the same rules as the rest of Division I-A and Division I-AA teams. Murphy, Siedlecki, and their staffs can contact recruits a fixed number of times during specific weeks on the calendar. Recruits can make a certain number of official visits to campus, trips which the school pays for either in part or completely. These rules theoretically put Murphy and Siedlecki on a level playing field with all other Division I-AA programs.

But then come the challenges from the Ivy League.

First and foremost, each football player admitted to the Ivy schools must pass muster on academics alone. If the head coach at a major college football power has the opportunity to sign one of the top high school recruits in the country, that coach will find a way to get the player on his roster regardless of his academic stats. A resume with 1,600 yards rushing in a season means a lot more to a Division I-A coach than 1600 on the SATs. Not so in the Ivies.

In the Ivy League, all prospective football candidates must first file an application with the admissions office. The coaches might forward a recruit's academic statistics to the admissions office to get a feel for whether or not that candidate has a shot at getting in, but in no way do the coaches influence the admissions office's decision. They only consult the admissions office to save time—they don't want to chase players that will never get in based on a substandard academic record. There's no other way in than through the admissions office. No player gains admittance as a favor. He must earn it as a student.

The Ivy League has remained true to the original tenets upon which it was founded, and therefore top priority is to keep a balance between academics and athletics. The Council of Ivy Group Presidents, the governing body of the Ivy League, consists of two-thirds academic participants from the Ivy schools (the school presidents and an at-large faculty member from each school who has no ties to the athletic departments) and one-third representatives focused on athletics (the athletic directors). The council sets all Ivy League policy, including guidelines for recruiting. While other college conferences might have a council with representatives of each school, they also employ a commissioner who wields the most power. Few make efforts to impose stricter limits and guidelines within their conference than the NCAA minimum requirements. The Council of Ivy Group Presidents adheres to NCAA guidelines as well, but places much higher standards—academically and otherwise—on its student athletes.

And unfortunately for Murphy and Siedlecki, they direct special rules at the football teams. Rule changes implemented in July 2002 further hampered an already difficult recruiting process for the two coaches.

During the preseason Murphy and Siedlecki learned that the Council of Ivy Group Presidents reduced the maximum number of recruits for the 2003 season from thirty-five to thirty (only eleven years after lowering the number from fifty to thirty-five). Murphy and Siedlecki also would not be allowed to retain all of their assistant coaches. Starting with the 2003 season each coach could only have seven full-time and three part-time coaches on staff; down from six full-time and six part-time coaches. At least two coaches had to go.

The coaches were baffled. It seemed that Ivy League officials wanted to make it harder for the coaches to field a team even though the players fulfilled academic obligations year in and year out. But Ivy League officials insisted that the changes resulted only from a continued attempt to keep a balance between student athletes and the remainder of the students on campus.

Jeff Orleans, the executive director for the Council of Ivy Group Presidents, said that "as the pool of qualified applicants for Ivy institutions continues to grow, Ivy institutions want to provide admissions offices with as much discretion as possible. The Ivy presidents periodically reviewed admissions in football since the current admissions structure was created in the early 1980s, and they concluded that we could maintain competitive and safe football activities with a few less players."

No matter the reason, starting with the Class of 2007, Siedlecki and Murphy would have to make do with five fewer slots on their rosters. With one mandate from the Council of Ivy Group Presidents, the recruiting competition stiffened.

And getting players through the admissions office is only one piece of the complicated Ivy League recruiting puzzle. Another way in which the Council of Ivy Group Presidents maintains a system of checks and balances between athletics and academics is the Academic Index. According to a December 1996 Ivy Group press release, "In football, the overall Academic Index pattern of matriculated student-athletes must have a specified relationship to the Academic Index patterns of the school's previous four matriculated classes." Drafted in the hallowed halls of academia, in plain English the system boils down to this: the football players (and all other athletes) must be, on average, as smart as all the other students in their school's previous four classes. And each year, the average student at Harvard and Yale gets smarter.

The Academic Index pattern is commonly referred to as the "band system." Each student's academic stats are boiled down to one number, and then the spectrum of numbers, from highest (e.g., smartest) to lowest, is divided into bands (much like the grade divisions of A, B, C, etc.). These schools have a 10 percent acceptance rate, so the Harvard or Yale football player who lands in the bottom band would likely have some of the best numbers at many other colleges. But Siedlecki and Murphy can't take many of those players. Each coach gets a certain number of recruits in each band, but 70 percent of all recruits must fit in the *top two*. Cream of the cream of the intellectual crop.

The band system theoretically puts all the Ivy schools in the same situation. Each coach must adhere to the bands based on his school's average Academic Index. While all the Ivy schools are notoriously difficult to get into, admissions to some are more difficult than others. Since the Ivy League adopted the band system in 1993, the success of one school stands out. Over the ten years that the band system has been in place, the Penn Quakers have won the Ivy League championship five times. Because Penn's incoming class size is nearly double that of all the Ivy schools except Cornell's, the average Academic Index is lower. The band system appears to create a distinct advantage for Penn, but Jeff Orleans believes the system is fair.

"First, we all understand that the schools are different in many ways, and that these differences make different schools more or less attractive to different applicants," Orleans said. "Secondly, when folks are candid, they'll acknowledge that they can define a set of advantages and disadvantages both for their own school and for each of the others. The folks at Penn likely would remind you that most applicants—including most athletic applicants—who are accepted at both Penn and Harvard or Yale choose Harvard or Yale, so *those* schools have an advantage. If the advantage claimed for Penn is that it can take a few athletes with slightly lower SATs, they would argue that it is offset by the 'draw' of Harvard or Yale."

Siedlecki also downplayed Penn's alleged advantage in the band system. "Penn has had twenty-four fifth-year players over the last four years. The next highest number in the league is six. I think that is a far greater advantage than the fact that their bands are lower than ours," he said.

So not only do Murphy and Siedlecki have to get their players past the admissions office, but they can't all be hovering at the bottom of the class. Given these stringent restrictions and the small number of talented football players who clear both hurdles, it's easy to see why the Ivy League coaches compete fiercely for the top prospects in that subset. Murphy and Siedlecki look at opposing team rosters and see many names they tried to secure for their own squads. In the Division I-A ranks of college football prospect lists, the number-three- and number-six-rated quarterbacks might not be separated by a wide talent margin—it may not make a big difference to a Division I-A coach to lose the number three quarterback prospect to another big-time football power if he can get the sixth-ranked player instead. The coach who lost out in that scenario may never even play against the one that got away.

But losing an Ivy recruit matters enormously to Murphy and Siedlecki. The skill level drops considerably between the top three or four players available at a given position and the rest of the field. Also, Murphy and Siedlecki know that they'll have to compete against the recruits that they can't persuade to sign. And if this isn't enough, there's also another element to Ivy League recruiting that Siedlecki and Murphy face. Say a player has perfect SATs, sports an academic index off the charts, and rivals Eddie George in running ability. The admissions office loves him and the coaches adore him. He still has to want to attend an Ivy League school *and to do so on his own dime* (unless he qualifies for need-based financial aid). The Ivy League doesn't offer athletic scholarships, only grants based on need. It adds up to quite a few hurdles for the coaches to overcome. One obstacle, however, stands out more than any other. An A. The extra A in Division I-AA.

Overall, the Ivy League sports teams flourished under the original 1954 Ivy Group Agreement, when the eight schools created the Ivy League. The member schools continued to compete at the Division I level in most sports, even in the face of the highest academic standards in the country. Football, however, suffered. Still the highest profile sport for all the Ivy League colleges and their alumni supporters, the caliber of play has declined significantly over the forty-seven years that an official Ivy League champion has been crowned. In 1982 the NCAA relegated all Ivy League football teams to Division I-AA from Division I-A.

During his thirty-two-year tenure as Yale's head coach, Carm Cozza saw firsthand the decline in the skill level of Ivy League football.

When Cozza started coaching in 1965, Yale wasn't that far removed from being synonymous with national big-time college football. It always had been. Yalie Walter Camp's innovations helped evolve the sport from its infancy. Bulldog gridiron great Albie Booth had thrilled fans nationwide in the Depression era. Clint Frank and Larry Kelley had won back-to-back Heisman Trophies in 1936 and 1937. Major networks ABC, CBS, and NBC had televised one Yale game each season nearly every year since 1948. And just five years before Cozza's arrival Yale had ended the season ranked in the top twenty in both the Associated Press and United Press International polls. Cozza didn't have much trouble convincing players to attend

Yale. His first recruiting class included three future NFL draft picks: tight end Bruce Weinstein, quarterback Brian Dowling, and 1969 rookie of the year running back Calvin Hill. But by the time Cozza retired, things had changed. Yale's only national attention came on the day of The Game, a spot for Yale in the AP or UPI national poll results was impossible, and Cozza battled the other Ivy League coaches for players from a limited pool of qualified students.

"The I-AA designation really had a negative effect on recruiting efforts, especially with the elite student athletes," Cozza said. "We started losing guys to schools like Stanford and Northwestern once Yale went to I-AA."

These days, if football is more important than academics, players can take their game to a higher level of play in Division I-A. Any player with NFL aspirations can see a path to the pros more clearly by playing in the Big Ten or SEC than by playing in the Ivy League. If grades and a good job count as much as good football, players can get a degree from some of the country's best academic Division I-A institutions such as Duke, Stanford, or Northwestern. Murphy and Siedlecki have to count on some of the more talented available players to consider life after football and the advantages of a degree from Harvard or Yale.

It boils down to this: in order to keep their jobs, Murphy and Siedlecki have only to find extremely smart, talented athletes who want an Ivy degree and don't mind playing in I-AA. Oh, and who don't care that they can't play in a high-profile bowl game. Because unlike Ivy League athletes in other high-profile sports like hockey and basketball, Ivy League football teams aren't allowed to compete in any playoffs or bowl games. It seems like an impossible, unenviable task, one that gets more difficult each year. Indeed, the Ivy League may push the sport into a position from which it can't recover.

But that's just what the newly formed Ivy Football Association hoped it could help avoid.

In 1997, Stanislaw "Stas" Maliszewski, the president of the Princeton Football Association, former two-time All-American guard, and

1966 Princeton graduate, discussed his alma mater's football booster organization with the Yale Football Association's Don Scharf before the Yale-Valparaiso pregame reception. Maliszewski realized that he and Scharf had similar issues and problems, and that it was unlikely that the two were alone. He decided to contact other members of the Ivy League football community. After several conversations, Maliszewski decided to form an independent organization to promote and celebrate the Ivy League schools' unique history and contribution to football's development. Bob Hall, an All-Ivy selection who captained the 1965 Brown football team and played against Maliszewski, loved the idea and jumped on board. Hank Higdon, captain of the 1963 Yale football team, soon joined them. Together, the three founders of the Ivy Football Association brainstormed a plan.

"The Ivy Football Association's short-term goals include gaining eligibility for postseason play and securing television contracts that allowed for each team to play in a televised game at least once per season," Higdon said.

On the surface it didn't seem like much of an agenda, but the IFA faced an uphill climb. The Ivy League strives to keep professionalism out of its sports programs, and increased television coverage invites the potential for schedule changes, additional media interference, and a perceived focus on athletics over academics. Any postseason bowl play would tamper with the neat little package in which the Ivy League football schedule exists—for example, an Ivy League team that reaches the national Division I-AA championship game would have to play an additional four games and finish the season just before Christmas.

Maliszewski, Hall, and Higdon knew they would need a good deal of help from influential members of the Ivy football community to see their goals realized. They decided the best way to raise awareness and to further the organization's cause was to hold a biennial banquet honoring prominent former Ivy League football players for their off-the-field accomplishments.

The Ivy Football Association feted one player from each of the Ivy

League schools at its second dinner in January 2003. The dinner moved to The Waldorf-Astoria in New York City after the first celebration in 2001 oversubscribed at a smaller venue. The black-tie event's list of honorees was extremely impressive: Paul Choquette Jr., Brown '60, chairman and CEO of Gilbane Building Company; Allison Butts, Columbia '64, CEO of Next Wave LLC; Charles F. Knight, Cornell '57, chairman of Emerson Electric Company; Henry Paulson, Dartmouth '68, chairman and CEO of the Goldman Sachs Group, Inc.; David Pottruck, Penn '70, president and CEO of Charles Schwab Corporation; Kenneth Wolfe, Yale '61, former president and CEO of Hershey Foods Corporation; George P. Shultz, Princeton '42, former secretary of state under President Ronald Reagan; and Tommy Lee Jones, Harvard '68, Academy Award–winning actor. Yale graduate and New York governor George Pataki served as honorable chairman of the event and Eli alumnus Jack Ford of ABC fame was the master of ceremonies. Over one thousand people attended. Though a fledgling organization, the IFA clearly had friends in high places, and the event wasn't merely a high-powered social affair despite its star-studded lineup.

"The purpose of the dinner is to honor and recognize the nonathletic accomplishments of those who benefit from playing football in the Ivy League and who represent the thousands who have benefited from participating in an environment with a rigorous academic approach, and yet a rigorous football program as well," Higdon said.

The 2002 mandate that reduced recruiting class size and eliminated some coaching staff members is just the type of action the IFA would like to defeat in the future. Coupled with the fact that each year the admissions hurdle forces applicants to be smarter than the last year in order to receive an offer, the IFA fears that the reduction of football players and coaches will put Ivy League football in peril, that the changes may lead to further degradation or elimination of football at the subvarsity levels. IFA members even worry that top student athletes may shun the Ivy League altogether.

"Those student-athletes at the lower end of the ability spectrum might opt for New England Small College Athletic Conference schools such as Amherst or Williams if the level of play continues to diminish. Those players of higher athletic ability may turn to Division I-A schools like Stanford, Duke, or Northwestern," Higdon said.

Higdon, Maliszewski, Hall, and their IFA supporters acknowledge that putting Ivy League football teams in playoffs and national tournaments may not be readily embraced by Ivy League football purists. Ironically, the biggest draw of the Ivy football season is a problem for the IFA's push for more exposure.

"One of the biggest obstacles is the sanctity of Harvard versus Yale," Higdon said. A fine line separates nourishing tradition from extinguishing the future. Meddling with The Game could potentially create a strange rift between the IFA and the very coaches whose teams they support.

"We finish our season every year in front of over fifty thousand rabid fans. It's like a bowl game. Why would we want to go and play in front of ten thousand people the following week against a scholarship school?" said Tim Murphy. "It would be anticlimactic."

After all, how do you follow The Game with a mere playoff game?

7

Clash of the Titans

JACK SIEDLECKI LOST MORE than a quarterback when Alvin Cowan broke his leg at Cornell. He lost the heart and soul of his offensive unit. Cowan yelled, Cowan swore, Cowan galvanized the younger players. The Bulldogs believed in him and now their leader was reduced to a sideline cheerleader on crutches. Soft-spoken, reserved Jeff Mroz proved an able signal-caller in his winning performance after Cowan went down, but Siedlecki knew that the team needed the fiery energy that the junior offered. He worried that Mroz simply lacked Cowan's innate ability to marshal the troops.

As a sophomore, Mroz found it difficult to portray himself as a leader. Many of the other players were older, with more experience, and many of them had longstanding relationships with Cowan. In the Cornell game, Mroz did the only thing he could think of: he let his playing do the talking. The situation for the upcoming week differed. Mroz had seven long days to think about starting. He met the day with anticipation rather than nervousness.

"The week leading up to the Holy Cross game was a great week for me, not because of the heightened media attention or that I was more recognized around campus, but because it was my first start," Mroz said. "The reason I came to Yale was to be the starting QB early in my career. All the years of hard work finally paid off." Mroz looked forward to playing in front of two fans in particular—his parents.

The week of his stunning performance at Cornell, Mroz's parents attended Princeton's game. His brother Dave was the backup quarterback for the Tigers. But not only did the Mrozes miss all of Jeff's action—Dave never got into the Princeton game.

Harvard victim Holy Cross traveled to the Yale Bowl on October 5, facing a host team with a 2–0 record. Mroz did his part to make it an inhospitable stay for the Crusaders. He threw ten complete passes on eighteen attempts for 118 yards. Two touchdowns. No interceptions. He played steadily and executed well, building his team's confidence in him, but the performance didn't make him the team's new inspirational leader. Sophomore running back Robert Carr shouldered that load.

As in the Cornell contest, Carr again was the story of the game. He had shone in Ithaca after Cowan left the game, and continued his one-man ground assault against Holy Cross by posting his second game of rushing 200-plus yards. Quite a feat, considering that since Yale started keeping records, no one had done such a thing. The powerful running back ran thirty-eight times for 219 yards and one touchdown.

Siedlecki saw Carr further filling the leadership void on offense with each yard he gained. "He's an infectious type of kid," Siedlecki told the *New Haven Register*. "For a kid, as young as he is, to be the leader that he is, that says a lot and more."

Jason Lange provided the Bulldog defense with all the leadership it needed, though his position on the line couldn't have been more low profile. His consistent play in the trenches permeated the defensive ranks. The more pressure he and his defensive linemates put on the opposing line and quarterback, the easier they made the secondary's job. Lange's performance in the Holy Cross game resulted in three interceptions for the Bulldogs. Safety Don Davis and cornerback Greg Owens each had a pick, and Lange, not to be outdone, recorded the third. "The secondary really stepped up," noted Lange. "When Holy Cross threw the long ball, we always managed to be there."

One statistic in particular pleased defensive coordinator Rick Flanders. Holy Cross's star receiver, Ari Confesor, caught only six passes for 47 yards. Against Harvard's defense, Confesor had two touchdowns and 318 all-purpose yards. In all, the Yale defense held Holy Cross to 132 yards passing on fifteen of thirty-two attempts— not bad considering that Holy Cross entered the game averaging nearly 200 yards passing per game. Two Holy Cross touchdowns came through the air, but Flanders had known teams would still be able to score on his inexperienced pass defenders. He just had to see to it that it didn't happen too often, and the pass defense showed that they could contain a potential game-breaking receiver like Confesor. Staring down a pass-oriented Ivy schedule, Flanders felt comforted by the 28–19 victory.

He and the Bulldogs faced a different threat the following week versus Dartmouth.

Yale celebrated its three-hundredth anniversary as a university in 2001, and the Big Green of Dartmouth crashed that party, beating host Yale 32–27. The 2002 Bulldogs ventured to Hanover, New Hampshire, on October 12 with revenge in mind. Carr's legs, Mroz's arm, and a pass defense ranked ninth nationally in Division I-AA despite a host of injuries rounded out the Bulldog weaponry. Settling the score looked like an easy job. Dartmouth had lost its first three games and ranked dead last out of 123 Division I-AA teams in defense.

But the power of pride can't be discounted. Prior to the game, Robert Carr led the nation in all-purpose yards per game and was second in rushing with 186 yards per game. Pregame discussions buzzed with the speculation that Carr might match the Ivy League record of more than 200 yards rushing in three consecutive games. Cornell's Ed Marinaro, *Hill Street Blues* actor and Heisman Trophy runner-up, accomplished the feat over two seasons in 1970 and 1971. The Big Green bristled at the thought of allowing such an accomplishment.

The defense keyed on Carr and the running game, holding the explosive back to 108 yards and a touchdown on thirty-two carries.

Marinaro's record stood, but Carr still had four games rushing for over 100 yards on which to build. The lost record didn't bother Carr. "I don't like to look at statistics. I don't like to think of myself as an individual," Carr said after the game. "I don't think I'd be where I am if it weren't for the other guys on the team."

And there were indeed highlights from some of those other guys. Mroz continued to improve, throwing thirteen completions on twenty-three attempts for 246 yards and posting his best game since he took over as starter. The sophomore punctuated his performance with a 42-yard touchdown pass to Jay Schulze in the fourth quarter to close within three points of Dartmouth, 20–17. After nearly three complete games, Mroz still hadn't thrown an interception. The offensive line couldn't protect Mroz the entire game, though, and the Big Green sacked the sophomore four times.

Yale's pass defense again succeeded in keeping the ball away from a premier receiver. Junior Casey Cramer owned Dartmouth's records for catches and receiving yards by a tight end, with eighty-one receptions for 1,104 yards and eleven touchdowns. Cramer's 113 receiving yards per game leading up to the Yale contest put him third nationally among Division I-AA schools. The Bulldog defense, however, ensured that Dartmouth quarterback Brian Mann found tight end Cramer only four times for 53 yards. Bulldog junior defensive back Barton Simmons guaranteed that Cramer did not factor in the scoring when he deflected a pass in the third quarter that looked destined for Cramer and the end zone. Regrettably, no one would remember Simmons for that pass breakup or his nine tackles. His two punt-return fumbles stood out instead.

The first culminated in a Dartmouth touchdown. The second came with five minutes remaining in the game, just after Mroz's touchdown pass to Schulze. Simmons made an aggressive play returning a Dartmouth punt, trying to get good field position. "I should have let the ball go. I made a mistake that hurt us," he said. "It was a short, low kick. I thought I had room to run." More than anything, the latter fumble swung the game's momentum to

Dartmouth. Yale still had a chance to tie the game with seven seconds left, but Dartmouth's Clayton Smith blocked John Troost's low 35-yard field goal attempt. Dartmouth 20, Yale 17.

The loss rankled Siedlecki. His team had succumbed to the pressure in a close game, practically giving the win away. Siedlecki especially disliked losing on mistakes. The Dartmouth game gave the coach horrible flashbacks to the 2001 season and the team attitude he and his staff had tried so hard to change. Those Bulldogs had no bite at the end of the season, resigning themselves to a mediocre year before they even played all the games on their schedule. The coach and his staff had taken great pains in the off-season to reform the team, introducing extra conditioning efforts that included several seven o'clock in the morning runs each week. Siedlecki hoped that the additional effort would train the team to work harder in order to avoid failure.

Jason Lange ably led the defense, but Siedlecki still needed someone to fill the leadership void on offense. Mroz and Carr had shown that they could occasionally do the job, but Siedlecki needed consistency. Hard-charging, excitable consistency.

"I'd be kidding you if I didn't wish that Alvin Cowan was in there to grab somebody by the face mask, because that's what Alvin would have done. Jeff's a sophomore and he hasn't been in that role before," Siedlecki said after the game. Cowan couldn't reach any face masks from Texas, though.

"I had gone home that weekend to get some work done on my leg by a massage therapist in Austin," Cowan said. "I was listening to the game on the radio. I wished that I'd been there, looking back, but at that point I had to do whatever I could to get myself prepared to play. The team was really down after that game. They seemed to feel like they'd let one slip through their hands—and they had. Every bounce seemed to go Dartmouth's way and we didn't help ourselves by committing some costly errors."

One team member commented that the squad seemed emotionally flat during the Dartmouth loss, something incomprehensible to the demanding Siedlecki and his "get it done" style. "We only get ten games! How can you not be emotionally up for the game?" Siedlecki rhetorically asked during an interview. He knew the team had to bounce back the next week or the season would spiral down the drain just like 2001. Unfortunately, the Lehigh Mountain Hawks beckoned on October 19—not the creampuff school Siedlecki needed.

Even with two losses, Lehigh stood at number nineteen in the national Division I-AA rankings. Nearly unbeatable at home in recent years, the Patriot League school handed most Ivy League visitors a loss. This year, however, Lehigh faced severe adversity in the form of injured players. Three of those were quarterbacks, which meant the Yale defense faced number four on the depth chart, Kyle Keating. Siedlecki hoped his defense could rattle the inexperienced sophomore.

Mroz hoped the offense could capitalize on the situation. He believed that Yale had to win to gain back some legitimacy it had lost in the Dartmouth game. "Lehigh is such a good team that they're almost the measuring stick to see if you are legit," Mroz said in a pregame interview. "When Penn beat them, everyone started saying 'Penn's for real.' When Princeton gave them a game, people said, 'Princeton's got a good team.' It would be great for us to come up with a win against Lehigh. It would really open up some eyes around the league."

Mroz did his best to snag a win, completing twenty-four passes for 223 yards in a defensively dominated game, but his run of games without an interception ended. The Lehigh defense picked off two Mroz passes, including one in the end zone with eight seconds remaining in the game. Lehigh also sacked Mroz four times. The Mountain Hawks stunted Yale's running game as well. The defense contained Carr to 65 yards on twenty-two carries, preventing the running back from reaching the 100-yard plateau for the first time in 2002.

The Bulldog defensive unit did its part by forcing and recovering four fumbles, allowing the Mountain Hawks only one score in four trips to the red zone. In all, the pass defense allowed 106 passing yards on nine of fifteen attempts and Lehigh managed only 301 yards in total offense, their lowest output of the season so far. Simmons chipped in with two sacks and an interception. The defense's game pleased Yale captain Jason Lange. "I have very high expectations for our defense," Lange said. "We played well, and I think this is the caliber of defense that we can play and have to play."

Although both the Yale defensive and offensive units played well enough to win the game, Lehigh managed one more touchdown than the Bulldogs. The Mountain Hawks, with their fourth-string quarterback, won the game 14–7.

Two losses in a row. Now at the season's midpoint, the Yale record stood at 3–2 overall and 1–1 in Ivy League play. Still redeemable. Siedlecki, however, still worried that the year would slip away. In 2001 the team was in the same position and then finished a dismal 3–6 overall with a 1–6 record against Ivy opponents. The Lehigh game deepened his fears. "We played young. We have to grow up," he said. "The last five are Ivy games, five more tough football games." Yale couldn't have asked for a worse opponent the following week on October 26: Penn, the first Ivy team to beat Lehigh in Lehigh's last sixteen games against Ancient Eight teams.

Yale freshman David Knox immediately let the Penn Quakers know that the Bulldogs came prepared to play. The running back returned the opening kickoff ninety-six yards for a touchdown. Yale's defense seconded the motion by forcing Penn's big-threat wide receiver Rob Milanese to fumble after his first catch of the day on Penn's opening offensive series. The defensive struggle between Penn's second-ranked run defense and Yale's ninth-ranked pass defense continued throughout the first quarter, and Yale ended the quarter ahead 7–0. Then, Penn found its groove.

Quarterback Mike Mitchell began picking apart the Yale secondary. After he'd hit tight end Matt Michaleski with the tying score on an eighteen-yard touchdown pass, Mitchell stymied Yale's defensive backs with a trick play. Penn forced Yale to punt after

Michaleski's touchdown. On the first play, Mitchell pitched the ball to wide receiver Joe Phillips, who promptly hurled it to a wide open Erik Bolinder for a touchdown. After a field goal apiece, Yale went into the locker room down 17–10 at the half.

The second half was all Penn as Mitchell and Milanese connected again and again en route to a 41–20 win. Mitchell humbled the Yale defensive backs, finishing with 351 yards passing and three touchdowns. Milanese logged twelve catches for 140 yards and two touchdowns. The tandem simply overwhelmed the Yale defense, and Siedlecki made no excuses. "They have a couple of outstanding players who had one hell of a day, and we didn't have a lot of answers for them," Siedlecki said at the postgame press conference.

Flanders knew that Siedlecki wanted solutions for the likes of Mitchell and Milanese, and with Brown's Gessner, Princeton's Opara, and Harvard's Morris still on the docket, Flanders knew that he needed them fast. Yale's record stood at an even 3–3, but 1–2 in Ivy League games. The Bulldogs needed to make some quick changes to preserve any hopes for Ivy championship contention. Siedlecki hoped that Mroz, Carr, or another player would provide a spark to trigger the offense in the stretch run, because he now knew for sure that it wasn't going to come from Cowan. Doctors recommended that the junior spend the rest of the season on the sidelines.

● ● ●

No quarterback controversy raged in Cambridge in the preseason, but questions slowly began to emerge in September. First a Holy Cross defender slammed the record-setting Neil Rose in the field, and then he hurt his back on the bus ride to Brown. Rather than tiptoeing around the senior's delicate back injury, Murphy turned the reins over to Ryan Fitzpatrick.

Though Fitzpatrick was the backup, Murphy felt that he easily could have performed from game one as the starter. Fitzpatrick and Rose shared one trait: both were natural leaders. Just as he had with the technical quarterback duties, Fitzpatrick stepped right into the leadership role that goes hand in hand with the position. When a play came off as outlined in the playbook, Fitzpatrick executed. When a play broke down and it looked like an imminent sack, Fitzpatrick usually eked out some positive yardage. And he made it look easy. Fitzpatrick's instinctive confidence inspired the players around him. He simply wouldn't let the team down, and his teammates returned the favor.

Leading up to the third game of the season, Rose and Fitzpatrick did not know which quarterback would lead the Crimson on October 5 when the defending Ivy League champions met Lehigh, the defending Patriot League champions. Prior to meeting with a back specialist, Rose commented, "I haven't been cleared officially yet. There are a lot of things going on. If I had to bet on it, I'd say I'm going to play. The question is, will they let me?"

Good thing Rose didn't place the bet. Murphy named Fitzpatrick the starter. "My decision to start Ryan is because he played so well and because Neil has not practiced much," Murphy said after he made the announcement during the weekly football luncheon for members of the press. "If Neil was completely healthy, and he had more practices, he'd be our guy. He is our captain and our team leader."

Murphy made clear that Fitzpatrick's starting spot wasn't permanent. "From a loyalty standpoint, some people have short memories. I'm not about to bench a quarterback that completes ninety percent of his passes," he said. Murphy added that he'd still use Rose in the game if he felt Rose was ready and the doctors agreed.

Murphy said all the right things, but the press wasn't buying it. The writers believed that they had a juicy, unexpected angle for their weekly reports on Harvard football. They smelled a quarterback controversy.

Harvard traveled to Bethlehem, Pennsylvania, to fight the Mountain Hawks and, they hoped, to continue the Harvard winning streak. They had their work cut out for them. Lehigh despised losing at home and had handed the last twenty-six visitors a loss. The ray of hope that Harvard clung to was that they were the last team to leave Goodman Stadium with a win. But that was five years ago. Somebody's streak was about to end.

Fitzpatrick played almost flawlessly in the seesaw skirmish, completing twenty-two of twenty-six passes for 289 yards and no interceptions. More than half of those went to Morris, who had twelve catches for 129 yards. Fitzpatrick made up for not throwing a touchdown pass by running over the goal line on two occasions. Nick Palazzo scored three times and rushed for 68 total yards on twenty-five attempts. Not a lot, but he covered the critical ground.

The Mountain Hawks posted 408 total yards of offense, slightly under their season average after four games, which included a game of over 600 total yards against Buffalo. Lehigh's quarterback shortage stung the team, as Harvard's Mante Dzakuma intercepted each of the two Mountain Hawk quarterbacks who played. The Crimson defense also recovered two of the three balls Lehigh fumbled.

Harvard either led or was tied for the entire game with the exception of forty-eight seconds. The last forty-eight seconds. With under a minute remaining, Jermaine Pugh pushed his way into the end zone, bringing the score to 36–35 in favor of the home team and stopping Harvard's win streak cold.

Murphy took the loss in stride. "We made a living during the winning streak making plays when dealing with adversity," he said. "Today we didn't do too well with prosperity."

The coach did like what he saw in Fitzpatrick, despite the losing effort. "I think he's a very poised, courageous kid," Murphy said. "Like any sophomore quarterback, he'll be better when he's a senior. But I think he played well."

With the pressure of maintaining the winning streak gone, the Crimson focused on its next opponent, the Cornell Big Red. The quarterback question still simmered, but either way, Harvard looked to exploit a weaker Cornell team with its potent offense.

From kickoff to the final whistle, it was all Harvard in a soggy affair at the stadium on October 12. Fitzpatrick started the game again as

Rose's back continued to plague him. The sophomore took the opportunity to get himself into the record books right behind the record setter he replaced. He took second place in the single-game total offense category by amassing 417 yards, missing Rose's record of 427 by 10 yards. Fitzpatrick completed twenty-four of thirty-two passes for 353 yards and three touchdowns. He also led the team in rushing with 66 yards on the ground.

Fitzpatrick had some help. Morris posted another day of over 100 receiving yards by catching eleven balls for 165 yards. One catch was good for 54 yards and a touchdown. Rodney Byrnes had six receptions for 55 yards and returned a kickoff 89 yards for a touchdown. When all was said and done, Harvard reigned in the rain, 52–23. They scored three touchdowns in the final eighteen minutes, making the final score seem more lopsided than the game really was.

Any coach would be happy with a win of this magnitude, but the weak Crimson defense bothered the demanding Murphy. The Crimson record stood at 3–1, but each opponent over the first three games scored at least twenty-three points—not an impressive number. Cornell's star wide receiver Keith Ferguson accounted for more than half of both the Big Red's points and receiving yards with two touchdowns and 154 yards on twelve catches. Cornell never really threatened to win the game, but they made some big plays against the defense. And the Harvard defense had a major test coming up the next Saturday, October 19. Murphy had one week to work with his players on keeping opponents off the scoreboard, not an easy task against the Crimson's next visitors: crosstown opponent Northeastern.

Finally, both quarterbacks were healthy enough to play. Murphy told his signal callers that Rose would play the first quarter, Fitzpatrick the second quarter. The one who performed better would finish the game. Suddenly, Rose needed to win his position back from the upstart sophomore. The nonleague matchup provided a perfect opportunity for the competition. The fourteenth-ranked Huskies sought to knock off the Crimson for the first time, having come up short the first five times the schools played each other.

Rose took the field in the first quarter, eager to reassert himself. He owned the lion's share of Harvard's passing records. He led the team throughout its perfect season the year before. He was the captain. He didn't postpone a plum job in paradise to ride the bench.

After three running plays and a first down, Rose completed his first pass attempt to the man who had helped him fill the record books, Carl Morris. It seemed like old times for a minute, but then the quarterback's light touch evaporated. Rose hit Kyle Cremarosa, but the receiver dropped the ball. Rose misfired to Rodney Byrnes, and then to Morris.

Perhaps it was the rust, perhaps the pressure, but Rose threw nine more incomplete passes over three possessions before he homed in on a target again, a minuscule three-yard completion to tight end Matt Fratto. Hardly a showstopper. Rose ended his live-game audition with fifty-four yards passing on six of nineteen attempts, Harvard behind 10–0 midway through the second quarter.

Most of Rose's back pain was gone, but his sciatica still hampered his mobility. And now it wasn't only the physical problems that plagued him. "I knew I had been ineffective against the Northeastern defense, and it was because of my ineffectiveness that I felt so terrible," Rose said. "I wasn't contributing to the team like I was supposed to, like I had so many times before. I didn't feel any self-pity, though. A game was going on, my team was on the field, and I was bouncing on my toes in anticipation of the good things Fitz would do."

On Harvard's first possession with Fitzpatrick under center, he marched his team down the field confidently with a combination of passes and running plays. Fitzpatrick ended the series with a one-yard pass to tight end Adam Jenkins for a score. The sophomore easily manhandled the defense that had baffled Rose.

Rose wasn't thinking about what Fitzpatrick's quick success might mean to his status as the starting quarterback. "I think I was leading the cheering on the sidelines," Rose said. "It was great to see the team finally convinced that we could win. I never thought about my future role on the team. It didn't matter. During a game I lived in the moment. There was no tomorrow. Of course I wanted back in the fight to do some damage of my own, but I was ecstatic that we were back in the game."

So was Fitzpatrick.

On Harvard's first possession of the second half, Morris took Fitzpatrick's eighteen-yard strike into the end zone, putting the Crimson on top for the first time in the game. The lead didn't last. The Huskies' sophomore quarterback, Shawn Brady, quickly threw a touchdown pass to Cory Parks from twenty yards out. The score stood at 17–14 in Northeastern's favor. It stayed that way until late in the fourth quarter, when Fitzpatrick had one more chance to put his team ahead for good.

"To be able to march the team down the field and position us to win was really a turning point for me," Fitzpatrick said. "By putting me in the game and sticking with me, for the first time I knew Coach Murphy had confidence in me."

With thirty-nine seconds to play, Harvard sat on Northeastern's doorstep. Fitzpatrick had expertly moved the team eighty-one yards down the field in one minute and forty seconds and looked poised to finish off the Huskies with one final surge. He took the snap and rolled right along with Rodney Thomas. He pitched the ball to Thomas, who had nothing but green grass and chalk in his path. But Thomas couldn't handle the lateral and fumbled. Northeastern's Steve Anzalone pounced on the ball. Game over.

Despite the outcome, Murphy never wavered in his opinion that the option play had been the best choice. "The bottom line is we catch it and walk in," the coach said after the game. "There were two timeouts left. It was the right call. We just didn't execute."

The Crimson failed to capitalize on the most critical play, and in fact throughout the game the sloppy offense often hadn't connected the dots: Harvard dropped eight passes overall. The only consolation in the devastating loss was that it wasn't an Ivy League game. Harvard needed to execute much better against Princeton the following week, regardless of who was at quarterback, or Penn would take over at the top of the league.

It was the biggest game of the season so far in the Ivy League race, and Murphy again gave the starting nod to Fitzpatrick. The team seemed to gel better around Fitzpatrick than Rose, but Murphy refused to make the selection permanent. "Fitzpatrick will start, and nothing else is written in stone at this point," Murphy told reporters.

Rose took the decision in stride, but it needled him. "Coach Murphy told me that he would do the same thing against Princeton [as he'd done in the Northeastern game with the quarterbacks]. This time Fitz would start and I would have one series in the second quarter," said Rose. Rose planned on pulling out all the stops when his time came. As much as he respected Fitz, he wanted his job back. And he really didn't like the Tigers.

"All I cared about was winning against Princeton. A goal of mine was to never lose to Princeton," Rose said. "The animosity between the teams makes winning that game sweeter than most. That game is never as amicable as the Yale game. The thought of losing to Princeton, to me, was sickening."

Rose knew he'd get a shot at Princeton one more time. "I knew I'd get in there—how long depended on how I played," he said.

Or on how Fitzpatrick played. Princeton had Fitzpatrick's number on October 26, never letting him get in a rhythm. The Tigers stopped the passing game, allowing him only 26 yards on four of five completed attempts. They closed down the run, limiting him to 7 yards. In a role reversal, Rose came in to relieve the struggling sophomore.

Rose had been waiting for just such a chance. He needed to redeem himself.

The senior completed thirteen of nineteen pass attempts for 170 yards as he inked another record, this time with 375 career completions. The Crimson also scored on three of Rose's first four possessions. One of those passes gave Carl Morris enough yards to surpass the 3,000 yard receiving mark—only the third Ivy Leaguer to do so. Nick Palazzo took three balls into the end zone.

It was not, however, Rose or Morris who deserved the credit in the gritty 24–17 win. The core of Murphy's concerns—the defense— emerged as the deciding factor, forcing four turnovers. Harvard converted those turnovers into seventeen of its twenty-four points. Chris Raftery earned Ivy League Player of the Week on defense with twelve tackles, two pass breakups, and one interception.

With six games behind them and four to go, Harvard's record stood at 4–2. The win over Princeton let them keep pace in the Ivy League standings, sharing the top spot with Penn at 3–0. Murphy continued his cat-and-mouse game with two capable quarterbacks, insisting that the week-to-week rotation of Fitzpatrick or Rose was not by design. "Ideally that's not what I'd want to do, but I'd sure as heck rather have two outstanding quarterbacks than one," he said.

Fitzpatrick and Rose impressed Murphy with the way they handled the situation. "The things I love about both kids are, one, they're very good and, two, they're both selfless kids," said Murphy.

After an article about Rose and Fitzpatrick and the Harvard quarterback controversy appeared in the *New York Times*, the national media came calling. Producers from Fox Sports Net's *The Best Damned Sports Show Period* requested an interview with the two for a segment on an upcoming show. Murphy approved, and Rose and Fitzpatrick, both big fans of the show, jumped at the chance. The show's team of hosts, D'Marco Farr, Chris Rose, and Tom Arnold, interviewed them from the Los Angeles studio via satellite. Tom Arnold took a page from *Good Will Hunting*, immediately messing with the "smaht" kids.

"Hey Ryan, it's Tom Arnold," the comedian crowed, staring at the image of Fitzpatrick on the studio's three-foot flat screen. "Listen— your shirt. What, did you lose a bet, or what the hell, man?"

The sandy-haired sophomore defended his wardrobe choice, a short sleeve button-down shirt with African masks dancing against a pale green background. He bought it from a ten-dollar sale rack while shopping in Arizona with his mother, who told him not to buy it because he'd never wear it. He could think of no better way to prove her wrong than to wear it for his first national television appearance. "Neil told me we were gonna tag up and wear these cool shirts to the show, and he decided not to wear his. So I look real good," Fitzpatrick said.

Rose, sporting a gray Harvard athletics T-shirt under a light khaki jacket, threw his head back and laughed. He and Fitzpatrick had indeed discussed their wardrobes, but Rose didn't get a chance to go back to his room and change before the show. Just as he did on the field, Fitzpatrick quickly adapted to the situation, and the studio audience loved him.

Arnold followed up by asking if there were any girls at Harvard who looked like Reese Witherspoon, the star of the movie *Legally Blonde*. After a brief pause, the outspoken Rose deadpanned, "I wish." The audience roared again. With the quarterbacks loosened up, the talk turned to the on-field dilemma. D'Marco Farr commented that even though everyone was talking about Harvard's quarterback controversy, the two looked like they were friends.

Rose said that the two were great friends and cited his back injury as the reason the whole controversy started. He praised Fitzpatrick for stepping up to the challenge in the difficult role, and added that he just wanted to get healthy and contribute to the team.

Fitzpatrick said that coach Murphy made the decision week-to-week, but that Rose had been playing really well. He announced that Rose had just broken the record for total career passing yards the previous game and that, even though the decision was ultimately up to the coach, Fitzpatrick would go with Rose as the starter.

Controversy? It sounded more like an end-of-the-season awards show. Rose and Fitzpatrick came across as affable guys just happy that their team was winning games. Looking to stir up some competitive dialogue, Rose asked them who had the higher SAT scores. "I did," blurted Fitzpatrick. "Fifteen eighty. Missed twenty points on the English." Rose didn't object. They may have shattered the image of the dumb jock football player, but Rose and Fitzpatrick upheld the stereotype of top-tier Ivy League students.

Tom Arnold announced that he got a 560. "Is that bad?" he asked.

"Dude," Farr replied, "You get four hundred points for signing your name."

"Huh," Arnold said. "I guess that's why I went to Iowa."

The campus buzzed about Rose and Fitzpatrick's appearance on the show. The segment had spotlighted a program eager for the exposure—after all, these days Harvard players almost never appear on the national stage, unless it's the day of the Harvard-Yale game.

Such a media brush-off wasn't always the case.

🏈 🏈 🏈

In the early twentieth century, college football fans hungrily waited for the Sunday newspapers just to check out the latest Saturday afternoon Harvard or Yale scores. The Ivies were the teams to beat on the national college football landscape, and when the two powerhouses clashed in November, the anticipation hit Super Bowl proportions. Fans filled the bowl and the stadium to capacity each time, and extra tickets were scarce.

This national frenzy peaked in the early 1930s. Though each school had its share of superstars over the years, Harvard and Yale each boasted a marquee player at the same time for only three brief years, 1929–1931. The tandem of Harvard's Barry Wood and Yale's Albie Booth dazzled the American public, competing head-to-head in the biggest game of the college football season on three occasions. As the freshly minted American sports culture passed from its Roaring Twenties golden age of Babe Ruth, Jack Dempsey, Bobby Jones, and Bill Tilden, not even the desperate days of the Great Depression could suppress the two storied college athletes, especially when Harvard met Yale and Wood met Booth. The Game was the biggest annual college football spectacle in the nation, and it boasted the two most captivating men to play for Harvard and Yale before or since. They defined their respective schools, elevated their teams' fortunes on the gridiron, and were consummate leaders on and off the field. Newsreel features told of each man's heroic deeds on the gridiron in movie houses from coast to coast.

Albert Jones Booth Jr., the son of a foreman in the Winchester firearms factory, was born in New Haven, Connecticut, in 1908. Booth grew to be the neighborhood's premier athlete, but the 125-pound quarterback didn't just dominate the gridiron at New Haven's Hillhouse High School. He played basketball and captained the baseball team before serving as captain in all three sports during a postgraduate year at Milford Prep.

After a successful season spent building his skills on the freshmen team, Albie Booth arrived on the Yale practice field to begin his sophomore season standing 5′7″ and weighing a surprisingly sturdy 144 pounds. Though built for running, Booth was far from a flat-out speedster. He instead relied on a dizzying array of open-field moves. The deceptive ball carrier known as Little Albie, the Mighty Mite, the Mighty Atom and, most commonly, Little Boy Blue, beat defenders with the stop-and-start, the sidestep, quick pivots, and the spin-and-go. In the spirit of Red Grange, the Galloping Ghost of the University of Illinois and college football's ultimate star of the 1920s, Booth became famous for his game-breaking broken field runs. His diminutive on-field appearance in a sport that emphasized size and strength made him the perfect hero for the average-size common man. Booth stepped up to the plate mentally as well—he captained the freshman football, baseball, and basketball teams and three varsity football teams during his four years.

With an offensive attack modeled on the University of Southern California's power approach, the Bulldogs began Booth's storied varsity career by inserting him as a single-wing tailback in his sophomore year. He promptly ran wild. In just his third varsity game Booth's legend took shape. With Yale trailing 6–0 in the first half versus Brown, Booth engineered a pair of scoring drives highlighted by his own touchdown runs and extra point kicking conversions. Little Boy Blue had only just begun.

The following Saturday a favored West Point visited the Yale Bowl. A crowd of eighty thousand turned out to witness a duel between Army's Chris "Red" Cagle and Booth. In one of the greatest individual efforts in the history of Yale football, Booth rallied the Elis from a 13–0 deficit to a stirring 21–13 victory. He scored all the Yale points. He called all the plays and carried the ball thirty-three times for 223 yards. Booth played defensive back, did all the punting, and drop-kicked the extra points. Booth's 70-yard punt return for a touchdown still ranks among the most electrifying runs in Eli history as players literally collided head-on in his wake.

Word of Booth's mighty feats quickly spread beyond the packed Yale Bowl. The upset victory over Army catapulted Booth into the position of a national hero overnight, with wire services and newsreels making his name a household word. Fan mail flooded the local post office. Already engaged to be married, Booth forwarded the romantic letters from young admirers to his teammates, many of whom took on the name of Albie Booth for dating purposes. Booth's most shining moment cast him into the spotlight for the next three years.

Fans of Yale and Harvard ultimately measure Blue and Crimson heroes by their performance in the Harvard-Yale game, and Booth couldn't escape this scrutiny. Prior to his first varsity Harvard-Yale game, he missed two games with a leg injury. Booth's condition dominated the pregame media buildup to The Game. If he was unable to perform, a long-sold-out Harvard Stadium would house an expected record crowd of sixty thousand disappointed fans. The quarterback rested in the infirmary most of the week, managing to hobble to practice on Thursday. The training staff hoped for the best, but it seemed that number 48 could only muster enough energy to kick, not run.

Booth took a turn for the better on Friday, quelling fears when he led his team to the practice field. Although far from 100 percent physically, Booth refused to sit out the biggest game of the year. His name appeared on The Game's lineup on Saturday. For Booth, sheer will triumphed over simple pain.

Despite a Thursday snowfall, the entire city swelled with football fans in the days prior to the game. Hotels, cafes, theaters, restaurants, and nightclubs all reported standing-room-only business. The tenth intercollegiate undergrad ball at the Copley Plaza Hotel attracted a crowd of one thousand. New York mayor Jimmy Walker was reportedly heading to town. Fans swarmed to Cambridge by car, train, boat, and even by the New York airplane—the only aircraft in operation at the time. Store owners in Boston and Cambridge decorated their windows in crimson and blue to draw football fans into their establishments, much as businesses in Super Bowl host cities do today to capitalize on the event. People desperately tried to get a coveted seat in the stadium and scalpers collected money hand over fist, commanding fifty dollars (about six hundred dollars in modern times) and up for a pair of tickets.

The stock market had crashed a month earlier, but you'd never suspect a depression in Cambridge. Extra police roamed the streets, additional subways shuttled partygoers, and supplemental staff eased the crunch at hotels so stuffed with boisterous fans that No Vacancy simply signaled the start of doubling up and room sharing. The fans spilled over into the downtown streets, dancing and drinking until the wee hours. As was the tradition, the Harvard undergraduate clubs opened their doors for both members and returning graduates.

The media gave the crowds plenty to chew on. Author Damon Runyon brought his unique characters to a special story he wrote for the *Boston Globe* entitled "Hold 'Em Yale—A Tale of Something That Might but Won't Happen at Harvard Stadium Next Saturday." Booth, who already was penning his own nationally syndicated newspaper column, expressed his frustration at having lost to Harvard in football, basketball, and baseball as a freshman. Another loss would be unacceptable.

Unacceptable, but would it be unavoidable? The game opened with a scoreless first quarter, each team unable to get an edge on the other. After the Crimson blocked Booth's field goal attempt in the second quarter, Harvard quarterback Barry Wood engineered an eighty-two-yard touchdown drive, successfully added the point after, and kicked a field goal to offset a Booth touchdown pass to Hoot Ellis. A sluggish Booth made his countermove in the second half, busting a long, broken field return as he eluded several Crimson tacklers. Harvard's All-American center Ben Ticknor somehow fought through Yale interference to catch Booth by the back of the jersey. It proved to be the game-saving tackle, as the Bulldogs never managed to threaten again. Harvard won 10–6.

A moping and somber Booth spent the off-season dealing with thoughts of what could have been. Though worshipped by Yale students and fans, he had disappointed himself. Any exploits against other teams paled in comparison to his performance versus Harvard. Booth faced a long junior season before a chance at redemption.

Booth wasn't the only one who couldn't forget his sophomore year performances. In his junior year, Army vowed revenge for the 1929 loss to Yale, which was of course primarily a loss to Booth. Determined to avoid a repeat performance, Army coach Ralph Sosse pointedly challenged his team before the rematch. "I'm not telling you to go out and maim Booth! But you put him on a pedestal last year! Now go out there and knock him off it!" After intercepting a Cadet pass in the second quarter, Booth found himself flat on the ground. Three Army tacklers crushed him simultaneously, knocking him out of the game.

Booth's growing legend led to a physically tough 1930 campaign. Teams routinely ganged up on him. Tenacious in the face of punishing tackles, Booth often played through the injuries. Despite the bull's-eye on his back, Booth led Yale to a 5–1–2 record.

Meanwhile, the Crimson staggered through a 3–4–1 season. A disappointing record, to be sure, but a victory over Yale would carry Harvard through the winter and offer a little salvation. It would be no easy feat. The revenge-minded Booth and his Yale teammates eagerly awaited the Crimson invasion of a jam-packed Yale Bowl. They shouldn't have been so welcoming.

It became, quite simply, Barry Wood's finest hour.

Noted as the college game's premier passer, expertly utilizing a weapon that in many ways was still relatively new, Wood conducted a veritable aerial symphony. He combined with his lanky, fast left half-back Art Huguley on a pair of perfectly executed looping touch-down passes of 31 and 26 yards. Playing the entire game on both sides of the ball, Wood completed six of nine tosses for 111 yards. His numbers were truly prolific for his time.

His Bulldog counterpart fared far worse, finding himself the pri-mary target of the Harvard defense. Booth endured an afternoon of sheer misery, gaining just 22 yards on ten carries. On the defensive side, the 5'7" Booth's inability to cover the 6'2" Huguley only added to his woeful day. After the game, word spread on the streets of Cambridge that Booth was a good football player, but an overrated one. In the minds of the Harvard faithful, clearly Booth couldn't hold a candle to Barry Wood.

Wood, born on May 4, 1910, hailed from the nearby Boston sub-urb of Milton, Massachusetts. He fit the part of the archetypal All-American hero: tall, slender, handsome, and scholarly. The classic natural athlete, Wood was a gifted leader both on and off the play-ing field. His frequent ability to rise to the occasion and deliver what-ever the Crimson needed at the most crucial time inspired the utmost confidence from his teammates.

Similar to Booth, Wood established himself as a result of a memo-rable performance versus Army in 1929. The Crimson began the sea-son with two relatively soft games against Bates and New Hampshire en route to a highly ambitious schedule that included Army, Dartmouth, Florida, Michigan, Holy Cross, and Yale. After a pair of thrashing wins (48–0, 35–0), the Crimson jumped to a two-touchdown first-half lead over Army before a stadium crowd of fifty-seven thou-sand. Army surged back, led by All-American Chris Cagle's three touchdown dashes. With one minute remaining, Wood, inserted at quarterback, improvised. With the Crimson running attack stalled, Wood connected with substitute end Victor Harding for a dramatic forty-yard touchdown pass. Wood followed by drop-kicking the tying point. From then on, Wood and his dazzling passing ability personified the Harvard offensive attack. As Booth had done in his defining Army game, Wood very quickly became a national sports personality through newspapers and newsreels.

By 1931, the two were playing at the peak of their abilities, their careers careening toward the inevitable climax in November. The Eli fortunes spanned the gamut of emotions, with Booth positioned squarely at the eye of the storm. After shutting out Maine 19–0 in the opener, Yale suffered its only defeat, a third straight loss to the Bulldogs of Georgia. The following week Yale made its first western road trip in school history to commemorate the fortieth anniversary of Blue alum and coaching legend Amos Alonzo Stagg as mentor of the University of Chicago football program. Yale bounced back, delivering a 27–0 performance starring Albie Booth. A pair of ties the next two weeks versus Army and Dartmouth followed. A blowout 52–0 victory the following week over St. John's of Annapolis, Maryland, left the Elis in the enviable position of having two weeks to rest, recuperate, and prepare for Harvard. Also, for the first time since 1899, the Harvard game was not the season finale for Yale. Princeton held that position. Nevertheless, the Harvard game still represented the climax of the Yale season in the eyes of informed observers.

Meanwhile in Cambridge, change was in the autumn air. Eddie Casey, a two-time All-American back and star of the 1920 Rose Bowl team, had accepted the position of Harvard head coach. The rookie coach had an exceptional group of athletes under his tutelage that included the captains of four other varsity sports. After the disappointing .500 season the previous year, the Crimson were primed to make amends and excel in Wood's final gridiron season.

Harvard burst out of the gate with dominant shutout victories over Bates and New Hampshire at the stadium, just like in 1929. The following Saturday presented a much more formidable test. The Army game had been the turning point in each of Wood's first two varsity seasons, the game that built momentum for the Harvard contest. Wood saved his best for last in the 1931 contest at West Point.

The Cadets struck quickly with two first quarter touchdowns. Trailing 13–0, Wood seized the moment and the game for Harvard. On offense, he expertly guided the Crimson's two scoring drives with his precise passing. After the first touchdown Wood was in position to drop-kick the extra point. A low snap led to a fumble but the Harvard captain had the poise to pick up the ball, dodge a group of Army pursuers, and sweep left to the end zone for the point after. He later drop-kicked the second point after.

Clinging to a precarious one-point lead, Wood took over on the defensive side of the ball. His first game-saving effort was an open-field tackle of an Army back who had burst into daylight, streaking fifty-eight yards until Wood caught him from behind at the Crimson twenty-two-yard line. Then, on Army's last-gasp drive for victory in the final minute, Wood intercepted an Army pass inside the Harvard five-yard line. The stirring victory was only the beginning of a Harvard season that seemed destined for greatness.

Over the next four weeks the opponents fell like dominoes. The University of Texas made its one and only visit to the stadium and was rudely turned back to Austin, 35–7. Again Wood's brilliant passing dominated the Crimson attack. A 19–0 shutout win over Virginia was followed by more Wood heroics. The quarterback completed a forty-yard pass for the tying touchdown versus Dartmouth with four minutes to play and kicked the extra point for a 7–6 Harvard win. The stunning come-from-behind Harvard victory, however, wasn't the only story of the game.

CBS Radio's Ted Husing was a pioneering play-by-play sports broadcaster in 1931, an age when Harvard and Yale football was a plum assignment. From the U.S. Open to the World Series to heavy-weight title fights, Husing brought vivid images from momentous sports events into the living rooms of millions of Americans. The bold, outspoken broadcaster was known for interjecting his own commentary into his descriptions of the events unfolding before him, and, in a brief error in judgment, rendered himself perma-nently banned from the Harvard press box.

Just before Wood saved the day versus Dartmouth, Husing told the audience: "Barry Wood is playing putrid football today." The backlash was immediate and powerful. Telegrams flowed steadily into CBS headquarters blasting Husing for his offensive comment. Newswriters assailed Husing in papers from coast to coast. Harvard athletic director Bill Bingham sent a letter of protest to CBS President William Paley. Though Paley admitted that Husing had made a mistake, he turned the matter into a censorship issue. The support shifted to Husing's favor, but Bingham refused to back down, even after Husing tried to make amends. If CBS wanted an announcer in the broadcast booth during the years that Harvard and Yale played in the stadium, it would have to be someone other than ace sports reporter Ted Husing. (Bingham finally relented two years later and allowed Husing entry to Harvard Stadium for the intercollegiate track and field championships. Though Bingham in essence forgave Husing, Harvard didn't forget. A decade after the Wood slur, Husing requested a Harvard-Cornell program in order to prepare for an upcoming broadcast. He received it in an envelope addressed to Ted "Putrid" Husing.)

The Harvard football team, led by Wood, couldn't have been any less putrid. They finished their pre-Yale season undefeated and untied. The 1931 Harvard-Yale game represented the only possible stumbling block between the Crimson and a perfect season. Wood just needed to repeat the performance he'd given every time he'd squared off against Little Boy Blue, and another victory would be in hand. The background dramatics weren't lost on Crimson and Blue fans.

Once again throngs of football fans filled the hotels in and around Boston prior to Harvard's quest for perfection, welcome news for business owners during difficult financial times. The scene might have come straight out of the fall of 1929, except that now Wood and Booth were seniors. All ticket-holders hoped that the two had indeed saved their best for last. If they had, the fans were in for an incredible head-to-head battle in sold-out Harvard Stadium.

Not all of the seats held fans, however. Some unfortunate travel circumstances left more than 200 tickets unused.

A group of millionaire merchants and bankers that included Rodman Wanamaker III, author Eliot White Springs, and bankers Claude L. Cathings and Foster Rockwell had contracted the luxury liner *Pan American* for a pleasant, leisurely New York–Boston sail to see Booth and Wood compete for the last time. With wives and sweethearts in tow, 140 Yale men and 71 Harvard men embarked on their short voyage on Friday afternoon in weather that, had it not been a special party, would have kept them in New York Harbor. The captain piloted the boat out through thick fog and proceeded full steam ahead when he reached open water. At sunrise, there was no sun to be found. Soupy fog blanketed the ocean, forcing the captain to drop anchor and wait. With fewer than six hours until kickoff, the wealthy men realized that they might not make it to the game in time. From twelve miles off the nearest coastline, the rich and powerful took action.

Several radiograms went out to New York City and Boston. Before long, eight speed boats from the Woods Hole (Massachusetts) Coast Guard Patrol raced to the *Pan American* to bring the stranded passengers to shore. A special train awaited the prominent folk at Woods Hole, and the New Haven railroad gave the train the right-of-way all the way to Boston. But before the patrol boats reached the vessel and put the plan in motion, the fog lifted. The ship charged for Boston, but too many precious minutes had slipped away. The liner cruised off Cape Cod at two o'clock, the slated kickoff time. Forced to make do, the captain shut down the telegraphic radio and tuned in Rick Munday's broadcast from Harvard Stadium on two radios, one in the smoking room and one on the aft deck. The disappointed well-to-do fans—including Nick Roberts, who hadn't missed a game in thirty years and threw an annual barn party for the Yale team—were forced to listen to the game huddled around a radio, just like countless others who hadn't the money or connections to get a coveted seat. And what a game it was.

As the *Pan American* bobbed in the Atlantic surf, Barry Wood received the opening kickoff. His teammates clamored around him to form a protective blocking wall as the Bulldogs stormed downfield. When the combatants collided, Wood handed the ball to Jack Crickard, who swept around the mass and broke for daylight. He had only one player to beat—Albie Booth. Booth gamely engaged the much larger Crickard, but Crickard rolled over him with a stiff arm for good measure. Booth managed to trip him up in the process, allowing just enough time for Herster Barres to catch up to Crickard and make the saving tackle. It took another fifty-eight minutes of play for Little Boy Blue to fully realize how important his tackle was.

Harvard squandered its opening kickoff run to deep Yale territory, losing possession on downs. From that point on, the Harvard and Yale defenses rose to the occasion, Harvard stuffing Booth's running and Yale thwarting Wood's passing. The two teams raced up and down the field as Wood and Booth exchanged punts. Each team waited for the one opportunity to make its move and hoped for the other side to blink. Late in the fourth quarter, Yale got its chance.

On fourth down, Wood dropped back to punt. Yale end Tom Hawley shot right up the middle and blocked the attempt. The ball never left Wood's toe, and Yale's left tackle Johnny Wilbur recovered on the Harvard forty-five. Booth wasn't about to let his last chance at glory pass him by.

The Bulldog's legs had made him famous, and though he was no Barry Wood in terms of passing, he also had a decent arm. On the first play from scrimmage he rifled a twenty-yard pass to Barres for another first down. The Harvard defense stifled the Yale surge on the next two plays, but a Bulldog victory was still within reach. Yale turned to Booth to grasp it. On third down, in nearly the same spot from which Booth had missed two years ago in the Harvard-Yale game, Little Boy Blue sent a textbook twenty-yard drop-kick through the uprights for a field goal. With under a minute to play, Yale led 3–0. But Harvard still had one more chance.

Wood had saved the game before, and he'd had the edge over Booth since their first meeting as freshmen. The gun sounded on the final play of the game as Wood dropped back to air out a desperation pass from deep in his own territory. Before he could hurl the ball, several Yale defenders swarmed and smashed him into the turf close to Harvard's goal line. Game over. Victory, Yale.

The Yale fans stormed the field in a ceremonial snake dance, quickly felling the goalposts on both ends of the field as Harvard fans sat and watched in dumbstruck awe. The Bulldog backers splintered the posts into souvenir-size pieces, taking home chunks to commemorate Booth's heroic win. The Harvard fans seemed content to let them. Though Yale had beaten their acclaimed captain in his final football game, many Harvard fans admitted that they were just a bit happy for Albie Booth. After witnessing Booth's years of frustration, they felt he'd earned the right to celebrate.

A mob of fans chased Booth into the lobby at his Boston hotel following the game. The captain felt awful. On the biggest day of his career, the beginning stages of pneumonia clogged his lungs. Always gracious to the fans, Booth told one of his classmates, Stuart Ludlum, that he just couldn't stay in the lobby any longer without collapsing. Ludlum, who was more or less the same size as Booth and shared common features, began signing autographs for the fans while Booth slipped undetected into an elevator. The ruse worked until some Yale fans carrying chunks of the goalposts came to the hotel hoping to get the keepsakes autographed by Booth. They knew Ludlum wasn't who he claimed to be. By the time Booth made it back to New Haven he was gravely ill. Instead of lining up at the Yale Bowl one final time versus Princeton the following week, Booth struggled with pneumonia in a sanatorium. It took him months to recover.

The last Booth-Wood battle marked the end of a unique subplot to the annual Harvard-Yale games. Other football stars have played for Harvard and Yale since, but never two players of Booth's and Wood's caliber at the same time. And never again on such a national scale. Though the magnitude of the Booth-Wood matchups was rare, the level of leadership the two stars contributed to their respective teams was not. Whether a Harvard or Yale team is in the hunt for the Ivy League championship or just trying to get a single mark in the win column, strong leaders always emerge.

❧   ❧   ❧

Jason Lange filled the official leadership role as Yale's captain, and the most a Yale captain could do for his team was to lead them to victory over the Crimson. For all but a single game during the season Lange's efforts would be limited to mentions in the Connecticut papers—until Yale played Harvard. From coast to coast Harvard and Yale fans would anxiously await the results just as they had during the Booth-Wood years, only now fans wouldn't have to wait for wire service reports. They could watch the game via satellite or track the game play-by-play over the Internet. Lange didn't care if people heard the score from computers or newspapers or carrier pigeons. He just wanted to make sure the headlines said one thing: "Yale Beats Harvard."

The Professionals

THE YALE BULLDOGS NEEDED to put up or shut up when the Columbia Lions roared into the Yale Bowl on November 2. Three straight losses dogged the team going into the game, resulting in a depressing record (3–3, 1–2 Ivy) that matched the tally of the previous year—a year that ended in total collapse. A game against Columbia—a team that followed up a victory in its first game of the season with five consecutive losses—appeared to be the ideal contest after facing a series of tough opponents in October. On the other hand, Columbia had delivered the crippling blow to Yale's season in the same situation a year ago.

Siedlecki didn't put much stock in Columbia's sorry record. The Lions had suffered some lopsided defeats at the hands of Colgate and Penn, but they pushed both Princeton and Dartmouth to the brink, losing by a combined four points. Columbia also led going into the fourth quarter in three of the five games they lost. Though Columbia didn't have a top-tier receiver for quarterback Steve Hunsberger, he had still accumulated over 1,300 yards passing over six games. Rick Flanders's defensive backs had to stand their ground.

Defense turned out not to be the story. Jeff Mroz threw for over 300 yards and four touchdowns, two to wide receiver Ron Benigno and two to big tight end Nate Lawrie. Yale's defense did contribute, with Jason Lange spearheading the attack. The captain had two of

Yale's six sacks, including one for a 9-yard loss on second and goal from the Yale 7-yard line late in the first quarter, which deflated the beleaguered Columbia team. Yale capitalized on the momentum, and overmatched Columbia didn't stand a chance in the 35–7 Yale win. Observers could see that these Bulldogs bore little resemblance to the team that had squandered an opportunity at Dartmouth three weeks ago.

Siedlecki no longer thought Yale had a chance at the Ivy League title, though. The Bulldogs had lost to Penn and the Quakers now led the league once again. "Whenever you need help from others to win the title, I try not to get caught up in the projected scenarios," Siedlecki said. "Winning the game at hand is the only thing you can be concerned with."

But good things come from winning the game at hand. Mroz's teammates noticed that his confidence had finally peaked. Perhaps spurred by Alvin Cowan's announcement earlier in the week that the injured quarterback considered applying for a medical red shirt, Mroz seemed to have accepted that this team was his. And so did his teammates. Siedlecki finally had the confident leader he had hoped for on offense.

"Leadership is part of being a quarterback," Mroz said. "Being a sophomore and inexperienced, it was tough to come in and assume the leadership role by being a vocal leader. I just went out and competed. But I had a great group of teammates and they helped me make the transition. As the year went on I became more comfortable. I began to be more vocal and assumed more of a leadership role."

Jason Lange agreed. "With every game he played he became more confident than the previous one. At that point in the season, especially with the knowledge that Alvin wasn't going to return for the rest of the year, it was a tremendous boost to the entire team to watch Mroz play so well. I also think it really helped him personally, knowing that he could play at that level and compete," said Lange.

Even Cowan felt that Mroz truly proved his mettle in the Dartmouth game. "By the time of his performance in the Columbia game everyone knew what he was capable of," Cowan said.

The junior also pointed out another substantial fact. Cowan may have had the best debut at starting quarterback of any player in Yale annals, but he still only had a single game's worth of experience at the varsity level. Cowan thought Mroz had every reason to be secure as the starter. "He's not a backup quarterback," Cowan said. "He's a hell of a football player."

Siedlecki's Bulldogs passed a critical test during the pivotal game, reversing a slide that would have killed the season. Perhaps the Yale coach had successfully rebuilt the heart and attitude of his team after all, a task much more difficult than improving its ability to execute on the field. These Bulldogs weren't about to roll over and play dead like last year's team did after falling to 3–3. Good thing, because they would need all the heart they could muster the following week against a Brown team with one of the nation's best receivers.

Brown was in the perfect position to spoil Yale's upswing. Even more so than Columbia, Brown's record didn't adequately reflect the team's capabilities, especially with Chas Gessner in the lineup. A preseason All-American and Payton Award candidate, wide receiver Gessner rated first in Division I-AA in receptions per game and fifth in receiving yards per game when Yale visited Providence, Rhode Island, on November 9. Though Gessner played with a dislocated pinkie through most of October, he still posed a serious threat. Brown had the tenth-ranked pass offense in the nation, due in large part to Gessner and quarterback Kyle Slager.

As everyone expected, Brown came out throwing. Slager and Gessner stumped the Yale defensive backs. Gessner caught nine passes for 136 yards on the day, while Slager completed thirty-one of forty-two pass attempts for 364 yards. Late in the fourth quarter, with Yale clutching a 24–20 lead, Gessner caught an 18-yard pass for a touchdown. With the extra point, the score was 27–24 with under six minutes to play. Luckily for Yale, Slager wasn't the only quarterback having a good game.

With under two minutes remaining, Mroz threw his fourth touchdown pass of the day, one of his twenty-one completions. Wide receiver Ralph Plumb's catch seemed to put the game away for Yale, but Brown threatened again.

Though Yale's defensive backs couldn't contain the pass-happy Bears for the bulk of the game, they came through with a tremendous effort on Brown's final possession. The drive began inauspiciously. Slager took Brown down the field on four quick strikes, bringing them from their own 18-yard line to the Yale 12. But then Yale stalled Brown running back Joe Rackley on first down. Slager overthrew Gessner on second down. Owen Gilbert and Greg Owens each broke up a pass on third and fourth down respectively. Exploited for nearly sixty minutes, the defensive backs finally made the key stops to secure the victory.

"The Brown win was one of the happiest moments in my entire football career," said Lange. "The emotional nature of the game and the intensity of the final defensive stop, combined with the fact that my class had yet to beat them, made it overwhelming. It gave us an incredible amount of confidence going into the Princeton and Harvard games."

And no one was happier with the Yale win than wide receiver Ralph Plumb.

Originally from Portsmouth, Rhode Island, Plumb figured he'd stay close to home and play for Brown. The Bears recruited him, but the coaching staff insisted that the 6'4″, 211-pound Plumb play defensive back. Feeling that his talents better suited the wide receiver position, Plumb packed his bags and headed for New Haven. Lucky for Yale. Plumb led the Bulldogs in receptions on the season and galvanized the team with his fourth quarter score, drawing energy from his hometown crowd.

He hoped that he and Yale could build on this momentum and triumph over Princeton, the Bulldogs' next opponent. But defense ruled the 125th renewal of the Yale-Princeton rivalry, played out in a rainy Yale Bowl on November 16. Over three quarters of play the Yale and Princeton offenses accounted for a total of just three points, one field goal by Princeton's Derek Javarone. Princeton kept Mroz, Plumb, and Benigno at bay; Yale returned the favor by halting Tigers quarterback Matt Verbit and wide receivers Chisom Opara and B. J. Szymanski. In the fourth quarter, Mroz finally found his comfort zone and engineered a drive covering 85 yards and culminating in an 11-yard pass to Benigno, giving Yale a 7–3 lead. Though the game ended with this score, the fans hailed neither Mroz nor Benigno as the hero. Yale defensive back James Beck made the real play of the game.

With four and a half minutes remaining in the fourth quarter, the Princeton fans roared as the Tigers appeared poised to take the lead. Running back Cameron Atkinson broke through the Yale secondary and sprinted toward the goal line. Beck chased after him. Atkinson's spring sport was track, his event the one hundred-meter dash. An event in which he held a national ranking. Somebody forgot to tell Beck. Beck pursued at the perfect angle, found his footing on the chewed-up turf, and caught Atkinson from behind at the Yale 36. The defense quickly shut down the Tigers on the next three plays to regain control of the ball.

During this win over Yale's oldest rival Robert Carr quietly ran for 93 yards on twenty-one carries, by no means a memorable statistic. The distance was enough, though, for Carr to pass former Chicago Bears head coach Dick Jauron's single-season rushing total of 964 yards, set in 1970.

* * *

Yale wasn't the only school rewriting its own record books. As the final weeks sped by before the 2002 installment of The Game, Harvard also pumped out some amazing numbers.

Harvard traveled to Dartmouth's Memorial Field for its first game in November and hoped to spoil the host's homecoming day festivities. Snow blanketed the field prior to kickoff, threatening the anticipated offensive fireworks. On the Dartmouth side, quarterback Brian Mann ranked fourth in Division I-AA in total offense after six games and had led the Big Green to a 3–3 record. Juniors tight end Casey Cramer and wide receiver Jay Barnard were Mann's primary targets. The Big Green needed a big game from their potent trio to avenge their 2001 loss to the Crimson. They hadn't forgotten that game, in which Carl Morris took control by throwing a touchdown pass, catching a touchdown pass, and setting up a third with a 40-yard reception—all in a three and a half minute span, nullifying a three-touchdown Big Green lead.

Dartmouth's trio didn't disappoint.

Mann had an incredible afternoon, to the delight of the Dartmouth alumni. He connected on half of his fifty pass attempts for 382 yards. Barnard hauled in ten Mann passes for 124 yards and two touchdowns. Cramer matched Barnard's reception and touchdown totals, and outdistanced the wide receiver with 196 yards. On this, his career-best passing day, Mann surpassed Dartmouth alumnus Jay Fiedler in career completions (Fiedler went on to start at quarterback for the Miami Dolphins). The Dartmouth squad couldn't have put on a better offensive showing. But Harvard could, and did.

Early in the week leading up to the Dartmouth contest, Carl Morris appeared in a one-page feature in *Sports Illustrated*. The article, titled "Harvard Yardage," profiled Morris and his career at the nation's first college and discussed his potential in the NFL draft. Although Morris relished such national attention, friends and teammates joked with him about the dreaded *SI* curse. For years, many of the athletes who appeared on the magazine's cover experienced precipitous drops in performance after publication, oftentimes due to strange occurrences. Morris hoped the jinx pertained only to those who made the cover. Dartmouth prayed it didn't. Morris was right.

Despite Dartmouth's best offensive showing of the year, the Big Green defense froze in horror as Morris terrorized them once more. Neil Rose, who got the start over Ryan Fitzpatrick after his stellar effort at Princeton, connected with Morris for two touchdowns and broke seven Harvard records. Dartmouth focused on not letting Morris beat it deep, lining up as many as ten yards behind the line of scrimmage to neutralize the long-ball threat. They let him have as many of the short-route passes that he wanted—and the yards accumulated quickly. But they didn't make it easy. "I faced double-team coverage for about eighty-five percent of that game," Morris said. Even with the double coverage Dartmouth couldn't contain him.

Morris topped his own best numbers with a single-game high of 257 yards receiving and 21 receptions, a single-season receiving total of 1,068 yards, and single-season receptions total of 73. And he still had three games in which to add to his new records. Had he not been leveled by a scary hit that left him shaken and prone on the field with six minutes remaining in the game, Morris easily could have broken another record.

"I was running a slant route and Neil threw me a low ball that I had to slide down to get. I hit the safety helmet to helmet and was knocked out immediately," Morris said. "I was unconscious for four or five minutes and I don't remember anything that happened until about thirty minutes later." Morris needed only four more receptions to break the Division I-AA record for receptions in a game (24), shared by Brown's Chas Gessner and Mississippi Valley State's Jerry Rice. *That* Jerry Rice. But record or no record, Murphy wasn't about to sacrifice his star's well-being. He snatched Morris's helmet away to keep him on the sidelines.

Rose also outdid himself, setting single-game marks for passing yardage (443), total yards (449), and completions (36). Harvard's offensive line easily warded off the Dartmouth rush and gave Rose ample time to pick apart the defense on play after play. With Rose and Morris clicking, Fitzpatrick remained on the bench, even though he had led the Crimson in both passing yards and rushing yards going into the game. He took some snaps in mop-up duty at the game's end and Murphy even used the versatile sophomore as a wide receiver. After all, Murphy strove to put his best eleven athletes on the field as much as possible, and Fitzpatrick was one of them.

Rodney Byrnes was another. Byrnes took over rushing duties when Nick Palazzo left the game early after aggravating his nagging shoulder injury. Harvard's plays consisted primarily of passes, but Byrnes carried the ball eighteen times for thirty-nine yards. Like Palazzo's minimum output against Princeton, though, Byrnes got the most important yards when Harvard needed them. Twice Byrnes ran the ball into the end zone from a few yards out. Rose also threw him a touchdown pass for a twelve-yard score in the third quarter.

Dartmouth did manage to keep the score close enough to potentially come from behind at the end of the game. They scored late in the fourth quarter and attempted an onside kick to regain possession with sixteen seconds left and Harvard leading 31–26. Had it worked, the Big Green very well may have pulled off a homecoming day stunner, but the ball skittered harmlessly across the Memorial Field turf until it rolled into the sure hands of Dante Balestracci. The Harvard linebacker smothered the ball and the Crimson ran out the clock.

As pleased as Murphy was with Harvard's school-record eleventh consecutive victory over Ivy League foes, he noted some areas where the Crimson needed vast improvement. Freshman kicker Jim Morocco missed two field goal attempts and an extra point, and the defense let Mann, Cramer, and Barnard pile up receiving yards. Both were unacceptable. Harvard would face Penn in two weeks, and the Quaker combination of quarterback Mike Mitchell and wide receiver Rob Milanese had the talent to equal or surpass Dartmouth's yardage. Penn's stingy defense also would be much more difficult to overcome than the Big Green's.

Murphy had also been keeping a watchful eye on Yale.

The Game loomed three weeks ahead, and the Crimson coach noticed that young Bulldog Jeff Mroz seemed to be coming into his own, posting big numbers in tandem with wide receiver Ron Benigno and tight end Nate Lawrie. Like Penn, the Bulldogs wouldn't be pushovers. At least Murphy had a weaker opponent before the two biggest games on Harvard's schedule. The Columbia Lions, winless versus Ivy opponents, rolled into Cambridge on November 9.

Whatever adjustments the Crimson had made to the secondary during the week in practice didn't take hold during game play, at least not at the outset. Columbia quarterback Steve Hunsberger drew first blood in the opening quarter with a touchdown pass to Steve Cargile. The early score must have offended the Harvard defense, though, because that was all the scoring they allowed. Corner back Chris Raftery had eight tackles, an interception, and forced a fumble. Balestracci recovered the fumble Raftery caused, had ten tackles, and added a sack. In all, the Crimson sacked Hunsberger five times. When the Lions made it to the Harvard five for a first and goal, the defense stopped them on four straight plays. The outstanding defense created the extra cushion the offense needed to pull off the businesslike 28–7 victory.

Murphy again started Rose under center. After Rose's air show at Dartmouth, keeping him out of the lineup wasn't an option. Throughout the Harvard quarterback controversy Murphy maintained that he would go with the quarterback who was playing better at the time, and since Rose took over at Princeton he'd simply bested Fitzpatrick. Versus Columbia he further staked his claim.

Rose accounted for three touchdowns, running one into the end zone. He completed twenty-five of thirty-five pass attempts for 257 yards in the air, and ran for a total of 40 yards. Rose's running wasn't the only surprise in the Harvard ground game. Nick Palazzo's shoulder just wouldn't cooperate after an early in-game aggravation, so he retreated to the sidelines. Murphy wanted Rodney Byrnes to spend his time at wide receiver, so he called on freshman Ryan Tyler to fill in for Palazzo. Tyler debuted with a touchdown and over 100 yards rushing, becoming the first freshman in Harvard history to break the century mark in a game.

Carl Morris, fresh from winning the triple crown of player-of-the-week awards—The Sports Network National Division I-AA, Ivy League, and Coca-Cola New England Gold Helmet—delivered a typical performance. He caught his ten passes, scored his touchdown, and fell 2 yards short of 100 yards receiving. Morris simply did what fans, coaches, teammates and, now, NFL scouts had come to expect from him. Those expectations were high, but the undeterred wide receiver met them week in and week out.

Against Penn, though, the expectations rose even higher and took a different twist. After the *SI* piece and all the buzz about his

NFL potential, media attention didn't faze Morris much. Despite the amount of press reports, the breadth of the coverage was more or less limited to the Ivy League set. All that would change after the Penn game.

After Penn and Harvard's spectacular game in 2001, featuring Morris's now-famous 62-yard game-winning touchdown catch, someone on the ESPN *College GameDay* panel remarked that they should have broadcast the Harvard Stadium game, which decided the Ivy League championship. When it began to look as if the Harvard-Penn game would hold the same importance in 2002, *GameDay* producers confirmed that if the two remained undefeated prior to meeting at Franklin Field in November, the show would be there. As the season wound down, the pieces fell into place. Penn dispatched Princeton to go 5–0 in Ivy League play, and Harvard took care of Columbia for an identical Ivy League record. The deal was inked.

While Harvard practiced quietly in Cambridge, the Quakers dealt with the hoopla that inevitably surrounds *College GameDay* broadcast. A forty-eight-foot trailer arrived to encourage attendance and promote the program at Franklin Field, considered the oldest football stadium still in use since opening in 1895. Camera crews descended on campus, filming scenic shots and capturing footage for a feature on quarterback Mike Mitchell.

ESPN tagged Carl Morris for its Harvard player profile. The filming of Morris's piece didn't get the same amount of fanfare as Mitchell's did at Penn, though. By now Harvard people were used to seeing Morris with reporters and in front of a camera. After the piece aired, however, Morris discovered how many people actually saw it.

"I got calls all weekend from friends and family, many of whom I hadn't spoken with in a long time," Morris said. "Some of them didn't even know I played football. A lot of people I met later on at all-star games and NFL combines saw it and it was kind of an ice-breaker for us."

The leading pregame show for college football, *College GameDay* veered sharply from tradition in visiting the Ivy League venue. The show debuted in 1986 but shot its first broadcast on location in South Bend, Indiana, in 1993, at a game between number one Florida State and number two Notre Dame. Since then, the road show trio of Chris Fowler, Lee Corso, and Kirk Herbstreit normally traveled to Division I-A hotbeds like Gainesville, Knoxville, and Ann Arbor. The show at Penn was only the second one broadcast from a game that did not have national title implications. (The first was at a 2001 Air Force–Army matchup in Colorado Springs.) In eighty-five broadcasts, the show had never set up shop at a Division I-AA school. Producers weren't sure what viewers would make of the Ivy League spectacle, but they noticed that the show gained abnormal momentum the week leading up to the game.

"It turned out to be one of the best things we ever decided to do," said Mark Gross, coordinating producer for *GameDay*.

The crew erected a 900-square-foot stage in one of the end zones, draping a canopy over it in an attempt to combat what was turning into quite a soggy scene. It didn't help much. The rain blew in sideways, and the canopy couldn't raise the near-freezing temperatures. The miserable weather didn't dampen the spirits of the cast and fans, though. Rain-soaked supporters crowded behind the stage, jumping and waving their arms, hoping to thrust themselves onto a national television program witnessed by thousands of viewers. Their wishes were granted.

Maybe it was the novelty of seeing Lee Corso masquerading as Benjamin Franklin (white wig flowing, colonial garb flapping, and tiny glasses sliding down his nose), or maybe it was the incredible reach of the Ivy League alumni, but inexplicably the *College GameDay* pregame broadcast from Penn became the most-watched regular-season episode in the program's history. Approximately 1.52 million households tuned in for the Ivy League show, supplanting a preshow from a Florida–Florida State game that reached 1.49 million.

"I think the appeal was not only to the Ivy League alumni and fans, but to all the non-big-time traditional fans from schools that may not get a lot of recognition," Gross said.

The viewers weren't the only ones who enjoyed the broadcast. Corso, who puts on some kind of hat or costume during each show, answered a question about his most memorable outfit in a later interview for the *Pittsburgh Post-Gazette*. "The best show we ever did was the Harvard-Penn game. I dressed up as Ben Franklin, got a wig and glasses. I loved that," the announcer remarked.

When it came time to make his prediction for the game, Corso/Franklin didn't hesitate. "It's my school," he said. "Penn!" Herbstreit and Fowler agreed with him. ESPN viewers would have to wait to find out. Though ESPN broadcast *GameDay* from Franklin Field, they didn't have the game. It aired only on the YES Network.

Neil Rose got the start at quarterback once again. Rose was the last Ivy League quarterback to post a win against Penn, and Murphy hoped his Hawaiian hurler had more magic up his sleeve. If Rose could beat the dominant Quakers once more, he would have the starting spot for The Game locked up. Rose had good motivation going into the game. Penn, however, had a better motivator: revenge.

Penn jumped on the enemy from Cambridge right from the start. They pressured Rose and he fumbled early in the first quarter, followed by a Penn recovery. The Harvard defense prevented a touchdown by stopping Penn on three plays, but Penn's Peter Veldman still capitalized on the fumble with a field goal. After Harvard got two points back on a safety when Brian Garcia sacked Mitchell in Penn's end zone, Rose fumbled again. This time Penn did score on the return. Then they scored again. And again. And again. Penn put forty-one unanswered points on the scoreboard.

Murphy stuck with Rose for the first half before putting in Fitzpatrick in the third quarter. Fitzpatrick helped Harvard save a little face when he hit tight end Matt Fratto late in the fourth quarter, preventing the offense from a complete shutout.

While Rose floundered in the face of the dreary conditions and Penn's impossible defense, his Quaker counterpart flourished. Mitchell threw four touchdown passes and completed twenty-one of thirty pass attempts for 317 yards. Nine of Mitchell's tosses found an open Rob Milanese as the Penn receiver contributed to the pounding with 139 yards and a touchdown. Milanese had spent the week in the shadow of the other marquee receiver playing for the Ivy crown, but he burst into the spotlight on the field. The seventeenth-ranked Quakers destroyed the overmatched Crimson 44–9 to the soundtrack of the Penn crowd's chant, "O-ver-RA-ted!"

No one was sure if it was the *Sports Illustrated* curse delayed—the nasty tradition biding its time until the Payton Award candidate, number-one-ranked Division I-AA receiver and NFL prospect reached his pinnacle of national college football attention before overcoming him. More likely, however, the expert coverage by Penn's defensive backs was at fault. Morris ended a pitiful afternoon with a paltry three catches for a whopping 16 yards. That was all. Penn double- and sometimes triple-teamed Morris, never letting him factor into the game.

It wasn't hard to picture the scouts now second-guessing Morris's NFL potential. He hadn't dealt well with the pressure of a championship-caliber game and he didn't overcome the adverse weather. If a few Ivy League defensive backs could handle him, Morris would be swallowed whole by the secondaries in the pro ranks.

Morris was more concerned about what the loss at Penn meant to the team than what it meant to his future, and anyway he thought his NFL chances were unaffected. "I don't think that it hurt me too much because of the coverages that were run against me," Morris recalled. "Penn decided that we had to beat them on the ground exclusively if we wanted to win. I think the scouts saw that and understood that those weren't realistic looks."

Tom Hepler, general manager of Ourlads' Scouting Services, agreed with Morris's assessment. "If a player is neutralized, that says that the player is a star," Hepler said. "He's the weapon that must be contained. Players are always assessed on a whole body of work, never one game."

And Morris's body of work was incredible. Besides, there wasn't any way he was going to end his college career like that. He had one game to make amends. A resilient rebounding performance versus

Yale could silence the naysayers. He knew that networks around the country would show Harvard-Yale highlights, giving him a chance to erase the Penn game from people's minds. He could end the season on an uptick and make the NFL market bullish on Carl Morris. If he pulled off an incredible performance, it wouldn't be the first time a player shined in Ivy League play to catapult himself into football's premier landscape.

* * *

It all started with Yale's Pudge Heffelfinger. When William Walter "Pudge" Heffelfinger arrived at Yale in 1888, football captain Pa Corbin promptly put him in at guard. Heffelfinger stood 6'3" and weighed 200 pounds, a hefty cut above the Yale line average of 175 pounds, and Corbin wanted his new big man at the center of the action. Corbin also knew that Heffelfinger wasn't just big, he was a veteran. While in high school he played with the varsity team at the University of Minnesota, getting a jump on the school he assumed he'd attend because he couldn't afford any other. In May of his senior year, however, Heffelfinger's father told him that he found the money to send him to Yale.

Heffelfinger played like a dream. He was fast, agile, powerful, and intelligent. But he lacked one characteristic that would have made him the most feared man in the game—a killer instinct. Shy Pudge didn't speak up much. Corbin saw Heffelfinger's placid demeanor as a major deterrent to his new guard's capabilities. The captain set out to fix it, and not just for the team's benefit. Playing football with an easygoing disposition, no matter how big he was, could literally end up getting Heffelfinger killed on the field. The violent nature of the game during the late 1800s held no mercy for the mild-mannered.

Heffelfinger's teammates tried screaming at him to get him fired up, but Pudge remained cool and calm. Yale player Howard Knapp tried something different. If Heffelfinger didn't respond to the spoken word, perhaps he needed something in writing. Knapp acquired a pot of blood from a New Haven slaughterhouse and used a writing quill to pen a grisly message to Heffelfinger. No one knows what the letter said, but for some baffling reason Knapp's primal note struck a nerve. A very powerful, angry nerve. The idle monster in Heffelfinger emerged, much to the dismay of Yale's opponents.

Heffelfinger became a one-man wrecking crew, his main objective to neutralize the popular mass formations of the day. After a kickoff, when opponents huddled for the advance downfield, Heffelfinger zoomed in on the point man. A few yards before he made contact, Heffelfinger would leap into the air, catching the lead player in the chest with his knees and scattering opponents like bowling pins. No player before Heffelfinger had single-handedly cracked these formations, supposedly a surefire way to gain yardage. Not anymore.

Heffelfinger continued his assault on opposing players, tackling runners and providing crippling blocks on offense, his only protection a white bandage wrapped around his head to prevent cauliflower ear (the first leather helmets debuted in 1893, and they didn't become mandatory until the late 1930s). The first two Yale teams to reap the rewards of Heffelfinger finished undefeated. No opponent scored a single point during those seasons. Had the honor existed in his freshman year, Heffelfinger would have been a hands-down four-time All-American.

Heffelfinger had completed his higher education and had no further business at Yale, but four years of football in college weren't enough. He wasn't ready to give up the game. He was flat out too good at it. The guard found another place to play after he graduated from Yale.

Football had become one of the main draws for the athletic clubs that predated professional sports and sprang up in cities throughout the country following the Civil War. These athletic clubs sponsored teams and naturally tried to stock their rosters with the best players available. The catch was that the players had to be unpaid amateurs. The clubs formed The Amateur Athletic Union to govern the leagues in which the clubs played, and keeping hired guns out of the amateur game was one of the union's primary responsibilities. Even back then, however, money talked. To lure the premier athletes, the athletic clubs created indirect ways to reward players financially. The clubs gave jobs to some of them. Others received expensive watches as gifts, which the recipients usually pawned for cash. The AAU allowed clubs to reimburse players for out-of-pocket expenses, and a few players collected double expense money. The AAU constantly battled the inventive ways in which the athletic clubs funneled money to their amateur athletes, but for each practice it outlawed, the clubs thought of another.

The Chicago Athletic Association had a particularly strong football team, and one of the ways it kept its players loyal was through the double-expense-money ruse. The Chicago team convinced Heffelfinger to take a leave of absence from his new position as a railroad office worker to set out on a six-city tour with the Chicago team. For the former Bulldog who desperately wanted to keep playing, leaving the job behind was a no-brainer. Members of the Pittsburgh Athletic Club scrutinized the first game of Chicago's tour, a contest with the Cleveland Athletic Association. Heffelfinger wowed them in his debut. The PAC hurriedly offered $250 each to both the former All-American and another Chicago player, Knowlton Ames, hoping the two would join the squad in time to play against their big rival, the Allegheny Athletic Association. Ames declined, not wanting to risk his amateur status. Heffelfinger didn't want to risk his amateur status either. At least not for $250. He thought he was worth more, and so did Allegheny.

When the AAA learned that Heffelfinger rebuffed the PAC, they doubled the offer. Five hundred dollars for a single game—about $10,000 dollars today. Heffelfinger promptly took the cash. Really, why should he care about amateur status? The managers were willing to pay outright for his skills and the skills of other players. Under-the-table gifts were giving way to cash salaries, creating a new job for him—on the field. He didn't need to shuffle papers in the railroad office day after day. He could make money playing the game he loved. And Heffelfinger was worth every penny. Late in the game versus PAC, Heffelfinger forced a fumble, recovered the ball, and rambled twenty-five yards into the end zone for the game's only score. AAA 4, PAC 0. Professional football was born.

Heffelfinger remained a die-hard Yale fan during his pro days, often returning to his alma mater to help coach the line. In 1916, Yale coach T.A.D. Jones asked him to help prepare the squad for a game against Princeton. Jones thought the presence of the legendary Yale player would inspire his men. The forty-eight-year-old Heffelfinger agreed, on the condition that he be allowed to suit up and work out with the team. Jones warned his team to take it easy on the old man. He forgot to tell Heffelfinger to take it easy on the young ones.

The team chuckled at Heffelfinger, amused at the sight of an old man in uniform. They didn't laugh for long. On the first play in practice Heffelfinger tore through the offensive line, delivering blows unlike any the players had felt. Yale captain Cupid Black asked Jones for permission to get rough. Jones agreed. It didn't seem to matter. Heffelfinger blasted through unscathed once again, but this time guard Mac Baldridge cried out in pain. Heffelfinger had broken three of his ribs. Furious, the overzealous Yale men sought to teach the old man a lesson. After two more plays, four other players lay on the ground writhing in pain. Jones had to ask Heffelfinger to sit on the sidelines for fear that the legend would whittle his team down to nothing.

Heffelfinger continued playing football as long as his body would let him. At the age of sixty-three, weighing in at 265 pounds, he played nine minutes in a charity game for disabled veterans of the Great War in Minneapolis. No word on the injuries, although odds are Pudge dished out much more than he took.

After Heffelfinger's landmark payment, the athletic clubs proceeded to move closer to a full professional league. Teams inked deals with individual players. The Latrobe Athletic Club became the first team to sign all of its players to a contract. In 1920, a group of team owners each contributed $100 toward the formation of a professional football league. They elected a board, named the teams, and established rules for the American Professional Football Association. Later, in 1922, the board changed the name to the National Football League.

The players of the NFL's first decade didn't play solely for the money. In the early days of professional football, most of the men just wanted to keep playing the sport against the toughest competition available. They played for the love of the game, just as many of them had in college. Ironically, when one Harvard grad, Ralph Horween, finally started to make a fair amount of money by playing football, he used the proceeds to get out of the game. With the $275 he earned for his last game, Horween left the gridiron to go into the family business. The family's Chicago leather tannery, operated now by Arnold Horween Jr., is the exclusive provider of the leather used to make Wilson footballs, the official football of the NFL.

🏈   🏈   🏈

Since the dawn of professional football, Harvard and Yale have supplied players to its ranks. All the players can say that they made the jump from The Game to the toughest competition the sport has to offer, although some of them made a bigger impact than others. One veteran of The Game factored prominently in one of football's greatest all-time contests: former Bulldog Chuck Mercein went from the Yale Bowl to the Ice Bowl.

The Eli running back finished his college football career with respectable statistics. Over three years he carried the ball 240 times for 1,210 yards, a 5.2 yard-per-carry average. Mercein, who also excelled as a shot-putter on the track team, posted better numbers in his other duties as a kicker. In 1964, he set the record for field goals in a season, including a 48-yard boot. Mercein's numbers impressed the New York Giants enough to select him in the second round of the 1965 NFL draft, the twenty-ninth pick overall, the highest ever for an Ivy League graduate.

Mercein never bloomed to the Giants' satisfaction, though, and they released him in 1967 after two seasons. Then, "I almost signed with Washington," said Mercein. "Otto Graham, their coach, had coached me in a college all-star game versus the defending champion Cleveland Browns. I scored ten points in that game. I wanted to think about signing with Washington over the weekend and planned on giving them an answer on Monday." Before the weekend ended, Mercein got another call that changed his answer about Washington. It was Vince Lombardi. The Packers' running game was suffering due to injuries. Green Bay wanted a fresh set of legs to carry them on a run at a third-straight NFL championship. Mercein hung up after speaking with Lombardi and looked at his wife. "I said, 'Pack up. We're going to Green Bay,'" Mercein recalled.

The Green Bay Packers—the preeminent team in the NFL—added Mercein to its roster in November 1967 as an emergency fill-in. Both of the Packers' Hall of Fame running backs and offensive catalysts, Jim Taylor and Paul Hornung, had left the team, and the Packers needed help. Mercein couldn't have been happier. Bouncing from the hard-luck Giants to the NFL unemployment line to a full-time job with the championship-contender Packers . . . ahh, life was sweet. It was about to get sweeter.

After bullying their way through the regular season, the Packers won the Western Conference championship to secure a spot in the 1967 NFL championship game versus the Dallas Cowboys. As the defending champions, the Packers enjoyed home field advantage, a welcome consideration in their quest for an NFL-record third consecutive title. Nearly fifty-one thousand intrepid souls braved arctic temperatures to watch their champions take a shot at a new record. The thermometer dipped to minus fourteen degrees at kickoff, and the windchill made it feel like minus forty-nine. "At the beginning of the game I remember the referee trying to blow his whistle," Mercein said. "His skin peeled off his lip and he was bleeding. That was the last time any official used a whistle. For the rest of the game they just yelled 'Halt!' to stop the play." Even for a population accustomed to bitter cold, the conditions were nearly unbearable, but the burning desire to root the Packers on to victory outweighed the frigid Wisconsin temperatures. Dallas and Green Bay took to the frozen tundra to battle for the crown.

The Cowboy and Packer running backs had a tough time just staying on their feet. "The clumps of frozen field stuck to the ground and didn't move. It was like trying to run on a stucco wall," said Mercein. "Hitting the turf was like landing on rocks. Our wide receiver Boyd Dowler caught a pass and was upended. He landed on his head and got a concussion that knocked him out of the game."

The game seesawed back and forth as the steam-puffing heavyweights slugged it out in front of the rugged fans. With five minutes remaining, the hometown team trailed 17–14. Coach Vince Lombardi decided that the most effective way for the Packers to move the ball downfield was with short, wide swing passes to the running backs. Quarterback Bart Starr and running backs Donny Anderson and Chuck Mercein took the field with their marching orders. They needed to cover sixty-eight yards for a touchdown.

Mercein made two critical plays on the Packers' final drive of the game. On the first notable play, Starr passed to Mercein in the flat from the Cowboys' thirty-yard line. Mercein found enough traction and followed his blockers down to the eleven-yard line for a first down. When Lombardi called the former Yalie's number again with 1:11 remaining, Mercein crashed off-tackle through the left side of the line and rumbled down to the three-yard line. After Anderson took the ball to the one, the Packers were left with first and goal. Four shots to put the ball into the end zone for the record-breaking title.

Lombardi counted on Anderson to cover the last inches of icy terrain on first down, but Dallas's Doomsday Defense met the challenge, stopping the back cold. Anderson again pushed toward the goal line on second down with the same results. The Packers took their final timeout with sixteen seconds on the clock. Starr called the play in the huddle: Brown Right Thirty-one Wedge. That meant it was up to Mercein. Starr took the snap and Mercein plowed forward to receive the handoff, but it never came. Starr kept the ball and lunged into the end zone for the score.

Only Starr and Lombardi knew that Mercein wasn't going to get the ball. The icy field concerned Starr and he worried about Mercein losing his footing. A quarterback sneak made sense because Starr could take the snap with his feet firmly planted and then thrust forward. In the famous photo of the Ice Bowl's deciding tally, Mercein raises his hands signaling touchdown, or so it seems.

When Mercein realized that Starr kept the ball, he didn't have time to slow down. Mercein raised his arms to show the officials that he hadn't helped Starr over the goal line, which would have been a penalty. Even though Mercein didn't score the touchdown, his two crucial plays made the winning dive possible.

Mercein realized the toll the cold had taken on him as he began to thaw after the game. "I got kicked in the left triceps early in the game but didn't feel anything since my whole body was numb. I realized I had a massive hematoma on my arm," Mercein said. "The air was a natural ice pack that kept the swelling down."

The Ice Bowl has been consistently considered the greatest NFL game in the league's history, and ESPN featured it at number six on its list of all-time best games in sports history, let alone football. To this day Mercein receives mail each week about the Ice Bowl. Still, it isn't the most memorable moment of his lifetime love affair with football. "By far my greatest thrill in sports was watching my son Tommy, a Yale fullback wearing my number thirty, scoring two touchdowns versus Harvard in Cambridge in the 1986 game," Mercein said. "On that day I truly felt the pride my parents had felt for me. There he was playing for Carm Cozza—my old coach—scoring two touchdowns in The Game. It's the greatest feeling I've ever felt."

Mercein's pivotal role in the miraculous Ice Bowl comeback has made him one of the most celebrated alumni of the Harvard-Yale rivalry and an NFL hero. He proved that Pudge Heffelfinger's legend lived on, that Ivy Leaguers still belonged among football's premier players. Decade after decade Crimson and Blue players fought their way onto NFL rosters. They still do today, and some of them still make an impact.

Harvard's Matt Birk, an All-Ivy tackle, now reigns as a perennial Pro Bowl center. Growing up in the Twin Cities, Birk adored the Minnesota Vikings, and the purple and gold drafted the hometown boy in the sixth round of the 1998 NFL draft. Birk knew that the Vikings had produced a long line of All-Pro players at the center position, including Mick Tingelhoff, Kirk Lowdermilk, and Jeff Christy. Though being drafted by a team that held ball-snappers in such high regard was in and of itself a thrill for the Harvard graduate, he hoped to continue in the footsteps of his predecessors. He knew he had the skills, but Birk suspected one of his first challenges wouldn't be a physical one.

In Birk's rookie training camp, defensive coordinator Brian Billick brought up the center's alma mater. Billick announced that he didn't believe Birk went to Harvard and demanded to see the diploma. Birk took Billick's joke seriously and he wanted to shove the degree in the coach's face. He had the good sense, though, just to let the coach's comments roll off his back. He expected the Ivy League cracks. Few Ivy League players had made it to the NFL in recent years, and Birk wanted to erase the assumption of mediocrity. He soon made any doubters forget for what college he had played.

Birk served as Christy's understudy as a rookie and took over snapping duties when Christy left for Tampa Bay. He made the All-Pro team in his first season as a starter. The next season he repeated the feat. In three years the former economics major went from rookie obscurity to NFL stardom.

Like many Harvard and Yale players before him, Birk's interests extended beyond the field. Prudential Securities had offered Birk a position prior to draft day, and he aspired to be a Wall Street financial analyst in the event that pro football didn't work out. Birk cleverly parlayed his popularity with Minnesota fans and his financial acumen into an opportunity that let him continue his interest in providing financial advice, a weekly call-in program called *Matt's Money* on KFAN radio. Birk practiced what he preached by following one of the most basic rules of financial freedom—no credit cards in his wallet. Then again, Birk signed a $1.2 million, one-year contract, an amount that would render any sensible man debt-free. Birk did part with some money to buy himself a companion, a dog named Jake. The breed? A bulldog. Exercising his personal domination of Crimson over Blue.

Birk overcame the Ivy League stigma by excelling on the field, but the NFL didn't forget entirely that one of its stars was a Harvard graduate. The United Way of America used Birk in a commercial campaign celebrating its relationship with the NFL, poking fun at Birk's Harvard education and playing up the juxtaposition between burly meathead and competitive intellectual.

🏈   🏈   🏈

Following Birk's drafting in 1998, the Elis kept pace by sending their own to the big leagues in 2000. Not only did Eric Johnson make the league and sign with the San Francisco 49ers, the former Yale wide receiver earned honors on the NFL's All-Rookie team as a tight end. Johnson was accustomed to individual accomplishment, having been one-half of a tandem of Bulldog seniors who created an unforgettable masterpiece in their Harvard-Yale game swan song. Quarterback Joe Walland and Johnson's joint performance in the 1999 Harvard-Yale game was an instant classic and an immediate contender for the title of The Game of All Games. They did it all under unusually adverse circumstances.

In 1999, for the first time in nearly a decade, both Harvard and Yale entered the game with winning records, a stark reminder of just how hard times had become for the two schools. The combined thirteen wins between the two teams was the most since 1987.

Harvard Coach Tim Murphy knew that after workhorse senior tailback Chris Menick sustained a knee injury against Penn the previous week, Harvard's all-time leading rusher had played his last game. Thrown this bone, Yale's defensive coordinator Rick Flanders took a decidedly more pass-conscious approach in his defensive preparation. Yale coach Jack Siedlecki, on the other hand, struggled through a week of growing uncertainty. Joe Walland, Siedlecki's senior quarterback, spent the week's practices on the sidelines due to nagging injuries to his shoulder and thumb. On Friday it went from bad to worse—Walland showed up at practice with a high fever, and the trainers sent him to the infirmary. Wallard learned there he had tonsillitis. Walland did not make an appearance at practice until Yale's final workout on Friday. Nonetheless, Siedlecki believed unequivocally that his southpaw would be ready to play. He was so confident that he, perhaps foolishly, didn't establish a contingency plan. Siedlecki readied no other quarterbacks for the game, betting the house on Walland. The coach dreamed of pink, healthy tonsils.

So did Joe Walland. Ten hours before kickoff at the Yale Bowl, Walland lay in misery in the infirmary, his arms throbbing from the alternating piercing of IV needles. He had a fever of 103 degrees. He realized how bad the outlook was for his final game versus Harvard when nature called at half past three in the morning on the day of the game.

"I couldn't get up and get to the bathroom without help from the nurse," Walland recalled. "I had to hold her shoulder with one hand and the IV pole with the other."

He couldn't even get out of bed under his own power. How in the world could he scramble in the pocket? Without Walland under center the Harvard defense would hold all the cards. Yale had no other quarterback to throw the ball. The Crimson could focus on shutting down the Yale running game, specifically the fleet Rashad Bartholomew, and wouldn't need to worry about the pass at all.

At game time the temperature neared 60 degrees, much to the delight of the fifty-two thousand spectators. Walland barely noticed; he was more concerned with the mercury in a different thermometer anyway. Still dehydrated and burning up, Walland suited up in Yale's locker room at the Smilow Center. Starting at eight o'clock in the morning he popped pills like a trick-or-treater with a sack full of candy. "I was on some serious medication. I was taking pills to prevent dehydration and other pills to help bring the fever down," said

Walland, who looked as bad as he felt. "I needed fresh air. I was pale and had the sweats."

In uniform and ready to lead the Bulldog offense despite a fever that raged at 102 degrees, a sore thumb on his throwing hand, an aching shoulder, and an old-fashioned headache thrown in for good measure, Walland shakily took the field.

"I don't think Coach Siedlecki thought I would be able to play," Walland said, "but there was no way I *wasn't* going to play. It was the last game, the biggest game of my life. We had a chance to win the Ivy title. And it was Harvard."

Siedlecki hoped that Walland's mere presence would both inspire his teammates and force the Crimson defense to show some respect for the pass, thereby opening the rushing lanes for Bartholomew. Walland may have been deathly ill, but the Crimson didn't know that at first. And All-Ivy wide receiver Eric Johnson was as healthy as a horse, making Harvard take him into consideration on every play.

Unsurprisingly, Walland was extremely sluggish in the first half, both mentally and physically. Fans noticed the absence of his trade-mark precision passing. He couldn't time familiar routes with his cadre of receivers. Not even with Johnson, his favorite target. Late in the half, though, Walland began to click, and he marched the Elis deep into Harvard territory on Yale's first sustained drive. Yale didn't score, but it boosted Walland's confidence and gave Siedlecki hope. Walland's sudden ability to get the ball to his receivers indicated that the anti-biotics he took 24 hours earlier might have finally kicked in. Good thing, because Yale desperately needed Walland to pass.

"I kept taking the pills all afternoon and I drank a bottle of water during the game after each possession," Walland said. "At the begin-ning of the second half my fever broke." All the way down to 101 degrees. The quarterback began to feel better.

Speedy Rashad Bartholomew carried the ball twelve times in the first half for forty-nine yards. The Crimson had prepared for the quick tailback and the running game, just as the doctor ordered, and Harvard didn't let him bust any big runs. Even though the Crimson offense hadn't exactly been spectacular, as long as they contained

Bartholomew, Murphy reasoned that Harvard would leave with a victory. A seven-yard touchdown pass from quarterback Brad Wilford to running back Troy Jones accounted for the only Harvard score, but it was enough to offset the three points that Yale mustered.

On the first play of the third quarter, Bartholomew carried the ball for a two-yard gain as the Crimson defense again quickly descended. Siedlecki made up his mind. He had gambled by relying on an ill quarterback. It was time to let it ride. Harvard wanted to force Walland to pass by stopping the run. Siedlecki stopped the run for them. He added a fourth receiver and replaced Bartholomew with a blocking back, Konrad Sopielnikow. Sopielnikow hadn't carried the ball all season—and wasn't about to start in The Game. No more running, literally or figuratively. Let the chips fall where they may. Siedlecki turned Walland loose.

For the remainder of the game, Yale spread the field with four wide receivers. Walland barked commands from the shotgun based on Harvard's defensive scheme. Amazingly, the Yale offense began to move with consistency, chugging into field goal range after a sustained drive deep into Harvard territory. Yale lined up for the field goal, eager to put the Bulldogs within one. Instead, Harvard extended the lead to 14–3 when Shawn Parker blocked Mike Murawczyk's field goal attempt and Mike Brooks took the ball sixty-six yards for a touchdown.

"At that point I knew there could be no more pity for my situation," Walland said. "My total focus was on winning the game. Go time or no time. At my position I had to perform."

Remarkably upbeat, the indomitable Walland took the field again on offense. Unfazed by Harvard's special teams touchdown, Walland picked apart the Crimson secondary. He scattered passes around the field, mostly to Johnson but also to the other wide receivers, Tommy McNamara, Jake Borden, and Jake Fuller. Walland threw his way downfield and into the end zone, countering Harvard's score off the blocked field goal. Harvard 14, Yale 10.

"We were able to wear out their defense. I remember Kane Waller

[Harvard's All-Ivy cornerback] puking all over the field. Their defensive line was shuffling guys in and out to try to stay fresh," recalled Walland. "We had a group of thirteen seniors and everyone seemed to rally and dig down as a team."

Yale all but flashed the game plan on the scoreboard. Walland threw and Johnson caught. And there wasn't a damned thing Harvard could do about it. The Crimson ran only three offensive plays in the third quarter. The Bulldogs rode Walland's arm and Johnson's hands into the final quarter, but still trailed 14–10. Less than a minute into the fourth quarter, Walland hit Jake Fuller with a twenty-eight-yard strike in the end zone and gave the Elis the lead for the first time in the game, 17–14. Harvard wanted it back.

On the next series, the Crimson offense responded. A dormant unit put together its best drive of the game, covering eighty yards in six plays. Troy Jones regained the lead on an eighteen-yard touchdown run set up by a thirty-yard halfback option pass from Brent Chalmers to wide receiver Kyle Cremarosa. Harvard pulled ahead, 21–17, and also snatched the momentum.

After a game replete with offensive power, the Harvard and Yale defenses finally appeared in the fourth quarter. The Crimson defense forced a Yale punt on the next series, and the Yale defense matched its counterpart when Harvard punted on the succeeding drive. Walland got the ball back again, but Harvard defensive back Kane Waller intercepted an errant pass. Again the Yale defense responded and forced the Crimson to punt. The stingy defensive battle consumed the majority of fourth-quarter playing time. Walland and Johnson had 2:53 left to find their groove and fifty-eight yards in front of them.

Walland started throwing and strung together three first downs that brought Yale deep into enemy territory. On third and three from the Harvard thirteen, Walland scrambled for a first down by inches. He threw the ball on every play in the second half, yet now a Walland run had brought the Elis to the shadow of the Harvard goal line. Johnson caught his twentieth pass of the game on the next play, a six-yard completion. Second and goal from the Harvard four-yard line. The student sections emptied as the crowd of 52,484 got ready to storm the field in one final cathartic eruption.

Walland faded back and fired to the middle of the end zone in the direction of a tightly covered Johnson. Harvard defensive lineman Chris Nowinski deflected the pass, and the ball fluttered toward the back of the end zone. Johnson dove toward his twenty-first catch of the fading afternoon. He cupped the ball with his hands inches above the ground.

At first, no one knew if Johnson had made the catch. Time stood still as the officials looked at one another, none of them certain. Suddenly, the back judge's hands headed skyward. Touchdown. Pandemonium. Controversy.

"I'm not much of a physical specimen at five-eleven, so there was no way I could see," Walland said. "It was a sure touchdown if the ball hadn't been tipped by [Harvard defensive lineman Chris] Nowinski. I waited until I saw the official's hands go up."

In the postgame press conference, Coach Murphy initially expressed doubt and polled the media members. "I thought it . . . I'm sure it didn't . . . but I thought . . . it's probably wishful thinking on my part . . . I thought the ball hit the ground," Murphy said. "Did anyone else think that for even a second? Raise your hand if you did."

Had he been at the press conference, Nowinski would have been the first to agree with Murphy. He thought Johnson trapped the pigskin on its side after the ball hit the turf. "I don't want to be the kind of guy to moan after the game, but from what I saw, I didn't think it was a catch. It would have been one thing if he had his hands underneath the ball," Nowinski said. Not surprisingly, Yale, and Johnson, disagreed.

"I caught it. Let that be known. I caught the ball. My teammates knew it was good and so did I," said Johnson, though he admitted that the replay revealed a much closer play than the hero thought.

The controversy couldn't spoil Walland and Johnson's remarkable record-setting day. Walland broke five NCAA records. He passed an unprecedented sixty-seven times and his receivers caught forty-two of them for 437 yards and three touchdowns. Half of the completions landed in Johnson's hands. Johnson's twenty-one catches for 244 yards nearly doubled the previous Harvard-Yale game record of eleven receptions. He fell four passes shy of topping Jerry Rice's single-game Division I-AA reception record of twenty-four.

An elated Coach Siedlecki, not a man prone to hyperbole, sang Johnson's praises in the postgame aftermath. "He is the greatest player I've ever coached. This game will go down in history, no doubt about it. He's got the greatest hands of any receiver I've ever coached," Siedlecki said. "You watch him. You talk to receivers all the time about catching the ball with their hands. He can pick them right off his shoe tops. I've never seen a kid catch a ball like that. That was amazing."

Johnson's game-winning reception drew attention far from the Ivy League alone. NFL scouts saw the replays of what came to be known simply as The Catch and read about Johnson's exploits in sports pages around the country. Johnson proved himself a big-game player during his team's desperate hour of need, and many franchises wanted players who could do the same for them. The San Francisco 49ers took a shot on the Ivy Leaguer with a seventh-round selection in the 2000 NFL draft. Though Walland also played heroically in the 1999 Harvard-Yale game, the teams didn't come calling for him. At least not as a quarterback.

"There were some teams that were interested in me, but I'd have had to change positions to defensive back. I ran a 4.5 forty so I had to improve my speed," Walland said. That was a problem. On top of the smorgasbord of maladies plaguing Walland during the 1999 Harvard-Yale game, Chris Nowinski added a broken bone.

"In the third quarter I ran up the middle, and Nowinski landed on top of the back of my heel. My toes got bent back at the joint. I suffered a hairline fracture of my big toe and couldn't run for two to three months," Walland said. Though Nowinski—who went on to dispense theatrical pain for Vince McMahon's World Wrestling

Federation as Ivy League–educated villain Chris Harvard—couldn't stop Walland's pass from finding Johnson's hands, he managed to body slam Walland's hopes for the NFL. Walland couldn't improve his speed in time for the NFL combines with a broken toe.

Walland did play a year of professional football in Germany and he also worked out for some of the arena league teams, but in the end he decided to leave football behind. If he couldn't play in the NFL then he didn't want to continue playing at all. He'd rather be remembered for that improbable day at the Yale Bowl.

"Our goals every year were to win the Ivy and to beat Harvard," Walland said. "The fact that we could accomplish it all in one day was pretty special. But it wouldn't have made a difference if we were both 0–9. It's Harvard-Yale."

Walland and Johnson proved that it takes some combination of skill, luck, and timing to translate Ivy League glory into an NFL career. Some, like Johnson, make the pros and succeed. Others, like Walland, do not. The odds are against Harvard and Yale players seeing the Sunday stage: the Division I-AA stigma. The perception of inferior competition. The lack of national attention for the Ivy League. No chance of playing in the I-AA national tournament. For Harvard and Yale NFL hopefuls, the Harvard-Yale game is the last chance to prove that they are worthy of a professional football contract. Eric Johnson was one of the Ivy League's latest to beat the odds.

Carl Morris hoped to join him.

* * *

Morris had one last chance to make it happen, to impress scouts and recover from his dismal showing in Philadelphia. One more chance to show that his skills warranted his name on the jersey of an NFL franchise. Morris didn't need any additional motivation to have the game of his life to fulfill his NFL aspirations. It was Harvard-Yale during his senior year. He'd already planned on it anyway.

The Calm Before the Storm

T IM MURPHY MADE A DECISION after Harvard's horrific loss to Penn. He wasn't going to show his team the game film from the broad-daylight mugging in Philadelphia. Watching the Ivy League championship go up in flames wouldn't help his team prepare for the Yale game. Penn had gotten revenge, and barring a minor miracle—Penn losing to Cornell in the Quakers' last game—the Ivy season was all but over. Best to just forget about it.

But the year wasn't a complete wash. Harvard would enter Saturday's game against its ancient foe with a 6–3 record overall and 5–1 tally versus Ivy opponents. Murphy knew that Cornell was a long shot versus Penn, but if the Quakers did lose, he intended on doing his part to ensure that Harvard shared the Ivy title: he would post a win over good friend Jack Siedlecki's Yale Bulldogs. If Penn won, then Murphy would just have to be happy with second place. Second place is a bitter pill to swallow for any coach, but if the number two spot came as the result of beating Yale it would settle better in Murphy's stomach.

It was time for The Game, a one-contest season of its own.

The outcome of the Harvard-Yale game weighed heavily on Murphy. He wanted to give his seniors a going-away present that they'd all appreciate, one that none of them had: a win at home over Yale. Murphy knew from experience how much it meant to seniors to beat their greatest rivals one last time before hanging up the pads for good. Whether that win secured a championship or gave the team its only win of the season, the players wanted it. They needed it. And they worked for it.

Murphy changed the way he readied the Crimson during the week of the Yale game. Considering the enormity of the Harvard-Yale game outcome to the players and fans, Murphy's methods contradicted conventional wisdom. He didn't drill them harder on the field. He didn't force them to watch hours and hours of additional game film. He didn't attempt to inspire them with grand sentimental speeches about honor and pride. Murphy didn't prepare the team more for Yale. On the contrary, he did less.

During the course of the season Murphy and the other coaches might have had to issue reminders to the team: *Don't look past this opponent because of their record. We need to win to keep pace with so-and-so. If we win and that team loses we still have a shot at the title.* None of those prompts were necessary to get the team up for the Yale game. "Our players are focused and motivated without any additional input from the coaches," Murphy said. "They know what this game means."

In the incomprehensible event that a Harvard player was short on inspiration or didn't understand the magnitude of The Game before the team dinner on Thursday night, he undoubtedly did after.

Throughout Harvard's regular season the team held players-only meetings following Thursday practices. During the week of the Yale game the team replaced the meeting with a special ceremony. After the last practice, with the practice field lights turned off, the coaches lit flares around the field. The seniors walked their last lap around the gridiron, and the other players and coaches formed a receiving line that each player worked his way through to say a few words or to give a hug. "It was an emotional time," Neil Rose remembered. "Guys kept saying, 'I can't believe this is it.' Tears fell as they always do."

After the ceremonial last lap, the team and coaches gathered for the traditional Thursday-night dinner at Dunster House. They all ate together, but the coaches left after the meal. When only the players remained in the dining hall, the senior speeches began. Each senior shared his appreciation of the players and coaches, many shared stories, and some retold funny moments and the lessons learned from them. Rose, the captain, gave the last speech. "I thanked the coaches for giving me the best thing that ever happened to me: Harvard football," Rose recalled later. "I told them to never give up. I was a player who had to prove myself over and over again to the coaches. I talked to the younger players about this because when I was younger, I sometimes wondered if I would be as good and accomplished as I wanted to become. I questioned whether I had the strength for it. You'll never know if you give up." Rose addressed one player in particular during his speech, freshman quarterback and Hawaii native Todd LaFountaine.

"I wanted to tell him so much," Rose said. "He became like a younger brother, and I was so proud of him for all that he had done and will do in the future. I told him to stick to it, keep on working, and that he's in for a great, great ride. I told him that our people in Hawaii will be there supporting him, as they had so generously done for me. And I said I would be leading the cheers."

Rose recalled leaving his teammates with a final thought. "I told them, 'No matter what I do or accomplish in life, I will always consider being a Harvard football player—being one of you—my greatest honor and accomplishment.' And I still mean it."

The dinner left the players full, and it wasn't just the food. The emotional night filled them with enough drive, motivation, and inspiration to take on two Yale teams. Listening to such a tough group of seniors pour out their hearts and shed tears in the name of Harvard football stoked a fire in the underclassmen. Yale was definitely in for it. Between the seniors' yearning for one last moment of victory and the underclassmen's willingness to ensure that the seniors got what they wanted, there was no reason anyone could think of why Harvard wouldn't win.

But some fired-up Bulldogs in New Haven had a couple of reasons.

● ● ●

Jack Siedlecki would also bring a 6–3 team to Harvard Stadium on Saturday, although he didn't have a prayer of Ivy title hopes. Yale's

4–2 record versus league opponents left it out of contention. Despite that, the season's results so far didn't disappoint Siedlecki. Way back in September, preseason publications had pegged Yale to finish sixth, and a win over Harvard would mean a tie for second place. A tie—with the Crimson. Despite Yale's complex about coming in second to Harvard on various fronts dating back to the origins of the two schools, Siedlecki wouldn't mind sharing second place this time. Of course, to tie Harvard for second place, Yale needed to win. It wasn't out of the question. Yale had won three in a row. They wanted to make it four.

Siedlecki didn't veer from his scripted approach to each game, even when it came to playing Harvard. The way he prepared his team during the course of the season seemed to be working just fine. He did, however, notice a marked change in the air. "The atmosphere the week of the Harvard game is always electric," Siedlecki said. "Little needs to be said. It's my shortest pregame speech of the season, and I don't speak to the team a lot to begin with."

Siedlecki may not have strayed from his usual game plan preparations, but Rick Flanders had no choice.

Harvard posed an unappetizing double threat for Flanders and Yale's defensive backs. It all depended on which Harvard quarterback took the snaps. With Neil Rose under center Flanders needed to address the challenges posed by a classic pocket-passer—a slew of pass attempts to a skilled cadre of receivers. Even though Flanders knew that Rose threw like crazy when he drove the Crimson offense, he also knew that pass defenses rarely figured out a way to stop Rose when he got on a roll.

On the other hand, Flanders needed to ready his charges for Ryan Fitzpatrick. Fitzpatrick's stats on the year told a frightening tale of arms and legs. Fitzpatrick hurled eight touchdown passes in nine games and threw for over a thousand yards on the season. He also led Harvard in rushing, averaging four and a half yards per carry. Commit to pass coverage and Fitzpatrick would tuck the ball and scamper downfield. Commit to bringing defensive backs to the line to help stop the run and he'd zip passes to his sure-handed receivers. Flanders had his work cut out for him.

Flanders had known at the start of the season that the inexperience of his defensive backs would be a trouble spot for Yale. They'd suffered some key injuries in the preseason and Flanders relied on junior Barton Simmons to shoulder the leadership burden. The pass defense had mixed success. Some high points included sophomore James Beck's game-saving tackle versus Princeton and Greg Owens's swat of a fourth-quarter pass earmarked for Brown's Chas Gessner to preserve a win in Providence. But Yale's underwhelming interception totals for the season summed up the collective lows. Four interceptions in all. One each by four different players, and lineman Jason Lange had one of them. Three of the four interceptions occurred in the Holy Cross game. Flanders knew that Harvard coaches had Yale's pass-defense statistics. The Crimson would likely try to exploit Yale's vulnerability to the pass, especially when the Bulldogs had the nineteenth-ranked run defense in the nation for I-AA teams. And Harvard had just the man for the job. Carl Morris, the one challenge Flanders had been preparing his defensive backs for all season long. That meant a long day for the Yale pass defenders.

Despite the mixed bag of results versus the pass, Flanders felt his men would rise to the challenge. Facing Harvard always tapped a deep passion and sheer will to win. He'd seen it before in the likes of Joe Walland in 1999, and he'd see it again. Yale football players lived to beat Harvard football players, and they'd damn near die trying to do so.

Flanders had his plans for containing Harvard's prolific offense in place. Though the Crimson offense concerned him, Flanders thought Harvard's defense ought to be just as worried about Yale's offense. Rose, Fitzpatrick, and Morris may have gotten the bulk of the headlines throughout the season, but Jeff Mroz and company won just as many games and posted impressive statistics. Mroz threw thirteen touchdown passes and covered nearly 1,600 yards in the air, most of them to wide receivers Ron Benigno, Ralph Plumb, and tight end Nate Lawrie. The Yale offense also featured running back Robert Carr, who twice ran for over 200 yards and logged over 1,000 yards on the season. The Harvard defense needed to be just as prepared as Yale's. Mroz would make them pay if they weren't.

Mroz followed his coach's lead. He prepped for the Harvard game as he had all the other games that season. "I do what I have to do to get ready for the opponent we are going to face, regardless of who it is," Mroz said. "I realized the great tradition of the rivalry and its importance in college football, and I realized that the stadium was going to be packed, but the game is played on the field. Nothing else matters. And that is the approach I had going into the game—treat it just like every other game." Spoken like the true leader Mroz had grown into by the end of the season.

Mroz could chart his leadership progression over the course of the Yale schedule. "Early on in the year, I wasn't asked to do a lot or make a lot of plays. At the end of the year, I was making a lot more calls at the line of scrimmage and making a difference in games with big plays," Mroz said. "I felt a lot more comfortable in the huddle and felt a lot more like a leader. I no longer had to lead with my actions. I could also begin to let my voice be heard." But with success came higher expectations. "I always expect myself to be a difference-maker and to make plays, but at the end of the year, the coaching staff and my teammates were expecting that as well." His teammates watched their quarterback's transformation, and no one noticed Mroz's evolution more than the Yale team's elected leader.

"If you were to look back at the film from the Cornell game, where he was initially thrown in, compared to his last game that season, it might be hard to believe that they were the same player," Jason Lange said.

The Bulldogs were sailing smoothly under Lange's leadership on defense and Mroz's leadership on offense. They saw no need to change what they'd been doing the entire season, even if the most important game of the year loomed. They didn't have any special ceremonies or dinners or speeches. No distractions. They'd celebrate after the Harvard game. Business before pleasure.

Even though Alvin Cowan would be watching the action unfold from the coaching staff's perch in the press box, where his broken leg had relegated him, he understood Yale's approach to the Harvard game. "As a football player, you're used to routine, and we really didn't want to get out of that routine," Cowan said. The Bulldogs did their best to treat the week of the Harvard game like any other, but the students, fans, and media around them didn't, and the players couldn't help but notice.

"There's definitely a buzz on campus during the Harvard week, more so than other weeks. Students actually get into this game—unlike some of the other games," Cowan said. "They really get excited. They come and talk to you about the game, sell T-shirts, and make plans."

The Yale Bulldogs had a single plan, simple and concise, the season-long mantra: Beat Harvard. They were ready for the Crimson.

$$\bullet \quad \bullet \quad \bullet$$

Both sides dug into their respective camps during the week leading up to the annual battle. They schemed and plotted. Formulated game plans and mapped out strategies. After all, this was war. But it was an extremely *civil* war.

On Friday morning before the showdown, nearly one hundred former Harvard and Yale players met in the Murr Lounge in Harvard's Murr Center. A fire crackled in the rarely used fireplace, the red bricks barely charred. Several men paused at the fire to warm their hands when they entered the room, which overlooked a soggy Harvard Stadium peeking out beneath thick gray clouds. The steady rains had subsided although a light drizzle persisted. But cold, wet weather couldn't keep the Harvard and Yale representatives from this vital annual meeting. It wasn't a hostile tête-à-tête to hash out the rules for Saturday's game. It was a warmhearted cocktail reception.

Yale's Walt Levering and Harvard's Forrester Clark, both football players in college, met in the service during World War II. After the war the two men, both in the investment banking business, kept in touch on a personal and professional level. In 1948 Levering and Clark decided to meet for lunch on Friday before the Harvard-Yale freshman game. Each of them brought a few friends to the lunch, but anyone who attended had to be a veteran. Not of the war, but of the Harvard-Yale game.

"My father thought competing against Yale was the greatest thing he'd ever done," said Tim Clark. "He took special pride in competing on teams that beat Yale twice in twenty-four hours in different sports. After beating Yale in a regatta in Connecticut he traveled to upstate New York, where Harvard's polo team beat Yale's the next morning."

After several years, the rules on the lunch loosened. First, attendance opened to anyone who'd played football at Harvard or Yale whether or not they played in The Game. Next, they invited other Harvard and Yale alumni to attend. Finally, they even let outsiders interested in and supportive of the rivalry attend the lunch. In 1999, Yale officially named the lunch for Walt Levering. Harvard followed suit in 2000 and honored Forrester Clark in the same manner.

Before heading downstairs for lunch in the Hall of History, which features a huge mural mapping out Harvard athletics' timeline and showcases vintage Harvard sports memorabilia, Johns and Elis from several decades of Harvard and Yale gridiron history clinked glasses, shook hands, and talked football. Coach Murphy stopped in for a brief speech and took a few questions from the crowd, even answering those posed by Yalies. Nowhere in college football's great rivalries does a similar scene play out the day before the two squads meet on the field.

Wolverines and Buckeyes raising glasses together? To smash each other, maybe. Tides and Tigers ribbing one another about old losses? Perhaps cracking each other's ribs. Aggies and Longhorns breaking bread? Breaking necks, more likely.

Yale's Levering Luncheon and Harvard's Clark Luncheon demonstrate how much the men who've played in The Game respect it, and the get-togethers only further the time-honored tradition of The Game. In a rivalry as old and storied as this one, each year inevitably marks an anniversary or milestone, and 2002 saw two historical Harvard-Yale game moments recognized. One of them centered on neither Harvard nor Yale, but rather a fraternity from Harvard's neighbor, MIT. In 1982, members of MIT's Delta Kappa Epsilon (Dekes) pulled off a prank that made stealing a rival's mascot look like child's play.

They exercised the prank with military precision. The week before the ninety-ninth Harvard-Yale game, Dekes dressed in camouflage stole into Harvard Stadium under cover of darkness and buried a device in the stadium turf, carefully replacing the sod. During eight prior covert visits across the Charles River, the Dekes had run wires through the guts of the stadium, tucking them into a gap in the cement track that encircled the field at the time. The wires plugged into a power source in the stadium that would give life to a prank conceived and constructed over two years' time. Harvard security and grounds crew members had thwarted two other Deke attempts to leave MIT's stamp on The Game, the first in 1948 and the second in 1978—but in 1982 the Dekes went undetected.

The attack came during the second quarter of The Game. The ground shook violently. Players, coaches, and fans stood still as a huge black rubber bladder emerged from the turf. Below the surface of the field vacuum motors and Freon gas inflated the orb. When it reached its full capacity the balloon stood nearly six feet tall. Three letters repeated across its girth. M-I-T. The Dekes had done it.

While officials scratched their heads and tried to think of a way to get rid of the giant balloon, it suddenly burst. A white cloud of powder dissipated into the air. Problem solved.

The game resumed and Harvard romped in a 45–7 victory that made headlines. The coverage wasn't for the Crimson, though. It was for MIT. CBS aired footage of the Dekes' prank nationwide. The fraternity has since made other attempts on "hacking" the Harvard-

Yale game, including the launch of a rocket trailing an MIT banner as Yale attempted a field goal in 1990. Though successful, it paled in comparison to the 1982 gag. But the twentieth anniversary of the notorious balloon prank failed to overshadow the fiftieth anniversary of another classic moment in Game history.

Yale's Charlie Yeager loved football. He played a version with six players to a side while attending Milford Academy in Connecticut, but at 5'5" and 138 pounds Yeager knew he wouldn't play at Yale. Instead, he stayed involved with Yale football as the team manager. In 1952, Yeager's senior year, 1943 Heisman Trophy winner and Notre Dame alumnus Angelo Bertelli joined Yale's coaching staff. Before long Bertelli was throwing passes to Yeager during each practice, and the manager eagerly received them.

Yale head coach Jordan Olivar watched Bertelli and Yeager and marveled at the effort Yeager put into the simple game of catch. Olivar thought the little guy deserved a chance, and he told Yeager that he'd put him in for an extra point attempt during the Harvard game—provided, of course, that Yale held a sizable lead. Yeager thought Olivar wanted him to kick and promised to practice.

"No," Olivar said. "We'll throw the ball to you. Work on your pass-catching."

Word spread and the idea became somewhat of an inside joke for the Yale football team. Yeager kept at it, though. Before the team boarded the bus to Cambridge, Olivar told Yeager to grab some equipment.

The cards fell into place on Saturday, and Yale led 27–7 at the half. Olivar told the scrawny manager to suit up. When Yale returned to the sidelines for the second half, the addition of number 99 went unnoticed by the Crimson, who had their hands full with the players on the field. In the third quarter Yale shut the door on Harvard for good with a fifty-seven-yard touchdown pass that made the score 40–14.

Olivar waved Yeager onto the field.

The play called for Yeager to run a short pattern into the end zone off a fake point-after kick. Harvard suspected nothing, because unlike today, the two-point conversion didn't exist. Any successful end zone efforts, whether kicking, running, or passing, earned one point. Teams always kicked. But not this time.

Yale quarterback Ed Molloy, who usually held for placekicker Bob Parcells on field goals and extra point attempts, took the snap. He rose from his crouched position, looking for the manager. Yeager got popped coming off the line, but Yale guard Pete Radulovic steadied him and pushed Yeager into the end zone. Molloy scrambled with a pack of Harvard players on his tail. He ran for the end zone.

"He could have run it in by himself," Yeager recalled. "He spotted me toward the back of the end zone and just flipped the ball to me."

Yeager caught the lob and ran as fast as he could, even though he was already in the end zone. He really didn't want to get hit—those players were twice his size. But Yeager found that the only players chasing him were his own. Harvard didn't understand Yale's ensuing celebration until the public-address system reported the improbable: Yale's *manager* had scored the insulting forty-first point.

"I can still hear the awful groan from the Harvard side and the cheering from the Yale side," Yeager said.

Harvard players and fans had mixed reactions to the stunt at the time, and still did fifty years later. Said star halfback Dick Clasby, "It was going over the line a little bit, but I don't think Yale meant it to be embarrassing." Harvard end Paul Crowley agreed. "Kind of a dumb stunt," he said. Harvard graduate and former mayor of Cambridge Frances Duehay called the play "inexcusable," while Harvard's then student manager John Kelso confessed that he was "a little amused" at Yeager's fifteen minutes of fame.

Fifty years later Clasby may have downplayed Yeager's catch, but the summer after it happened he schemed to retaliate if the chance presented itself. Tim Clark's sister, Nina, followed in the athletic family footsteps of her grandfather, father, and brother. She captained Radcliffe's field hockey team and grew up riding horses. She was perfect for Clasby's project.

Forrester Clark, Tim Clark, and Clasby built goalposts on the Clark family's farm in Hamilton, Massachusetts, and set to teaching Nina how to kick field goals. They practiced all summer until they felt Nina could kick an extra point in a game. Clasby and Clark couldn't wait to see the faces on the Yale players when Nina removed her helmet after booting a ball through the uprights following a Harvard score. It was a surefire way to pay them back for Yeager's catch. Unfortunately, not everyone agreed.

"Nina was definitely capable of kicking an extra point," Tim Clark recalled. "But Lloyd Jordan, the coach at the time, wouldn't allow it."

Yeager's famous score had a lasting effect on the rivalry, and it also provided former Bulldogs with an addition to their arsenal while trading barbs at the annual luncheon. Each year, after the dishes are cleared, representatives of each school speak to the group. In 2002, Tim Clark told one of his favorite anecdotes.

Clark, a reserve player on the 1957 football team, suffered through Harvard's darkest day in the history of the rivalry. Yale pounded the Crimson 54–0 at the bowl. Clark entered the game at the end as Harvard's final substitute. When the beating ended, Clark's father sought his dejected son out on the field.

"My father looked at me and said, 'So, let's see. You were the last player used in the worst loss Harvard's ever had against Yale. I guess that makes you the worst football player in Harvard history,'" Clark recalled, laughing.

After some quick math someone from Yale happily pointed out that 2002 not only marked the twentieth anniversary of the MIT balloon and the fiftieth anniversary of Yeager's catch, but also the forty-fifth anniversary of that game, the most lopsided contest in the rivalry.

There's always something to celebrate or commemorate surrounding The Game, sometimes creating controversy. In 1974, Harvard decided to recognize another football milestone. The only problem was that it was a milestone two other schools claimed and celebrated five years earlier.

Football historians widely accepted the November 6, 1869, Princeton-Rutgers game as the nation's first football game. The National Football Foundation and College Football Hall of Fame established the game's unquestioned credibility as the sport's first by celebrating college football's official centennial during the 1969 season. The series of commemorative events included a reenactment of the proceedings in period uniforms, a postage stamp, and a parade that turned into an antiwar rally attended by twenty thousand people.

But Harvard sports information director Dave Matthews believed someone fudged football's birth certificate.

Upon further review Matthews realized that Harvard could make a strong case that its match with McGill University on May 14, 1874, was the first football game. Harvard and McGill played by rules that were a combination of Boston football and McGill's Canadian rugby, which closely resembled the modern game. The kicking game played by Princeton and Rutgers more closely resembled soccer—players couldn't throw or run with the ball. When combined with the fact that the nation's colleges adopted the Harvard-McGill descendant, a rugby-like game played in the inaugural Harvard-Yale game in 1875, even the staunchest Eli had to admit that Harvard had a point.

"We saw all the other schools celebrate their centennials between 1969 and 1974 and thought about how we could stimulate some interest for our one hundredth season," Matthews said. But Matthews took the celebration further than just commemorating Harvard's one hundredth season. He and his staff conceived a special commemorative logo, and the text within the design caused a commotion. It read, "The Real Football Centennial." Harvard staged a reenactment with McGill as part of the celebration.

The college football community didn't take kindly to Harvard's commemorative concept. "It pissed everyone off," Matthews recalled. "Especially Princeton." Harvard's commemorative tagline threatened to stir up debate about the origins of the game, and Princeton and Rutgers didn't want to hear it. The National Football Foundation (NFF) didn't want to hear it either. The NFF operated the College Football Hall of Fame in South Bend, Indiana, and all the exhibits told the accepted story of football. No one wanted a debate. The NFF, Princeton, and Rutgers hoped that Harvard's centennial would pass quickly. And quietly.

Matthews didn't press the issue. He'd done his research. He was comfortable that anyone interested in the origin of the sport would draw the same conclusion from the same research materials. As far as Matthews and Harvard were concerned, Princeton and Rutgers played soccer in 1869, not football. Harvard had plenty of firsts. If Princeton and Rutgers wanted to believe that they played the first football game, let them. Matthews was willing to let it go. But someone at Tufts University in nearby Medford, Massachusetts, wasn't. He was just getting started.

Rocky Carzo arrived at Tufts in 1966 as the new football coach. Shortly after his arrival he heard about an early football game played between Harvard and Tufts that Tufts won 1–0. The Harvard-Tufts game piqued his interest, but Carzo didn't have time to research it. His coaching duties took precedence. Carzo had taken the coaching reins from Harry Arlanson. In 1974 Carzo succeeded Arlanson again, this time as Tufts athletic director. Sorting through some materials left behind by his predecessors, Carzo came across a file filled with research notes. What Carzo discovered compelled him to make time to research the Harvard-Tufts game.

Inside the folder Carzo found a letter from Eugene Bowen, the student manager of the 1875 Tufts football team. In the letter of March 24, 1949, Bowen recounted the story of the Tufts-Harvard football match of 1875.

"I can tell some of the early history of football at Tufts. In substance: The McGill University of Montreal football team, known as the 'McGills,' described themselves as the 'champions of America,' and then the Harvard team went to Montreal and won from the McGill team," wrote Bowen.

I was manager of the Tufts team in 1875. As to whether we challenged Harvard or Harvard challenged, I am not sure, but believe we must have challenged. Anyway, a game was played at Jarvis field in Cambridge. The lawnmower was unknown on the Hill then, the grass growing until the hay was cut and fed to the cows owned by the College. The milk was used in the dining hall—the basement of East Hall—for most of the students. Patrick McGuire was the farmer for Tufts. For the game at Harvard, the students "borrowed" horses and the hay wagon, the students climbing on the wagon, driving down North (Massachusetts) Avenue, with a growing number of urchins and others at leisure calling us farmers and hayseeds, jeering our progress toward Cambridge to play mighty Harvard.

Carzo read on. Bowen described the events of the game including how Tufts's Francis Harrington scored the touchdown that set up the game-winning point after kick, the only score of the game. He also described Tufts's elation at defeating the champions from Cambridge.

"Harvard fought hard and desperately for the remainder of the game but Tufts held on and we won. I never knew what became of Patrick's hay wagon after the game was over. However, we ran as fast as possible back to the Hill, broke down the attic door of Ballou and rang the college bell loud and hard," Bowen wrote.

Carzo had been sitting on a critical piece of Tufts football history for several years, and he couldn't wait to find out more. The coach knew Harvard had ruffled feathers in the college football world with its "Real Football Centennial," but he realized something. If Harvard and McGill had played the first football game, then Tufts played Harvard in the first game between two United States colleges. Carzo thought Tufts deserved the recognition, and he decided to push for it. Nineteen seventy-five marked Tufts's football centennial, and Carzo thought it a fitting time to throw Tufts's hat into the ring for its contribution to the development of the game. After seeing the backlash from Harvard's Real Football Centennial, he decided to take his time in building a case.

Carzo contacted Harvard athletic director Jack Reardon shortly after he found Bowen's letter. Carzo and Reardon discussed a reenactment of the first contest between Tufts and Harvard, as Harvard had celebrated the games versus McGill. "That didn't work out," Carzo said, "but they opened their resources to us regarding the game's background. Their records were very thoroughly detailed and well preserved." Tufts had some extensive records of their own and, combined with what they learned from Harvard's archives, the school put together a sixty-plus-page retrospective book chronicling the history of Tufts football. Over the next two decades Carzo continued to mount evidence supporting Tufts's place in football's evolution. He found an important ally during a speaking engagement at Kansas State.

Penn State professor Ron Smith, noted football historian and author of *The History of Big Time College Athletics,* suggested that Carzo look into the *Boston Globe*'s archives for more information. Carzo asked Smith to help with the research, and Smith agreed. Smith sent Carzo a letter in September of 1987 validating Tufts's assertion that its 1875 game versus Harvard marked the first football game between two United States colleges. In 1993 Carzo again contacted Harvard's athletic director. Billy Cleary then held the post in Cambridge.

Tufts had decided to rename its athletic fields in honor of Frederick "Fish" Ellis, the legendary Tufts professor, coach, and athletic administrator, recognizing him for his contributions to the college as one of Tufts's all-time greatest athletes. Carzo thought the high-profile event would be an ideal opportunity to acknowledge the Harvard-Tufts game from 1875. He sought Harvard's approval for the text on a commemorative plaque to be affixed to the captain's gate at the field's entrance and dedicated on the same day as the Ellis Oval. "I talked to Bill Cleary about the plaque and its dedication. They were one hundred percent in agreement with our thoughts on the subject," Carzo said. The plaque read:

An Historic Beginning.

Tufts University won the first game of American football played between two American colleges when it defeated Harvard, one goal to nothing on June 4, 1875.

At the time, college football was played strictly under rules similar to today's game of soccer. Harvard introduced the 'new' game featuring tackling and running, passing and kicking the ball. Tufts was the first team to agree to play Harvard in this style of the game which developed into American football.

The plaque also had two signatures: Rocky Carzo's and Billy Cleary's. Harvard stood on a united front with Tufts and its contention. The Crimson's decision to go on record about the significance of its game with Tufts bolstered Carzo's drive to seek recognition for the game on a grander scale. Carzo knew how the NFF had reacted to Harvard's "Real Football Centennial" in 1974. Harvard had pushed some sensitive buttons with its commemorative tagline, but it made no effort to rewrite the sport's history. To change the story of football, Harvard would have needed the cooperation of college football's longtime authoritative organization, the NFF. The NFF's main offices resided in New Jersey, the home state of the two schools that trumpeted their position as football's first players. The more Carzo read and researched the Harvard-Tufts game, though, the more determined he became to make Tufts's official, documented mark on football's developmental timeline.

"It's historically the most overlooked college football game ever played," Carzo said. "It's like United States history without the Battle of Bunker Hill. Our intention was never to knock out the Princeton-Rutgers claim, but to acknowledge our contention. We wanted it recognized as a very important piece of football's evolutionary history."

It took Carzo a few more years before he approached the NFF and the College Football Hall of Fame in 1998 about recognizing the Harvard-Tufts game as a link in the sport's origin. Preliminary discussions with the NFF didn't discourage Carzo, but they didn't honor his request right away. After some negotiations, the NFF agreed to add a display to the College Football Hall of Fame's exhibit on the beginnings of the sport.

Tufts designed a collage that incorporated the 1875 Tufts team photo with insets of Eugene Bowen and Arthur French, president of the Tufts Football Association. He replicated Bowen's letter in its original format and placed it to the left of the photos, also adding a story about the game printed in the *Boston Globe* on June 4, 1875. The caption on the collage read: "This Tufts College team played Harvard College in the first game of American football contested between two American colleges on June 4, 1875 at Jarvis Field in Cambridge, Massachusetts. It marked the first time American colleges competed in a game whose style and rules—including running with the ball—resemble what we recognize today as college football. It evolved from an early version of the game that resembled soccer. Tufts won the game 1–0."

The NFF finally added Tufts to football's evolutionary timeline in the College Football Hall of Fame in 2003, but they'd edited the original display piece Tufts had submitted, and it didn't quite showcase Tufts as Carzo would have liked. On a wall dedicated to the development of the game from 1875 to 1879, a wall primarily devoted to the Harvard-Yale game, the NFF added the 1875 Tufts team photo with the caption: "On June 4, 1875, Tufts defeated Harvard 1–0 in the first game after rule changes permitted running with the ball." Carzo wasn't thrilled, but he understood. "There is sensitivity to the preservation of the 1869 Princeton-Rutgers game," Carzo said. "The NFF does recognize our game as a significant development on the evolutionary track toward modern football, though."

"The Princeton-Rutgers game was not a football game, but a soccer game with a round ball that could be kicked, but not carried, without tackling," Carzo said. "Whatever it was, it wasn't football as we know it. I feel strongly that we should be acknowledged in order to help define the link between soccer, rugby, and the great modern strategic game of football. The Harvard-Tufts game demonstrates an important aspect of the hybridization of several different games played by some-what different rules. Our game is very much relevant in showing how modern football developed from a Model T to a Jaguar."

Carzo doesn't believe that Tufts will get the recognition he feels it deserves from the current College Football Hall of Fame display, but he hopes to one day see a change. That isn't stopping him from con-tinuing to publicize the Harvard-Tufts game as the first between two American colleges. Tufts features the topic of its place in the evolu-tion of football in *Jumbo Footprints: The History of Tufts Athletics*, a pro-ject Carzo spearheaded. "A quest for the truth is a fundamental principle of any academic institution," Carzo said. "To deny our her-itage as an academic institution would be wrong."

Harvard's 1974 "Real Football Centennial," which drew more attention during the weekend of the Yale game than any other dur-ing the season, contributed to launching Rocky Carzo's quest for the truth. But the 1974 Harvard-Yale game produced something else as well. In all the rivalry's years, never have the two schools played a bet-ter football game. The deeper the Harvard and Yale teams went into the 1974 season, the more apparent it became that their annual matchup would be the game to decide the Ivy League champi-onship.

Carm Cozza had assembled a very special group of Bulldogs. From the outset of the 1974 season, the defense quickly gained a reputa-tion for being nearly impenetrable. Four members of the starting defensive eleven—defensive end Brian Ameche, defensive tackle Rich Feryok, middle linebacker John Cahill, and defensive back Elvin Charity—all achieved first team All-Ivy recognition. Line-backer John Smart was another dominating force. Opponents simply couldn't move the ball against the Elis, let alone score. Yale rolled through their first seven games to a perfect 7–0 record. Only Pennsylvania managed to score in double-digits in a 37–12 loss.

On the offensive side of the ball, quarterback Tom Doyle effi-ciently operated a versatile, powerful I-formation attack. First team All-Ivy selection Rudy Green led a deep group of running backs, including Don Gesicki and Tyrell Hennings. The offensive line stood with the best in Yale history, and guard Greg Dubinetz and tight end Bob Fernandez joined bookend offensive tackles Al Moros and Charlie Palmer on the line of scrimmage and as members of the All-Ivy first all-star team. At wide receiver the Elis had another weapon in Gary Fencik, who went on to greater fame as a Chicago Bears defensive back and cornerstone of one of the NFL's greatest defenses ever in 1985.

An offense that amassed more total yards than any Yale team since the legendary undefeated 1960 club was overshadowed by a defense that, prior to the Harvard-Yale game, allowed a best-in-the-nation 5.7 points per game and caused an amazing thirty turnovers. It was unquestionably Cozza's best team since Dowling and Hill left New Haven for the NFL in 1969. Many veteran observers around New Haven openly speculated about the proper place for this 1974 edition among the best Yale teams of the twentieth century.

Although a formidable team in its own right, man for man the Crimson's talent was a shade below their Eli counterparts. Harvard fans never left a game unsatisfied, though. The 1974 Harvard team featured one of the most colorful personalities and dynamic performers in Harvard football annals, quarterback Milt Holt. Holt and wide receiver/punter Pat McInally thrilled Crimson crowds each week. Every Harvard football ticket that year came with a heaping dose of pure entertainment.

Milton Ikaika Holt hailed from Honolulu, Hawaii. After attending Kamehameha High, Milt—nicknamed "Pineapple"—left the carefree lifestyle of his beloved island home for the rigidity of Phillips Andover Academy in Andover, Massachusetts, a noted training ground for Harvard students and student-athletes. Holt landed in Andover at the behest of a Yale alumnus who hoped that the talented left-handed slinger would take his considerable football and baseball skills to Yale after a postgraduate year of study.

In Hawaii, Holt had freedom: his own car, the world's most beautiful beaches, and a bustling nightlife. At Andover, a suburb north of Boston, he had the nineteenth-century discipline of a New England prep school. Upon visiting Yale, New Haven looked too much like Andover to suit the free-spirited southpaw. One look at the funky, bohemian Harvard Square of the 1970s sealed Holt's decision. Much to the chagrin of the anonymous Yale alumnus who helped get Holt into Phillips Andover Academy, Holt chose Harvard.

Before departing Andover, Holt turned down a professional base-ball contract offer to pitch for the St. Louis Cardinals. Holt, not a hard thrower, relied on his control and cunning to get hitters out. "I'm the only guy who throws a football harder than a baseball," he commented. As a junior in 1974 Holt was named a second team All-American on a district championship team that advanced to the College World Series. Although Holt made immediate contributions to Harvard baseball, he had to wait for his time to shine on the gridiron.

Harvard already had an All-Ivy quarterback in Jim Stoeckel, who led the Crimson to a 7–2 record in 1973. Holt had to wait patiently on the bench until his senior year. After Joe Restic named Holt as Harvard's starting quarterback for the 1974 season opener, the flam-boyant Hawaiian reacted like a sixteen-year-old kid finally given the keys to the family car. And the "Pineapple" kid was ready to take Coach Restic's multiflex offense for a joyride.

Out of the gate Harvard reeled off an impressive streak, winning six of their first seven games. Holt culminated the run with his best performance of the season, throwing for three touchdowns and run-ning for another as the Crimson dispatched Princeton 34–17. The Ivy League recognized Holt's efforts by naming him Ivy League Player of the Week.

Holt, with the signature Joe Namath white cleats, shaped up as Restic's prototypical signal caller. "Milt could break all the tenden-cies and go against the odds," Restic said. "I could adapt with him right on the sidelines, which made it difficult for a defense to know what we would do, even if they studied us."

Indeed, Holt had evolved into a defensive coordinator's night-mare. Opposing coaches couldn't anticipate his tendencies or pre-dict Harvard's offensive schemes. The impulsive quarterback was just as likely to run on third and ten as he was to pass on fourth and one. A solid offensive line, anchored by imposing offensive tackle Dan Jiggetts (who later enjoyed an outstanding eight-year career with the NFL's Chicago Bears) along with center Carl Culig, allowed Holt ample opportunity to pick from an impressive array of tall targets. Tight end Pete Curtin at 6'5" and the wide receiver tandem of Jim Curry at 6'2" and Pat McInally at 6'7" all had good hands. The high-octane Crimson offense scored twenty-one or more points in all but one game leading up to the showdown with Yale.

Defensive tackle Bob Shaw, a two-time first team All-Ivy selection, led a defense that also had its moments. Rugged linebacker Eric Kurzweil anchored a hard line, and Mike Page, Fran Cronin, Joe Sciolla, and Bill Emper maintained a big play presence in the secondary.

Game day for the 1974 Harvard-Yale game, the culmination of Harvard's season-long "Real Football Centennial" celebration, dawned clear, crisp, cold, and windless. A perfect day for the annual late November ode to The Game. A sellout, standing-room-only crowd of more than forty thousand packed the stadium on the banks of the Charles River. Faces in the crowd included CBS news icon Walter Cronkite, Billie Jean King of women's tennis fame, and Massachusetts senior senator Ted Kennedy, who scored the only touchdown in Harvard's 21–7 loss to Yale in 1955. The celebrity attendees picked a good day to see a football game.

Yale hastily showed the fans why college football pundits favored them to win. The Bulldogs capitalized early in the first quarter on a Holt fumble at the Yale thirty-six. Yale quarterback Tom Doyle wasted no time. He threw two passes to wide receiver Gary Fencik that covered sixty yards. Halfback Rudy Green, the Eli captain, found the end zone from a yard out to give Yale the lead. The touchdown stunned the Crimson. Holt took the field to get the equalizer, but the jittery Crimson offense sputtered. Yale continued to thwart the Harvard offense.

The Harvard defense tried to return the favor but came up empty.

Five minutes into the second quarter Green crossed the goal line again. Yale placekicker Randy Carter converted on his second extra point attempt after missing the first, and Yale led 13–0. With the best defense in I-AA college football, Yale seemed destined to win. The Bulldogs had every right to be confident.

Harvard desperately needed Holt to respond. Yale was poised to run away with the game, Ivy title, and bragging rights. On Harvard's next series, the mercurial quarterback regrouped. He settled in and tossed three quick completions to tight end Pete Curtin and wide receiver Pat McInally, bringing the Crimson deep into Yale territory. Holt completed the drive with a two-yard touchdown pass to McInally. The touchdown did more than bring the Crimson within striking distance—it restored Harvard's confidence.

Yale had been blanked for seven straight quarters in The Game, dating back to the second quarter of the 1972 game at the stadium. But Yale then scored seventy-six straight points, for Harvard a grim reminder of Walter Camp and the domineering Bulldogs of the late nineteenth century. But no Harvard team of that era had a quarterback quite like Holt.

On the next Crimson possession, Holt went to work again. Restic dug deep into Harvard's phonebook-thick playbook. Shortly before halftime Holt took the snap and lateraled to McInally. McInally faked the run, pulled up, and heaved a perfect pass to wide receiver Jim Curry. Curry broke double coverage, caught the ball, and got some help from Mother Nature. It had rained earlier in the week and the soggy field hadn't dried completely. The nearest defender in the Yale secondary, Mark McAda, slipped. Yale finally caught Curry with one yard to spare. The razzle-dazzle flea-flicker play covered forty-six yards. It also led to another short Holt touchdown pass to tight end Pete Curtin, and running back/placekicker Alky Tsitsos successfully converted his second extra point of the day. Harvard took a skinny one-point lead, momentum, and a mountain of confidence into their Dillon Field House locker room at halftime. Yale's defense wasn't invincible after all.

Goliath had stumbled, and David still had stones to sling.

In the second half the respective defenses started to assert themselves. Restic, noted for his offensive acumen, had devised a defensive game plan designed primarily to stop the run. Harvard went with a six-man defensive front. They clogged the middle with four tackles and essentially played a goal-line defense all over the field. A bold move, but the strategy took hold.

The Crimson stifled Yale's marquee running back Rudy Green, holding him to just forty-five yards on twenty carries. The hard-hitting Crimson defense made sure Green earned every one of his yards. The Crimson seemed to relish meeting any Yale running play head-on. Indeed, aside from Green's rushing yards, Yale found room in the Harvard defense for just one more—the Bulldogs rushed for only forty-six yards during the game's second half. But an impotent running game didn't keep them from progressing on offense.

Harvard dared Yale's quarterback to throw, and Doyle accepted the challenge. The Yale signal caller had waited a long year to have his chance to start versus Harvard. The previous November Princeton had done a number on Doyle, forcing him to give way to senior backup Kevin Rogan, who had never started a varsity game. Doyle watched Rogan rocket from obscurity to Yale football immortality. Yale piled up 523 yards of total offense in the 35–0 shellacking of the Crimson in 1973. Doyle made it unscathed to the end of the season this year, and now it was his turn.

Doyle teamed with wide receiver Fencik to establish Yale single-game records for receptions in a game and receiving yards in a game—the quarterback threw for 237 yards and ran for 31. The Harvard defense never came up with an answer for Fencik, who finished with eleven receptions for 187 yards. Although Doyle and Fencik racked up the yardage, neither team scored in the third quarter. Even without scoring Yale managed to damage the Crimson when they leveled Holt. The quarterback remained in the game but his ears rang from the ferocious blow.

A nervous energy buzzed throughout the jam-packed stadium in the fourth quarter. Everyone suspected that the game hinged on the next mistake in the epic ebb-and-flow contest. The crowd waited for one of the teams to waver, each play capable of changing the tide for the final time. Yale and Harvard faced off in a staring contest.

Harvard blinked first.

A botched low punt snap never made it cleanly to the hands of the Crimson's wide receiver/punter Pat McInally. The ball skittered across the field and Yale recovered at the Harvard fifteen, but a costly holding penalty on the play set Yale back to the thirty-yard line. The Crimson defense stiffened and held Yale to a thirty-eight-yard field goal, but the damage was done. Yale regained the lead 16–14 and had time on their side.

With 5:07 remaining Holt led the Harvard offense onto the soggy stadium turf in the descending late-afternoon November twilight. First and ten at the Harvard ten yard line. Ninety yards and the league's best defense separated the Crimson from victory, a victory over Yale that would deny the visitors an undefeated season and an undisputed Ivy League championship.

Holt lined up under center and barked the snap count. Penalty flags flew. The Harvard offense didn't get the play underway on time. Delay of game. The Crimson's task grew by five long yards. With Holt still groggy Restic knew he had to reel in his southpaw quarterback. Restic called the plays, and Holt started making them. Holt completed a pass to McInally, and then a Tom Winn run got the Crimson offense some desperately needed room to maneuver.

Holt weaved his magic on the next play. He rolled left, ducking the clutches of two Bulldog pursuers and found halfback Steve Dart open for a huge twenty-six-yard gain and a first down. A well-executed screen pass to Dart followed and the Crimson picked up eight more. Now at the Yale thirty-seven-yard line, Holt wound up and fired a strike to a leaping McInally for nineteen yards. The chains moved again.

On first and ten from the Yale eighteen-yard line, Holt kept the ball the next two plays. Two option runs advanced the ball to the Yale twelve-yard line. Third and four with forty-nine seconds on the clock. Restic thought about a twenty-nine-yard field goal attempt. Never a sure thing. He decided to call one more play to at least get the Crimson closer.

Harvard Stadium hadn't seen drama like this since the 1968 epic. Restic seemed to have the 29–29 tie on his mind when he selected a play to improve Harvard's field goal chances. He called for the full-back draw. A wise choice. The play sprung wide open. Harvard full-back Neal Miller burst through a gaping hole in the previously impenetrable middle of the Yale defensive front. Mindful of the ability of Holt to pass or run, the play worked to perfection. As Neal Miller observed, "I figured it was just for field goal position but the hole opened up and I went all the way to the two." Yet another Harvard first down.

With the stadium crowd approaching a crescendo of pandemonium that compared with 1968, and the echoes of a century of clashes between the Crimson and the Blue ringing in the wind, Holt called his own number and gained a yard. Halfway to the Yale goal line. Harvard started with ninety-five yards to cover and now needed just one.

Now facing second and goal from the one-yard line, Holt called the Crimson's final timeout. The clock showed nineteen seconds. Restic thought about lining up for a field goal attempt for the win that was now shorter than an extra point try. "At that point, Milt was out of it. He had taken a shot to the head and was not thinking clearly. I put up one finger and he saw two. I put up two and he saw three," Restic recalled.

Restic sent Holt in with two plays, neither one a field goal. "We decided it would be less of a gamble to let Milt roll out to the left again. If he could run it in, good. Otherwise he throws the ball away and then we try the field goal," Restic said. "I kept telling Milt to make sure he did not get trapped on the field with the ball in his hands. We had no timeouts. We called a roll out, and I remember asking him to repeat to me what we were going to do."

Satisfied that Holt understood, Restic sent him in. The Hawaiian took the snap and rolled out, raising his left arm as if to throw. Yale blanketed the Crimson receivers. Holt spotted an opening, tucked the ball safely in his left arm, and followed the blocks of running backs Steve Dart and Tom Winn. An alley opened to the end zone. Holt sprinted and then dove across the goal line.

As in 1968, the crowd gathered along the edge of the field as the Crimson surged downfield. It took the officials five minutes to clear the field so Harvard and Yale could play out the final fifteen seconds. Alky Tsitsos hit the extra point, setting the final score at 21–16. The last few seconds ticked off the clock without incident. The jubilant Crimson fans' celebration gathered momentum and the goalposts fell.

On the Yale side it was the most unseemly of flashbacks—only worse. This time they couldn't take consolation in a tie. They lost out on a perfect season and had to share the Ivy League title.

Holt's final drive as Crimson quarterback resulted in a command performance and placed him in the pantheon of the great performers that had graced The Game. His flair for the dramatic had raised the bar by which all future heroes of The Game would be measured. He had marched the Crimson ninety-five yards in fourteen plays against a Yale defense that is still cited as one of the Ivy League's all-time best.

The Harvard seniors savored the win. They'd lost to Yale as sophomores and juniors. Now they could take their place alongside the other Harvard teams that had shattered the dreams of an undefeated Yale season. The postgame observations of the two coaches articulated the 180-degree discrepancy in the emotions of their young men.

"I feel for my seniors, especially Gary Fencik," Yale coach Carm Cozza said. "But Harvard deserved to win, and I know everybody in the stadium got his money's worth."

"Stop the clock, stop the calendar, stop the world right now. This is it now!" gushed an ecstatic Harvard coach Joe Restic at the postgame press conference. "This is by far the most satisfying win since I came to Harvard."

Reporters had to look for copy from players other than the normally affable, always quotable Holt. They asked him questions about the winning drive but Holt had no answers. Sporting a traditional Hawaiian lei of native flowers and looking dazed in the commotion of the cramped Harvard locker room, Holt simply replied, "I don't remember it." The third quarter hit Yale laid on him did more damage than Holt had let on. Holt may not have remembered, but the forty thousand-plus fans on hand would never forget.

◆ ◆ ◆

Neil Rose, Harvard's latest Hawaiian quarterback, knew about Holt's incredible performance in the 1974 Harvard-Yale game. It was a legendary feat in Harvard football history, something Rose knew a thing or two about. Rose had rewritten the record books for future generations of Crimson quarterbacks to chase. Rose also had his share of noteworthy single-game performances. He wanted to add one more game to his greatest hits list. A swan song by which he'd be forever remembered, a game like the one Milt Holt pieced together nearly three decades ago against a formidable Yale defense. Jason Lange and Yale's defense stood in his way.

The night before Harvard and Yale were to meet at the stadium, Lange wasn't too concerned with Rose or how well he'd do against the Crimson in his last game as Yale's captain. Lange had bigger worries.

He didn't know if he'd be able to play at all.

10

Playing the Game

JASON LANGE'S STOMACH FELT FUNNY. He expected but-
terflies on Friday afternoon, during the last practice before the
last game of his last year in college, but this uneasiness and
nausea seemed different. Worse than ordinary jitters and jangly
nerves. More like the flu.

He tried ignoring his body, but the pain grew so intense that he
had to retreat to the locker room. Time to face facts. An awful stomach virus had made an untimely visit, crippling the powerful lineman. A disbelieving Lange abandoned the locker room and practice
field for the hospital.

"While the rest of the team was fine-tuning in preparation for
the game, I was getting an IV put into my arm in hopes that I could
recover from the serious dehydration I had," Lange said. He
missed giving the team his customary Friday post-practice speech,
the first snag in Yale's attempt to adhere to its routine. A minor
thing, but there would be major problems if the virus bothered
Lange on Saturday. The Yale defense couldn't afford the captain's
absence from the lineup. They needed his skill and leadership on
the field.

Lange tried to put the team at ease later that evening, addressing
them in the hotel lobby after dinner. He kept his speech short in
order to give himself as much time as possible to rest. Lange battled

dehydration through the night—the team doctor pumped two more bags of saline into the senior's parched body.

Fortunately for Yale, the treatment worked. By morning, Lange felt better. A little tired, but ready to play. When Lange trotted to midfield for the coin toss at half past twelve, the health woes that nearly stole his chance to beat Harvard one last time were a distant memory.

Icy wind tore through Harvard Stadium on Saturday, November 23. Cold, gray, and dreary—it was not a beautiful day for football. But you'd never know it from the looks of the stands. The howls and hollers of 30,323 supporters serenaded Lange and Rose as the two converged on the officials at the fifty-yard line and exchanged handshakes. The referee showed the coin to the captains before flipping it into the air. As the visiting captain, Lange made the call. "Tails!" he shouted. The referee snatched the coin and flipped it onto the back of his left hand. Tails. The visitor's side bellowed as Lange deferred and Harvard took the ball. Lange chose to defend the goal at the closed end of the stadium horseshoe. The referee instructed the players to shake hands one more time and wished them both luck. Even this final handshake between the captains seemed more momentous than that of other games.

Lange and Rose stepped forward. Lange offered his hand, Rose shook it. Both captains looked each other in the eye and nodded. Rose then patted the top of Lange's hand with his left, adding a meaningful mark of sincerity and respect to an otherwise minor officiating task. Duty done, Lange and Rose broke to their respective sidelines to join their teammates in a massive huddle. The players bounced up and down in unison, rapping one another on shoulder pads and helmets and shouting a primal scream. A roar swelled from the capacity stadium crowd. The referee's whistle pierced through the cacophony, instructing the teams to take the field for the kickoff.

It was time to play The Game.

Yale's Andrew Sullivan, his bare foot white and chapped from the cold and wind, booted a high, short kick. Harvard's Chris Raftery caught it just inside the twenty and headed upfield before being blindsided at the twenty-six. Rose and the Crimson trotted out for their first offensive series.

"We had an excellent game plan and I had visualized the plan's execution a hundred times that week," Rose said. "I got almost a sense of déjà vu when I went up to the center and scanned the defense. I'd seen the defense on film, at practice, and within my own mind all week. The only thing different when I took the first snap was the color of the jerseys on the other side."

Rose handed off to Nick Palazzo, one of twenty-one Harvard seniors playing their final game for the Crimson, and Palazzo burst ahead for a three-yard gain. Palazzo surged ahead for five more yards on second down at the Harvard thirty-five. On third down, Palazzo got to the outside and picked up the needed yardage and more. It looked like he'd be busy all day. Three plays into the game and Murphy hadn't even thought about experimenting with his quarterback's arm in the gusty wind. As long as Harvard could keep moving the ball on the turf, Rose would stay grounded.

But after Yale stuffed two more Palazzo runs, Murphy called a pass play. Rose took the snap and dropped back. One, two, three, four, five. Plant the back foot. Fire! The attempt was a third-down ten-yard pass to wide receiver Kyle Cremarosa, on a right-to-left slant in the middle of the field. Yale's secondary coverage forced Rose to throw the ball into thick coverage, however, and Cremarosa couldn't handle it. Harvard's first drive stalled at its own forty-five. Palazzo had only tasted some brief running success before Lange's line snapped to attention and held fast.

"It was extremely important to start with some intensity on the opening defensive series," Lange said. "We wanted to come out strong to boost our confidence and intimidate the Harvard offense."

Now it was Mroz's turn on offense.

"I went through my mental checklist from the time I stepped into the huddle until I took the first snap," Mroz said. "I didn't want to get caught up in the moment of the game. There was too much to think about."

Yale picked up where Harvard left off—firmly planted on the

ground. Yale's star running back Robert Carr did the honors for the Bulldogs. Carr rushed to a Yale first down after three successive running plays. He also handled the ball on the next two plays, but the Harvard defense managed to contain him. Coach Siedlecki didn't seem to want Mroz to sling passes any more than Murphy wanted to test Rose—the coach even called Carr's number on third and ten from the Yale forty-five, almost always a passing situation. No luck. Yale punted, putting Harvard back on offense.

Harvard continued running Palazzo, and Lange stayed busy. Palazzo brought Harvard down to its own forty and again Murphy ran him. He bounced off an initial stop and tried to get outside, but Lange lunged off his block and took Palazzo down for a loss. Harvard faced third and five and ran yet again, but this time Rose took off looking for the first down yardage. The quarterback draw play didn't fool Lange. Yale's captain flung his Harvard counterpart to the ground, promptly bouncing up and stepping over a flattened Rose. "It always felt good to get to the quarterback," Lange said. "And there was a little bit more competition with Rose because of the time we spent getting to know each other during the photo shoot."

The punt-fest continued. With six minutes remaining in the first quarter, neither team had come close to scoring. In fact, the Harvard and Yale offenses hadn't even gotten the ball past midfield yet. The weather was partly the culprit—the conditions forced both teams to keep the ball on the ground, making the defensive plan easier. It looked like victory for either side would rest in the legs of Palazzo or Carr. That was fine with Yale defensive coordinator Rick Flanders. He didn't particularly want to test his pass defense, although it was hard to gauge the secondary's success so far. Harvard had only thrown the ball once.

The whipping wind frustrated Rose. His best weapon for guiding his team to a win was his arm, but Murphy wasn't about to go to a passing game. The wind was just too unpredictable. One gust could send a Rose pass into the wrong hands. It was early, but one mistake could still make the difference.

"In all my years of playing I'd never played in wind that strong. It was the first time the cold affected me. I had always prided myself in not wearing sleeves on the game field, no matter how cold," Rose said. "I liked to send a message that this Hawaiian was going to play as if he were home in eighty-degree weather. But the cold and wind bothered me too much, so I put on sleeves before the game."

But if Rose couldn't pass, then Carl Morris couldn't catch. And Tim Murphy needed to get Morris, his best athlete, involved in the game. He tried a different tack, and Morris got his first touch of the game on a Yale punt with five and a half minutes to go in the quarter. Morris collected the high kick and made it two yards before the Yale special teams squad swallowed him.

Rose then completed his first pass of the day to Rodney Byrnes, firing the ball to Byrnes at the line of scrimmage. Byrnes found an opening and brought Harvard into Yale territory for the first time, just across the fifty-yard line. Murphy tried to get Morris involved in the action on the next play. Rose handed off to Palazzo, who broke for the left sideline and then reversed the play by handing off to Morris. The play developed quickly, but not fast enough to beat Lange.

Lange blew past the Harvard offensive line and into the backfield. As soon as Morris took the handoff, Lange was there. The nose tackle reached for Morris and got just enough of the speedster to take him off balance and slow him down. Morris then ran right into Yale's Rishard Banks, and Harvard's razzle-dazzle netted a thirteen-yard loss. They got five back when Yale jumped offside on the next play, but a Harvard holding call on the following play brought the Crimson back to the spot of Morris's failed reverse. First the cold and wind, now penalties.

The first quarter ended scoreless, but the teams began the second with renewed energy. No more tentative tries. It was time to make some moves and take some chances. Yale struck first.

Carr busted a long run to put Yale into Harvard territory. Following a short run by David Knox, Mroz lined up in shotgun formation and took the snap. He scrambled under pressure and spotted 6'7" tight end Nate Lawrie wide open. Mroz threw to Lawrie for a first down, but Harvard answered by dropping Knox for a five-yard loss. Carr took a pitch on the next play and barely made it to the line of scrimmage, leaving Yale with third and fifteen. Siedlecki did opt for a pass this time.

Mroz took the snap from under center and dropped back three steps. He had Lawrie in his sights all the way. The huge tight end hustled down the middle and Mroz let the ball fly even though Harvard's Raftery had Lawrie covered. Lawrie and Raftery both went up for the ball. They both caught it, but Lawrie wanted it more. He wrested the ball from Raftery's grip to sustain Yale's best drive of the day. "We had Nate split out wide to take advantage of his size. I knew he was much bigger than the cornerback. If I put the ball up there to him there was a good chance that he'd be the one to come down with it," Mroz said. Completing a pass in such tight coverage took guts, and the toss revealed how clearly Mroz now believed in his own abilities and those of his teammates. The play brought Yale deep into Harvard's end at the fourteen-yard line.

Yale went back to the ground attack. After three straight Carr runs Siedlecki had a big decision to make. Fourth and one. Yale needed a yard to get into a first and goal situation. Points had been tough to come by so far. A field goal would give Yale three welcome points, but a field goal was risky. Even from twenty-five yards out the wind could wreak havoc on the ball's flight path. Siedlecki called a timeout to mull it over.

Yale decided to go for it.

Save for some loud yelling on a few big plays, the crowd had been relatively quiet. Harvard and Yale had given the sellout audience little to cheer about. No points on the board. A cautious, grinding running game. Penalties. Punt after punt after punt. At last, a little drama.

If it had been up to Mroz, he never would have used a timeout to discuss the available options. He didn't want a field goal. "We had come that far and we weren't going to be stopped," Mroz said. "We had a skilled offensive line and I knew they'd get a strong push off the line of scrimmage. I told Coach Siedlecki to let me keep the ball on a QB sneak."

Siedlecki didn't want a field goal either. He just wanted to talk the play over with his team to make sure they got the first down. Yards had been scarce so far, and a new set of downs this close to the Harvard goal line might mean the ball game. No time to play it safe. "We went for it a lot on fourth down during the season," Siedlecki said. "It was part of our aggressive offensive philosophy."

Harvard knew what was coming, but they couldn't stop it. Quarterback sneak. At 6′5″ and 215 pounds, Mroz had the size and strength. He took the snap and plowed forward behind his center to the Harvard two. The gamble paid off. Carr took the handoff and blasted into the end zone on the following play. Yale players jumped and hugged on the sideline, and student fans wildly waved house flags in the stands. A bad snap on the point after ended placekicker John Troost's point after streak of thirty-five in a row. Yale led 6–0.

The touchdown rattled the Crimson, so Siedlecki tried to shake them up more on the ensuing kickoff. Yale lined up for the kickoff as usual, but Sullivan didn't unload. The Bulldogs attempted an onside kick instead, nearly recovering, but Harvard retained possession. Yale had taken a shot at getting the ball back right away and paid for it by giving the Crimson a short field to work with. Rose took over at his own forty, hoping to match Yale's march to the end zone.

"The early touchdown didn't bother me. Events early on in a game never did," Rose said. "I guess I always expected—even wanted—the other offense to score first. It made the game more exciting."

The drive got off to a bad start.

On Harvard's first play from scrimmage, Rose looked downfield for his fail-safe receiver, Morris. But Yale had double coverage on Morris, as they had throughout the game. Rose tried to thread a pass through anyway. He knew he just had to get it close and Morris would do the rest. Unfortunately, Rose lost his grip in the middle of the throw and floated a wobbly duck just out of the reach of Yale linebacker Ken Estrera that fell short of Morris. Then Estrera and Lange teamed up to stop Rose cold on a keeper on the following play.

Facing third and ten with the offense sputtering, Rose showed the resiliency that had brought him to this point in his career. The quarterback surveyed the coverage and called an audible. He dropped back into the shotgun, took the snap, and hit Byrnes as he streaked across the middle. Byrnes turned up field and Yale finally caught up with him at the Yale thirty.

"It was good to finally get the ball moving," Rose said. "After every play I became more convinced that we would have to make fewer mistakes than Yale in order to win. It wasn't like other games where mistakes could be made and we could come back. The weather wouldn't allow us to make mistakes."

Rose focused on the end zone. The coach was letting him throw, and that's what he did best. Palazzo wasn't gaining yards as he had earlier in the half. Yale had done a good job of handling the running back, so Rose knew that he had to beat the Bulldogs with his arm. Unfortunately, Yale knew it too.

Buoyed by the long pass to Byrnes, Murphy sent another pass play into his senior signal caller. Rose called the play, took the snap, and looked for his favorite target. Yale had Morris triple-teamed, but Rose thought he could zip the ball to him before the defensive backs could get a hand on the ball. Rose threw. For the second time, he lost his grip on the ball. This time, Estrera was in the right place. Estrera batted Rose's ill-fated pass attempt into the air, dove, and made the interception. The Yale fans went wild once more.

The interception made defensive coordinator Rick Flanders happy, but Estrera was a linebacker. "The rush on that play and Rose making a poor decision to throw were more key than the pass defense," Flanders said. His defensive backs still hadn't been tested.

Rose jogged off the field and went right to Murphy, who had bad news. Rose was through for now.

"I told Neil that the weather conditions gave Fitzy a chance to be the difference in the game," Murphy said. "Though he wanted to play, he understood."

"I wanted to play and lead the team to a win," Rose said. "In my heart I knew I could. I thought I'd have one last shot, one last series to do good things. But Coach Murphy wanted Fitz right away, and in he went. I knew Fitz's legs were something Yale wouldn't be ready for."

Murphy had to go with the quarterback that gave Harvard the best chance to win. He wore number 14.

Fitzpatrick had little time to warm up. Yale's offense couldn't make anything out of the turnover, and the Bulldogs punted after three plays. Now it was the sophomore's turn to make something happen. The quarterback change didn't surprise Fitzpatrick.

"Coach Murphy told me before the game that he'd use me at some point," Fitzpatrick said. "He told me that I had the potential to be a big factor in the game because of the weather."

When Fitzpatrick trotted onto the field to take over, Flanders made defensive adjustments. "Fitzpatrick made us commit an extra guy to the run," Flanders said. "Especially in the one back offense, because there are really two running backs in the game with him at quarterback. We had to treat him like a tailback."

And that tailback immediately made an impact.

Fitzpatrick, the Crimson's leading rusher, ran three times on his first drive, once for a first down. The Yale defense loosened up as Fitzpatrick started spreading the field with outside runs. The Bulldogs still had Palazzo's number, though. Lange and company allowed minimal gains on two Palazzo rushes. Next, Fitzpatrick went to the air. Being chased out of the pocket, he dove and flipped a short pass to tight end Matt Fratto for another six yards. After the short pass completion, Fitzpatrick went deep to Morris. Yale had single coverage on Morris, but the wind provided the defense Yale needed. The ball sailed out of bounds. Flanders's defensive backs swatted away Fitzpatrick's next two passes, including one attempt on fourth and seven from the Yale thirty-five.

Yale got the ball and stole the momentum, running two quick plays and draining the remaining time in the first half. The Bulldogs took a six-point lead into the locker room. Not a huge lead, but enough. They only needed one more point than Harvard to leave Cambridge with a win. Lange liked Yale's chances.

"Six-zero was hardly a commanding lead," Lange said. "We just wanted to focus on keeping them off the board with our defense and giving our offense opportunities to generate more points."

Lange had the defensive front under control, and Flanders thought that his unheralded defensive backs held their own. They had completely taken Carl Morris out of the game for one half. But they had some help.

"I was being double-teamed for most of the game, but I was accustomed to that. I was generally able to find openings in double coverage," Morris said. "The main reason for the low passing stats was a direct result of the high winds. By the time they reached the field they were swirling in all directions."

Flanders didn't care what the reason was for Morris not yet factoring into the game. He just hoped Yale could hold him off for one more half.

Harvard kicked off to Yale to start the second half and Yale took over at their own twenty. Mroz hustled onto the field with his marching orders, but he couldn't execute. On three quick plays, Yale failed to convert a first down against the rejuvenated Harvard defense. The punt team replaced the offense, and then Harvard got the break they'd been looking for.

Yale punter Ryan Allen bobbled the snap and didn't get the kick away. He made a futile effort to pick up the first down but the Harvard defense closed in quickly. Fitzpatrick had excellent field position to work with when he took over at Yale's thirty-yard line. Harvard needed to capitalize on the gaffe.

Fitzpatrick handed off to Palazzo for a five-yard gain, and followed up with a screen pass to fullback Collin Blackburn for another five yards and a fresh set of downs. Fitzpatrick took the ball to the fifteen on a quarterback keeper on first down. Palazzo punched through the line on second down for an eight-yard gain and another first down. Another quarterback keeper put the Crimson at the Yale four-yard line. Murphy told Fitzpatrick to keep the ball again, and the sophomore darted through the weak side of Yale's line and into the end zone for six.

The drive covered thirty yards on six plays. And Fitzpatrick made it look easy.

"Fitzpatrick had a much different style of play than Rose. He tucked the ball and ran with it, putting pressure on the front seven to contain him," Lange said. "We really weren't ready for the switch."

Harvard kicker Anders Blewett booted the extra point and Harvard took the lead, 7–6.

Yale responded to the Harvard touchdown with a whimper. Mroz completed a short pass to Lawrie for three yards, and Robert Carr ran into a Crimson wall at the line of scrimmage on second down. A false start on third down pushed Yale back five yards more. Mroz faced a tough third and eleven. He took the snap, dropped back, and misfired to wide receiver Ron Benigno. Three and out. A weak punt by Ryan Allen gave the Crimson favorable field position.

The momentum belonged to Harvard, and the home team wanted to ride it into the end zone for an expanded lead. Fitzpatrick took the snap at Harvard's forty-yard line. The offensive line protected him from Yale's pass rush. He looked for Carl Morris on the right sideline. Morris had beaten defensive back Greg Owens on one-on-one coverage and Fitzpatrick lofted the ball twenty-five yards. Morris hauled it in and the race was on. Strong safety Steve Ehikian sprinted back to help and knocked Morris out of bounds at the eight-yard line. Morris's second catch of the day netted him fifty yards. It also showed Flanders what happened when you make even the smallest mistake when defending against Morris.

"We were in the coverage we wanted, but our cornerback hesitated for one split second within the first ten yards. The ball was thrown perfectly and Morris made a great play," Flanders said.

"It was a big play because they had begun to bring their defense down to stop the run," Morris said. "That play reminded them that they couldn't leave the receivers alone."

Morris was glad to finally contribute in his last game, and he knew that Fitzpatrick made Harvard much more difficult to defend. Still, he couldn't help but feel bad for Rose. "Neil had a tough year battling through injury," Morris said. "When we made the switch to Fitz I'm sure it was tough on him. I knew what kind of competitor Neil was. The hardest part was knowing that if he hadn't faced all the injury problems that year we could have done the same thing just as effectively with him in there."

Morris made the big play of the drive, but Fitzpatrick did the rest on his own. He kept the ball on first down and ran to the five. On second down he dropped back but Yale's secondary had regrouped. He had no open receivers. Fitzpatrick didn't need them. He angled ahead and bolted into the end zone untouched. Blewett shanked the extra point attempt, leaving Harvard with a 13–6 lead.

Yale continued its downward spiral, the offense floundering once more in the face of a Crimson score. The Bulldogs led off at their own twenty-yard line after a deep Adam Kingston kickoff. Knox took a swing pass to the twenty-seven. Carr pushed ahead for the first down. Mroz then ran into trouble when the Harvard defense blitzed on a Yale naked bootleg play and the Bulldogs surrendered eleven yards. Ralph Plumb caught a Mroz pass to make up nine yards, but Yale still needed another twelve. They tried Carr on a draw play, but the Crimson wrapped him up after another short gain. Yale was forced to punt one more time. And the more Yale kicked, the better the starting field position became for Harvard.

This time Harvard started on its own forty-three-yard line. Fitzpatrick went to Morris on the first play from scrimmage. Morris had broken for a long reception on the previous offensive series, and Murphy tried to make it happen again. This time around Fitzpatrick and Morris connected on a ten-yard slant. As soon as Morris's cleats hit the turf he changed direction and sprinted from right to left toward the goal line. Ehikian didn't catch up with Morris until the eighteen, finally whipping the senior sensation to the ground. Yale had provided the coverage Flanders wanted, but Morris eluded a tackle with pure athleticism.

"We had been hitting slants consistently, but the defensive backs had been creeping up on them, limiting our ability to run after the catch," Morris said. "When I jumped to catch the pass I was already thinking about how I could get away from the coverage to run downfield. My body just reacted."

Rose celebrated on the sidelines. Deep down he felt that Harvard would win, even before the game started. Now everything seemed to be going according to plan. Well, with one notable exception. He wasn't the quarterback throwing the ball to Morris. Rose wished he was in the game, but he tried to push those feelings aside. A Harvard win took precedence over everything else.

Fitzpatrick followed Morris's big play with another of his own. Murphy called for another quarterback keeper to the weak side and Fitzpatrick shot toward the end zone. Yale's Barton Simmons had been knocked down and he reached for Fitzpatrick's legs, but the sophomore hurdled Simmons at the eight and made it to the three. Fitzpatrick rested on the next play and handed off to Palazzo, who made it to the brink of the end zone at the one-yard line. He came through on second down, chalking up another six points for Harvard. Blewett got back on track and hit the point after kick.

In ten third-quarter minutes, Harvard had put up twenty unanswered points. The Yale defense looked helpless. "Harvard took advantage of our kicking game and Morris made two big plays. Yes, with Fitzpatrick in, the switch was going to produce yards and first downs. But those plays were why they scored," Flanders said. If Yale didn't stop Morris and Fitzpatrick in a hurry the game could get completely out of hand. Mroz, who wasn't ready to roll over, came out firing.

He found Lawrie open at the Yale thirty-three. Lawrie caught the ball, but lost it as he hit the ground. Harvard defensive end Mike

Armstrong recovered and started toward the end zone, but then slowed when he heard the referee's whistle. The field judge called it a fumble, but the linesman ruled Lawrie down. Yale had dodged a bullet by retaining possession. Mroz threw another completion to Plumb for a first down. Next came a seven-yard strike to Benigno. Then another to Plumb across midfield for a first down. Knox collected a swing pass for four more yards. The string of completions ended when Lawrie dropped a short pass. Then Mroz misfired to Plumb on third and three and the Yale drive ended. The Bulldogs were forced to punt, but at least Mroz had been able to sustain a drive. And finally the punt worked to Yale's advantage, for the first time of the afternoon. The special teams unit downed Allen's kick at the Harvard three. Good thing, because Harvard's twenty points had demonstrated what happened when the Crimson started with good field position.

Murphy had found a way to get Morris into the game. Fitzpatrick played flawlessly. Harvard's offensive line had Yale's pass rush under control and executed blocking assignments with precision when Fitzpatrick kept the ball. The Harvard offensive machine was on cruise control, and Yale's defense needed to stop it.

At least the Bulldogs had the Crimson backed up deep in Harvard territory. Harvard tried to run Palazzo to give Fitzpatrick more room to run the option, but Lange and his linemates dug in and stopped him on first and second down. On third down, Harvard botched the snap. Fitzpatrick corralled the ball before the Bulldogs could grab it, but the drive was over. Kingston had to punt from the back of the end zone. He delivered a weak kick and Plumb took it to the Harvard thirty-four as the third quarter expired.

Yale had fifteen minutes to make up a fourteen-point difference.

The Harvard defense thwarted Yale once more, and after three plays from promising field position, punter Ryan Allen entered for his eighth kick of the game. Allen had pinned Harvard at the three on his last try. This time he left them with ninety-nine yards to cover.

With shadows stretching long and thin across the stadium turf as the sun dipped lower in the November sky, Fitzpatrick began moving his troops. On first down he plunged ahead for two yards to give himself room to breathe. One more time on second down for a couple more. He faked a draw to Palazzo on third down and finally made it past the marker.

Fitzpatrick continued marching down the field. He was chewing up precious time, but Yale didn't panic. The Bulldogs got the ball back with ten minutes to go after a Kingston punt. Mroz *had* to get Yale downfield for a score in order to have a chance. And he had to do it quickly.

Mroz warmed up with two passes to Lawrie and then went deep. Plumb had Raftery in one-on-one coverage, and Mroz let the ball fly. Plumb caught it at the two, only to have Raftery strip the ball from his clutches before he had possession. Incomplete. Mroz kept his cool. After Carr didn't convert on third and four near the Harvard twenty, Siedlecki didn't need a timeout to weigh his options. Mroz needed two yards to keep the drive alive. He took the snap, dropped, and hit Lawrie square in the chest with a bullet for the first down.

After a false start penalty, Mroz pump-faked left, looked right, and fired. Harvard had Benigno in double coverage, but somehow the pass found him. He made a clean catch and kicked the goal line pylon as he went out of bounds. The officials signaled the touchdown, and Troost kicked the extra point to put Yale within striking distance.

After a simply terrible third quarter highlighted by long Harvard gains and twenty Crimson points, Mroz and his refusal to give up had miraculously managed to help Yale cut the lead to seven points. The Bulldogs still had hope, but Harvard would make them fight their way back if they wanted the win.

"I thought we had a chance. We had a successful drive and we were finally moving the ball through the air as well as the ground," Mroz said. "We had two great fourth quarter comebacks in the previous two games against Brown and Princeton."

Alvin Cowan had watched the entire game from the press box with the coaches, but he decided to cheer his teammates on from the sidelines for the last five minutes. The injured junior didn't anticipate the emotions he felt as he stood on the field. "Prior to the game I thought I'd gotten through all the feelings of disappointment," Cowan said. "But it was the first time I had been down on the field during a game since my injury. The disappointment came back." That didn't stop the pumped-up leader from firing up his teammates, pushing them to fight harder.

Yale got one more chance. Harvard had an opportunity to seal the victory by converting on fourth and two near Yale's twenty, but the Crimson couldn't capitalize. Fitzpatrick took the snap and dropped back. He didn't see Yale's Mark Patterson in pursuit, however, and Patterson sacked Fitzpatrick for a loss. The Bulldogs took over for one last shot at their own twenty-yard line with forty-two seconds on the clock.

The crowd rose to its feet to witness Yale's last gasp.

Mroz's first pass fell incomplete near the Harvard sideline. On second down he hurled the ball down the middle of the field to Benigno. The receiver couldn't snag the ball, but for good reason. He had Harvard defensive back Xavier Goss clinging to him like Saran Wrap. Penalty flags flew. The officials moved the ball fifteen yards from the line of scrimmage, helping the Bulldog cause. Yale had a first down at its thirty-five, with thirty-one seconds left to cover sixty-five yards. A false start pushed Yale back five more. Mroz went for it all on the next play.

The quarterback rolled right with the snap, reached back, and flung a desperate ball deep down the right sideline, in the direction of Benigno. But the pass fell into the hands of Harvard defensive back Benny Butler instead. Butler dropped to the ground. Harvard didn't need any more points. Only the formalities remained.

"There wasn't much time left in the game," Mroz said. "We had a lot of field ahead of us and a short pass wasn't going to get the job done. I underthrew the receiver and it got picked."

The Harvard side of the stadium went wild. Crimson students spilled over the stadium wall and onto the field to celebrate. They'd have to forget the time-honored tradition of tearing down the goalposts, though. Eight mounted policemen waited just outside the end zone, saddled up and ready to keep the uprights intact. The crowd screamed even louder when Rose trotted out from the sidelines for the last play. Murphy wanted to give Rose one last time on the field where the quarterback had shone so brightly. "If possible we try to get all the seniors into the Yale game at the end, but it's difficult," Murphy said. "The Harvard-Yale game has a tendency to go down to the wire." This year, Harvard had the game wrapped up and Murphy sent as many seniors as possible onto the field. Fitzpatrick didn't mind.

"My first thoughts after the game were for Neil and how great it was for him to go out with a win," Fitzpatrick said. "He was so unselfish. It didn't matter to him that he didn't play as much as he'd hoped. He was just so happy that we won."

"I actually didn't want to go in for the final set of downs," Rose said. "I thought Fitz should have taken it. He did a wonderful job and it should have been him taking the knee and hugging the game ball in his arms."

Rose lined up under center for the last snap. He called for the ball, dropped to one knee, and flipped the ball to the nearest official. Harvard 20, Yale 13.

The mounted police moved into position as the crowd flooded the field. The rivalry may have mellowed with age, but the Crimson stands relished the win the way their ancestors had more than 119 years earlier. Harvard had yet again wrestled its ancient foe into submission. The hometown fans were headed home happy, certain that things were as they should be. Morris couldn't stop smiling.

"I was pleased to be able to help the team through a tough game and finish the season off the way we had set out to," Morris said. "After we had lost to Yale freshman year, my classmates on the team vowed that we wouldn't lose our senior year. Beating Yale was also something we felt we had to do after losing to Penn the week before."

The loss ate away at Jason Lange.

"It was a really tough loss for the team," Lange said. "Not just because it was to Harvard, but because the game seemed very much in reach. The loss didn't really hit me until later."

The Crimson whooping and hollering died down surprisingly quickly, the most raucous of fans streaming into the night to pick up where the pregame tailgating left off. The heated high of the Harvard victory mingled with the regretful dismay of the Yale loss, mutating into a subdued aura that permeated the stadium with a kind of wistful melancholy. The Game was over. For the seniors, it was over forever. The year-long anticipation of this afternoon evaporated when the game clock ran out. Even the satisfying comfort of victory couldn't stop a sense of loss and sadness from setting in for most of the Crimson who'd never play organized football again, and for the Yale seniors the loss only rubbed salt in the wound. The Game had been the final stop on a journey that had started as many as fifteen years ago when these same players signed up for their first years of Pee Wee or Pop Warner football. Now it was time to quit playing. The seniors weren't eager to leave the stadium.

Neil Rose worked his way through the crowd looking for friends. He paused for a snapshot with some young fans, kneeling down to sign an autograph for another. Josh Staph, one of the heroes from the 2001 game, raced toward Carl Morris and jumped on him. Morris laughed, shook his hand, and talked with Staph and some other guys for a minute or two. Morris then moved to the sideline and searched the crowd: several friends and family members had flown in to watch Morris in his final appearance, and he wanted to see their reactions to the win.

On the Yale side, Jason Lange's father, a professional photographer, captured the final moments of his son's career. The elder Lange wished the photos showed a happier Jason, but he knew his son would want to remember this time despite being consoled rather than congratulated. Another Yale football dad sought out Jason Lange in the aftermath, offering his condolences and wishing the captain well. Lange's father took some shots of Jason with New York governor George Pataki, whose son Ted was among the football ranks but had taken the year off.

Even if Rose, Lange, and Morris had wanted to leave the stadium as soon as possible, they would have been out of luck. All foot traffic on the field funneled through a single gate at the open end of the stadium. The mounted police worked the edges of the crowd like cowboys herding cattle, gradually guiding the masses to the gate. Rose, still all smiles over his team's win, reflected on his last season as he shuffled to the gate with the rest of the herd. He'd miss most aspects of playing football: the camaraderie of a team, the long touchdown passes to Carl Morris, even scurrying away from the massive linemen that chased him from the pocket. Letting go of that part of his life wasn't going to be easy. But he wouldn't miss what happened when those linemen caught him. He definitely wouldn't miss the injuries, the unimaginable back pain, and long hours on the trainer's table. Finally, Rose made it to the exit. Security personnel stationed there to control the bottleneck waved Rose through, releasing one of Harvard's greatest quarterbacks from The Game. Happy and fulfilled, Rose wandered out into the world.

Epilogue

THE GAME MIGHT BE OVER, but good luck to the player who quickly tried to put Harvard football behind him. Especially with the bellowing sound of "10,000 Men of Harvard" pulsing through the air, courtesy of the Harvard University Band playing at a roaring volume normally reserved for outdoor rock concerts. Inside the clubby, wood-paneled dining room of the Harvard Club of Boston, the Crimson football team gathered for their annual breakup dinner. Neil Rose would never forget the sight of the entire Harvard Band marching down the steps at the Harvard Club, paying tribute to the hard work and sacrifices of the Crimson players, staff, and coaches.

The season had been a success, but Harvard didn't repeat as champions. Cornell couldn't overcome mighty Penn to give the Crimson a share of the title. Penn finished unblemished in the Ivy League at 7–0, and Harvard finished second with a 6–1 record.

The team awards followed dinner and Rose received the Robert F. Kennedy Award, given to the player with the highest level of desire, determination, and willingness to work. Coach Murphy passed the captain's mantle from Rose to defensive standout Dante Balestracci, officially ending Rose's days as captain. His days as a Harvard student soon followed suit.

The senior finished exams in January, packed his belongings, said his goodbyes, and hopped on a plane for the long flight home. Rose looked out the window and watched the Boston skyline grow smaller as the plane climbed. He'd miss Harvard. And football. His days on the football field rounded out his education the way an Ivy League classroom never could. Rose learned about teamwork, determination, competition, and dedication. He also learned about frustration, disappointment, and dealing with pain. Lessons he'd carry with him for the rest of his life, and hopefully pass on to his own kids someday.

Rose's family greeted him at the security checkpoint outside the arrival gates of Honolulu International Airport. He wanted to be close to his friends and family—they were the main reason he traded the promises of Wall Street for his sunny homeland. Rose quickly settled into his new life as a college graduate, eager to start his career at Cadinha & Company after taking a few weeks off. After working in finance during the spring of 2001, Rose decided he'd join the firm after he returned for good from Cambridge. He had received several verbal offers to work in New York City, but he knew he'd have to spend a lot of time paying his dues in a big corporate environment. Cadinha & Company offered a more entrepreneurial environment, and he'd be working with people interested in his success. Rose wanted to be an investment analyst like his mentor, and the path to his goal was shorter at Cadinha & Company. Rose knew he'd have more responsibility and welcomed the challenge. He thrived on challenges.

"I knew that after four and a half years of Harvard and football the real world would be sweet," Rose said. "I felt so empowered, so prepared for whatever the world could possibly throw at me. Investment management had to be a piece of cake compared to practicing in the dark, wet New England morning. No boss or colleague would push me as hard as Coach Murphy and Coach Mills had." Honolulu was getting back a hungry son, someone trained by the best and ready to run.

On a typically warm Hawaiian morning, with the sun shining into his Honolulu condo, Rose thought about his friends who worked in New York City and Boston, who had gone through their own morning routines five hours earlier. Suits and ties for them, more than likely. Rose dressed in slacks and a not-too-flashy aloha shirt. The only businesspeople who wore suits in Honolulu were lawyers due in court. He drove from his condo to the office in a new Lexus—his first big purchase—where a reserved parking space awaited him. The short drive to the office made Rose smile. Back East, buses, subways, and commuter trains awaited those who took public transit. Traffic and parking space battles angered those who drove. People everywhere. Let 'em have the big city firms on their resumes.

Rose arrived at work and made his way to his office, a fourteen-by-fourteen-foot space with a view of downtown Honolulu and the Koolau Range of mountains behind the city. Save for two tall houseplants on two corners of his L-shaped desk, the office was bare. Rose had bigger things on his mind than decorating. He devoted most of his spare time to studying for the first of three Chartered Financial Analyst tests. When not sifting through mountains of papers and thick textbooks, Rose honed two other areas important to his new career in business: golfing and eating. Both were invaluable in wooing new clients, although Rose's initial forays on the greens were terrible.

In the world of investing, past performance is not an indication of future results. In Neil Rose's experience as a football player the axiom couldn't be further from the truth, and it seemed that his success on the football field translated well to the pristine Hawaiian golf courses. He'd only been golfing for a few months and had already shaved several strokes off his handicap.

🏈 🏈 🏈

Jason Lange's season ended in mostly the same fashion as Rose's had at Harvard, in a flurry of tradition following Yale's surprising third place Ivy League finish at 4–3. He attended the annual Yale football banquet, where he received the Frederic Woodrow "Woody" Knapp

Memorial Trophy for typifying the cheerful disposition, leadership, and devotion to others that characterized the accomplishments of Woody Knapp's life at Yale. Lange also passed on his captaincy to the next worthy man—Alvin Cowan. But the similarities between Rose's and Lange's post-football careers ended right there. Lange, who was scheduled to graduate in May 2003, had decided to take a semester off from Yale. All his football eligibility was gone, but he was hoping he could make another famous Yale team, the Whiffenpoofs. The renowned singing group held auditions in the spring, so Lange decided that he wanted to stick around.

Each year, Yale junior men audition for one of the fourteen coveted spots on the oldest and best-known college a cappella group in the world. The all-senior Whiffenpoofs started as a quartet in 1909, meeting at the same time and place each week. Long before *Tuesdays with Morrie* came Mondays at Mory's—at six o'clock in the evening sharp. The group swelled to its current membership total and still sings at Mory's Temple Bar in New Haven each Monday night. But the Whiffenpoofs venture far from New Haven, touring throughout the world and singing at special events and fund-raisers. They've even performed at the White House, something Lange had already done with one of Yale's other ten male a cappella groups, the Baker's Dozen. But the Whiffenpoofs were the best a cappella group on campus, and that's the one Lange wanted to join.

The stakes for Lange were higher than for other men that auditioned for the Whiffenpoofs. "I had taken a big gamble by taking a semester off," Lange said. "If everything didn't pan out as I had planned than there would have been no reason to postpone my final semester." If Lange didn't make the Whiffenpoofs, he had delayed graduation for no reason. About forty singers battled with Lange for a spot.

Lange's plan did indeed pan out. The Whiffenpoofs tapped him to join the group as first tenor. Lange immediately noticed a difference between the Whiffenpoofs and other a cappella groups of which he'd been a part.

"Compared to the Baker's Dozen, being a Whiffenpoof was much more like a job," Lange said. "There was an aura of professionalism that exists in everything we did. Things were much more laid back in the rest of the a cappella community." Before the end of Yale's academic year, the new Whiffenpoofs held three short introductory concerts. The real season for the Whiffenpoofs would begin in the fall. Until then, Lange needed to busy himself with other challenges. He put his free time to use for a charitable cause, one that made him want to shed some of the girth that had worked to his advantage as a nose tackle. At close to three hundred pounds, Lange thought that Habitat for Humanity's sixty-three-day, four-thousand-mile Habitat Bicycle Challenge bike trip might be a tad tricky.

Lange interned with Yale's development office while he trained and raised the required four thousand dollars in pledges. After six months of training, a leaner Lange finally pedaled out of New Haven on his new Cannondale R400 road bike on June 1, 2003, traveling with the twenty-five other riders that made up his Habitat Bicycle Challenge team. He had lost nearly one hundred pounds.

Lange's team took a southern route. In the next two months they biked through Connecticut, New York, Pennsylvania, West Virginia, Kentucky, Illinois, Missouri, Kansas, Colorado, Utah, Nevada, and California. The length of each day's ride varied, depending on the difficulty of the terrain. One day the team rode forty miles, another day over one hundred. Volunteers hosted the riders in small towns along the way, often at churches or town recreational facilities.

The outdoor journey came with some natural hazards, and the Chicago-born Lange was vividly reminded of the nasty midwestern weather one afternoon on the Kansas plains. "We were on our way to Emporia, enjoying the flatness that Kansas has to offer our tired legs, when the blackest, darkest clouds began to form on the horizon directly in front of us," Lange recalled. "The sky changed from a beautiful sunny afternoon blue to a horrific scary black. Our only choice, considering we were in the middle of nowhere, was to ride on through the storm until we reached something that might resemble shelter." Lange's team plodded through the storm for several minutes of hurricane-like winds, stinging rain, and violent lightning before they arrived at a small town. A local woman offered her house as shelter, telling Lange that several bikers had come by earlier and had moved on to a church around the corner. It looked like the weather was letting up, so Lange and the others made their way to the church. But the storm hadn't completely passed.

"As I was attempting to get directions from a different woman that I'd flagged down in her car, an enormous bolt of lightning struck within fifteen yards of me," Lange said. He reacted as most people would. He dove from his bike, landing in a deep puddle of dirty rainwater. Lange jumped so fast that he'd forgotten that clips securely held his feet to the pedals. The bike stayed attached to his feet. "There I am lying in the middle of a gigantic mud puddle, straddling my bike, squirming something like a turtle on its shell—so I was told later—when the woman I was talking to looks down at me and says, 'Welcome to Kansas!' She drove off without another word." A dazed Lange finally righted himself and walked to the church. Not one of his prouder moments of the ride. He experienced one of those while in Colorado.

Lange had raised money for Habitat for Humanity prior to leaving on his trip and spread the word about the program along the way. In Colorado, he got to get his hands dirty while helping to build one of Habitat for Humanity's homes. "We only got to do work on two occasions for Habitat. Because I had never worked with Habitat before, I was luckily selected to be one of ten people who got to work on a house in Boulder, Colorado," Lange said. "After we had finished for the day I found it absolutely amazing. One other rider, Adam Nyborg, and I helped these two other regular Habitat volunteers cut, frame, and finish an entire section of the roof. At the end of the day, while staring at the roof, I felt an enormous sense of pride."

Lange's proudest accomplishment on the trip, though, was the finish. With four thousand miles of America's roads behind him,

Lange crossed the Golden Gate Bridge and completed the trek. He no longer looked like the burly football player who had graced the Harvard-Yale game program cover. A curly, wavy, sun-lightened mane framed his tan face, replacing the high-and-tight haircut he wore during football season. The gut was gone.

Lange's parents met him at the finish line. Triumphant, the senior hoisted his bike overhead and had his parents take a picture of him with the Golden Gate Bridge and San Francisco Bay as the backdrop. He'd conquered the highways and byways traversing the American landscape, contributed his donations to a pot of pledges that totaled over a quarter of a million dollars, and literally helped put a roof over a needy family's head. It was a remarkable experience that Lange would never forget, but he didn't want to sit on a bike seat for a while. He looked forward to seeing sights in a more conventional manner while touring with the Whiffenpoofs after he returned to New Haven.

The Whiffenpoofs' 2003 Winter Tour took Lange to Argentina and Brazil as well as to southern Florida for a few concerts. Lange and the rest of the group also spent some time in front of television cameras for all the major networks. The Whiffenpoofs had a cameo on ABC's *Jeopardy!,* where they appeared as a clue to one of the questions, and then later sang the game show's "think" music during the final round. NBC invited them to Rockefeller Plaza to sing on the *Today Show.* CBS's *60 Minutes* featured the Whiffenpoofs singing at Mory's. They even parlayed their singing success into a role on the WB's *Gilmore Girls.* The characters on the show have strong ties to New Haven—one of the main characters attends Yale, as did her grandparents. Producers of the show invited the Whiffenpoofs to take part in an episode in which the characters tailgated at the Harvard-Yale football game.

The Whiffenpoofs not only gave Lange a chance to experience the life of an actor, it gave him the opportunity to perform as a recording artist. The Whiffenpoofs recorded an album, and the preparations kept Lange extremely busy. But Lange balanced his

Whiffenpoof duties with his coursework to stay on target for his May 2004 graduation. "It was my hardest semester of my Yale career. I think it had something to do with being in the 'real world' for a year. It really gave me a different perspective with which to approach school," Lange said.

With diplomas in hand, in the summer of 2004 Lange and the rest of the Whiffenpoofs embarked on the culminating concert series of their a cappella careers at Yale, a three-month world tour. When Lange returned, his days at Yale were over. From football to charitable causes to the Whiffenpoofs, Lange had squeezed as many life-changing experiences as he could out of his time at Yale. New challenges loomed in the real world, beginning with a position as an investment banking analyst in New York City.

●　●　●

Both captains from the 2002 Harvard and Yale football teams left football behind after the end-of-season banquets and awards ceremonies. Lange and Rose had gone as far as they could, and wanted to, on the gridiron. Carl Morris, however, wanted to play some more, and for the first time in his life he wasn't in control of whether or not he'd get the chance. That decision rested with the coaches in the NFL. But Morris had a few more opportunities to impress them, and he wanted to shine. He worked with Chip Smith, an Atlanta-based strength trainer, in an effort to improve on his speed and jumping ability over winter break.

In January, Morris played in the East-West Shrine game and caught two passes for forty-two yards in the East's 20–17 victory over the West. The next month he played in the Hula Bowl with the nation's best college football players in Honolulu, Hawaii. Rose joined him, and the Hawaiian loved the experience of playing in front of his hometown crowd. He threw a twenty-one-yard touchdown pass in the second quarter, and he even had fun at the practices.

"Even though I hadn't thrown a ball since the Yale game, I was throwing harder and better than before," Rose said. "I attributed a lot of that to being the only guy there not looking for a job." Rose did feel that he could make it as a starter or backup somewhere, but he didn't think football could fulfill him. Cadinha & Company was the right choice. Although he didn't want to play in the NFL, he still had to go through the motions at the Hula Bowl practices. "Personnel from all of the NFL teams poked, prodded, weighed, and measured the players. Players were like cattle as they waited in line shirtless and sweating from the heat of the basketball gym. Men in polo shirts scribbled on clipboards, looked up at the next specimen, nodded, and scribbled some more," Rose recalled.

Morris, however, felt differently about the prospect of playing in the pros, and he treated every play in practice as a chance to add to his already impressive resume.

"Carl did wonderful at the Hula Bowl practices," Rose remembered. "I didn't think that any of the other receivers were as complete and fundamental as Carl. And none were nearly as aggressive."

Morris didn't do too poorly in the game either. Morris caught two passes for twenty-seven yards, but a play he made in the second quarter showcased his versatility. On the first play after the North recovered a fumble, leading 7–0, Texas Tech quarterback Kliff Kingsbury pitched the ball to Morris. Instead of taking off downfield, Morris launched a pass to Grand Valley State wide receiver David Kircus. Kircus caught Morris's pass and took it into the end zone. A thirty-nine-yard touchdown pass for Harvard's all-time leading receiver in front of a national audience. And, more important, in front of NFL scouts.

Morris's last chance to show NFL scouts that he belonged in the pros came at the combines, the final test for players looking to play on Sundays. Prior to the combines Morris returned to Atlanta for more workouts with Chip Smith. But Morris's final exams at Harvard went a lot better than the testing at the combine at Indianapolis.

Morris competed against one of the best college wide receiver crops in recent memory, and he posted below-average numbers for his position. Morris ran a 4.65 forty-yard dash—but he needed to be closer to the four-second mark to stand out. Officials registered the better of his two vertical leaps at thirty-three and one-half inches. The average NFL-caliber receiver could hit thirty-five inches. The results didn't discourage Morris. "All I can say is, football isn't played on a track," Morris said after the combines. "I don't think my time in the forty is going to hurt me that much. I think I'd be a good possession/slot receiver, and I do a good job of reading defenses and finding holes in zone coverages."

Morris hoped that the NFL scouts saw things his way. It seemed like they might. Several NFL teams expressed interest after the combine and invited Morris to work out in front of their coaching staffs. The Baltimore Ravens, Washington Redskins, Minnesota Vikings, and the defending Super Bowl champion New England Patriots all took a second look before draft day in April. Morris couldn't tell what the teams thought, and he nervously awaited the draft. Two weeks before the selections, reports in the *Boston Globe* put him on the defensive.

Globe columnist Ron Borges included an item about Morris in his professional football notes column on April 13. Borges reported that Morris made excuses for poor performances in the forty-yard dash and vertical jump. Borges claimed that Morris told scouts that he wasn't prepared for the workout at Boston College because he'd just returned from a trip to Cancun with his agent, and that he hit the Vertex machine with his hip on a disappointing twenty-eight-inch leap. "What was this guy thinking?" Borges wrote. "If you run 4.68 in the forty at the combine, as Morris did, you'd better be able to jump. If you show scouts you can't do either, your stock will plummet. 'I heard he was planning a draft day party,' one NFL scout said. 'It better be on the second day of the draft. And late in the day.'" Several websites posted the information about Morris. They couldn't resist taking a shot at a lazy, cocky Harvard football player who actually thought he could play wide receiver in the NFL. Morris could handle NFL scouts questioning his physical test results, but he wasn't about to quietly ignore comments that portrayed him as entitled and undisciplined.

Especially when they were so bizarre.

"A friend told me about the article and I was outraged by the lies," said Morris. "I have never in my life been to Cancun, or anywhere else for that matter, on spring break. I spent spring break at a friend's house. I made no excuses at the pro workout. I posted a better forty and shuttle time than I did at the combine. I did hit the machine on my vertical jump, but the scouts told me not to worry about it because I had two good jumps at the combine. I never had a draft party planned."

John Veneziano in Harvard's sports information department immediately came to Morris's defense. He called Morris to get his side of the story and then called Borges at the *Globe*. Veneziano pointed out the errors in the story, but he failed to convince Borges that his sources on Morris were wrong about the trip and the draft day party. Borges's carefully worded corrections in the next week's notes column didn't make Morris look any better.

"Word has filtered back to this corner that Harvard wide receiver prospect Carl Morris was unhappy with a note last Sunday referring to his most recent personal workout for NFL scouts. Among his complaints was that his forty time at the combine was misreported as 4.68. He is right. It was 4.69, according to one of the four clocks put on him," Borges wrote. Later in the report Borges noted that two stopwatches clocked him at 4.65. He also took the opportunity to report Morris's subpar vertical leap and to compare Morris to I-AA receiver Tyrone Calico, who had a low forty of 4.34 and a vertical leap of thirty-eight inches yet was considered a second-tier prospect. Borges also quoted an anonymous scout who said of Morris, "He's a productive kid but he's slow and he didn't jump well. That's what's killing him. He's a late second day pick." Finally, Borges finished the column with a tongue in cheek, "Hope that clears up any confusion." Borges had made Morris look even worse.

"The things that bothered me most," Morris said, "were that none of the allegations in the first article were even remotely true and the fact that this man would go out of his way to write these lies about a college kid who he had never even met." Or spoken to. As much as Morris wanted to tell his side of the story to Borges, numerous people advised him against contacting the reporter.

Morris dropped the issue. He couldn't do anything else. On the morning of the draft he sat down with his roommates and turned on ESPN—just as planned. But by the sixth round, the network hadn't flashed his name on the screen. To anyone charting Morris's progress on television, it didn't look good. But ESPN didn't have any cameras in Morris's living room.

"I started receiving phone calls from teams in the beginning of the sixth round," Morris said. "They were calling to let me know that they were interested in picking me up as a free agent. About seventeen teams were calling me, and when the draft ended it was complete chaos." Calls poured in from around the league on three different cell phones. Call-waiting beeped on every call. Morris's roommates answered for him as he listened to offers and put the interested parties on hold as necessary. Morris weighed the different offers with his agent and made his decision.

"After the dust settled I went with Indianapolis. They made me the best offer and seemed to show the most interest in getting me to their facility," Morris said. In 2003, he signed with the Colts as a free agent. He traveled to Indianapolis to begin working out with NFL stars like quarterback Peyton Manning, running back Edgerrin James, and wide receiver Marvin Harrison. The prospect of playing alongside those Colts appealed to Morris. But they weren't his teammates yet. Morris still had to survive a few rounds of roster cuts.

One Indianapolis receiver was particularly glad to have Morris in camp. "He went to Stanford and studied business and economics also," Morris said. "At breakfast we ate together and read the *Wall Street Journal.* He would always say how good it was to finally have someone to talk to about this with."

Morris did well, but several injuries in the Colts' first preseason game in Chicago ended his brief stint on an NFL roster. "Three of our running backs got hurt and we were down to Edgerrin James and one other back," Morris said. "The coaching staff met when we returned to Indianapolis and decided that they didn't want Edge to play very much in the preseason as he'd just come off of a serious injury. They needed to bring in more running backs in order to make it through training camp." In addition, Indianapolis already had a solid offense, and they were looking to improve on defense for the upcoming season. The cuts had to come from the offense, and a free agent wide receiver was easy to scrap.

"I left Indianapolis the following morning and drove ten hours home to Virginia," Morris recalled. Just like that, Morris found himself out of the NFL and unemployed. But he didn't have time to consider his options.

"I arrived at home and unpacked and waited for my family to get home. As soon as I finished unpacking my agent called," Morris said. "He told me to pack again. I had a flight to Philadelphia in three hours." The Eagles wanted him. His family drove him to the airport and he was off again.

But he didn't have a chance to get comfortable.

"I felt I was never given a fair shot to show my talent in Philly," Morris said. "I only got three or four reps in any given practice and I didn't get in on any preseason games. They released me three weeks after I got there." Morris was up for grabs once more. This time the phone didn't ring. Morris decided to head back to Cambridge where he could work and train with his Harvard strength coaches. He stayed with a friend outside of the city, and his life became routine.

"Each day I drove into Harvard for a workout, showered, and then went to work at a law firm. From the law firm I headed to a bar where I worked as a bouncer," Morris recalled. Certulo and Capone hired Morris as a file clerk where he updated the computer filing system. The time he spent away from football made Morris realize how lucky he'd been—no matter how briefly—to do something that he loved for a living. He longed for one more chance, but as the weeks ticked off the NFL calendar, Morris lost hope. Calls from friends still in the

NFL made it an even darker time for Morris. But in mid-December he got a phone call on his way into Harvard. The call he'd been waiting for. His agent told him that the Dolphins wanted him to fly to Miami for a tryout.

The Dolphins had had success with Ivy Leaguers. Starting quarterback Jay Fiedler graduated from Dartmouth. Morris liked the idea of having an Ivy League ally on the team to help fend off the inevitable cracks about his alma mater—he hoped this time it would work out.

A snowstorm delayed Morris's flight on December 8, 2003. He finally arrived in Fort Lauderdale around one o'clock in the morning and got to bed around three o'clock, five hours before the workout. Morris joined about seven other players for an hour-long audition. After the workout each man had a physical. Then they all hopped into a van and headed for the airport. "They dropped off all the other players and told me to stay in the van," Morris said. "I had to go back to the facility and fill out some paperwork. That's when I knew I'd made it."

After a stressful predraft period, two signings, an equal number of releases, and several months of waiting in limbo, Morris made the Miami Dolphins practice squad. Not a starting position, but a definite slot on the roster. The Dolphins had seen enough promise in Morris to keep him close in case they needed to quickly add a receiver to the team. It was one roller coaster of a ride, but Morris finally realized his dream of making an NFL team.

*   *   *

When Morris, Lange, and Rose left the stadium field for the final time, they graduated from The Game. The seniors went from players to fans in one tick of the clock. The final whistle may have ended the season for the coaches and underclassmen as well, but it also signaled a beginning, another twelve-month life cycle in the Harvard-Yale rivalry.

Jeff Mroz needed only two words to describe losing to Harvard. "It sucked," he said. Mroz didn't want to see anyone after the game. He walked to the locker room as fast as he could and spoke only to the seniors and then only to wish them well. Mroz just wanted to be alone. "I hate losing. I don't take it well," he said.

Mroz thought Yale had a chance at the end of the game, only to see his hopes dashed when the wind stalled a long pass he'd thrown to Benigno and it fell into the hands of Harvard's Benny Butler. The weather frustrated him all day long. "The cold didn't bother me at all, but I never played in such a windy game," Mroz said. "The referee had to stand over the ball between snaps so it wouldn't blow away. I'd rather play in a rainstorm than that wind. It took me a while to figure out how to cut through it."

Mroz would have to wait another year for a shot at Harvard again. Next year he'd be on his own turf at the Yale Bowl. He just didn't know if he'd be the quarterback.

One thing went through Alvin Cowan's mind when he watched his team lose to Harvard. He never wanted to see it happen again, especially when he had something to say about it. Cowan went into the off-season with all the motivation he needed, but he got even more at Yale's breakup banquet. His teammates elected him captain. One of Cowan's new duties was to see to it that Yale won in 2003. But before he recovered bragging rights for the Bulldogs, Cowan needed to strengthen his leg and survive eight other football games without injuring it again.

Cowan had begun rehabilitating his broken leg in 2002, even before he no longer needed crutches to get around. "Early on I got in the pool with a life vest on and ran, jumped . . . anything I could tolerate. I tried to do that every day, and I think in the end it really helped me get back to full speed," Cowan said. "I also worked out my good leg with squats and leg presses, and lifted weights for my upper body. I iced my leg four times a day."

Cowan worked on his leg the entire season, but it just didn't heal enough for him to make a comeback in 2002. "Once I was feeling better and got off the crutches, I tried to go out and run. Once I could run, I tried to cut. Once I could cut, I tried dropping back," Cowan said. "But by the time I could drop back without pain it was Harvard week. I was still only ninety percent. By that point I knew I was done. I still continued to throw the football every day to keep the strength I had in my arm."

Cowan's rigorous rehabilitation during his lost season and the ensuing off-season paid dividends. He arrived at Yale's preseason camp on two sturdy legs, ready to fight for the Ivy League title and defeat Harvard in the process. In 2002 Cowan had clawed his way to the quarterback position—Siedlecki had chosen him over Mroz in a close competition for the starter's role. Mroz played incredibly well in relief after Cowan's leg snapped at Cornell, and he got better and more confident with each game. But in 2003 Mroz was out of luck.

Most coaches have an unwritten rule about injured players. Whether an injury causes a starter to miss one play or the remainder of the season, the job is still his to lose when he's fit to play. Cowan's case fit these criteria, and in 2003 he made sure that he kept his job. He brought the Bulldogs into the Yale Bowl for the 120th playing of the Harvard-Yale game with a 6–3 record. He had also broken sixteen Yale football passing records.

The only quarterback competition Cowan saw in 2003 came from the other side of the line of scrimmage. Mroz got into Yale's first game, a 62–28 romp over Towson, and thus recorded his passing stats for the entire season. One completion on one attempt for twenty-six yards. Cowan stayed healthy, so Mroz stayed put on Yale's bench, waiting for 2004. So much for Yale's 2003 quarterback controversy.

Harvard didn't have one either. Crimson quarterback Ryan Fitzpatrick missed Neil Rose as a teammate, but Rose's absence eliminated the distracting weekly talk of the Crimson's quarterback situation. A focused Fitzpatrick ran the option all season long, except for three games lost to an injured hand, giving the Crimson a 6–3 record heading into the Yale game. His last challenge of the season was to finish as he had last year. A win over the Bulldogs.

Cowan performed incredibly at the 120th playing of the Harvard-

Yale game, a high-scoring affair that featured the Ivy League's two best offenses. The senior completed thirty-four passes on sixty-four attempts for a school record 438 yards and two touchdowns. Yale finished with 555 yards of total offense. It wasn't enough. Cowan nearly doubled Fitzpatrick's passing yard output of 230 yards, but Fitzpatrick doubled the host quarterback's touchdown pass total. Harvard won convincingly, 37–19.

Harvard coach Tim Murphy and Yale coach Jack Siedlecki went straight to work after the 2003 Harvard-Yale game, just as they had the year before and just as they will after the 2004 game. Win or lose, the coaches jump right back into the off-season fray. Heavy-hearted from a loss or relieved with a victory, they still have to do their jobs. Once The Game ends they've got vacancies to fill on their rosters. Recruiting takes center stage after the breakup banquets and awards ceremonies.

Murphy and Siedlecki spent the next two months crisscrossing the country in a hectic race to convince the best football players among the nation's top student-athletes to attend their respective schools. The rich tradition of the Harvard-Yale rivalry usually works its way into the conversation.

After all, in the grand sport of football it's the only game that matters.

Appendix

HARVARD VS. YALE

Date	Harvard	Yale
2004	35	3
2003	37	19
2002	20	13
2001	35	23
2000	24	34
1999	21	24
1998	7	9
1997	17	7
1996	26	21
1995	22	21
1994	13	32
1993	31	33
1992	14	0
1991	13	23
1990	19	34
1989	37	20
1988	17	26
1987	14	10
1986	24	17
1985	6	17
1984	27	30
1983	16	7
1982	45	7
1981	0	28

DATE	HARVARD	YALE
1980	0	14
1979	22	7
1978	28	35
1977	7	24
1976	7	21
1975	10	7
1974	21	16
1973	0	35
1972	17	28
1971	35	16
1970	14	12
1969	0	7
1968	29	29
1967	20	24
1966	17	0
1965	13	0
1964	18	14
1963	6	20
1962	14	6
1961	27	0
1960	6	39
1959	35	6
1958	28	0
1957	0	54
1956	14	42
1955	7	21
1954	13	9
1953	13	0
1952	14	41
1951	21	21
1950	6	14
1949	6	29
1948	20	7

DATE	HARVARD	YALE
1947	21	31
1946	14	27
1945	0	28
1942*	3	7
1941	14	0
1940	28	0
1939	7	20
1938	7	0
1937	13	6
1936	13	14
1935	7	14
1934	0	14
1933	19	6
1932	0	19
1931	0	3
1930	13	0
1929	10	6
1928	17	0
1927	0	14
1926	7	12
1925	0	0
1924	6	19
1923	0	13
1922	10	3
1921	10	3
1920	9	0
1919	10	3
1916*	3	6
1915	41	0
1914	36	0
1913	15	5
1912	20	0
1911	0	0
1910	0	0

DATE	**HARVARD**	**YALE**
1909	0	8
1908	4	0
1907	0	12
1906	0	6
1905	0	6
1904	0	12
1903	0	16
1902	0	23
1901	22	0
1900	0	28
1899	0	0
1898	17	0
1897	0	0
1894*	4	12
1893	0	6
1892	0	6
1891	0	10
1890	12	6
1889	0	6
1887*	8	17
1886	4	29
1884*	0	52
1883	2	23
1882	0	1
1881	0	0
1880	0	1
1879	0	0
1878	0	1
1876–1877	0	1
1875–1876	4	0

Yale leads series 64–48–8

*Harvard-Yale games were not played in 1943–1944, 1917–1918, 1895–1896, 1888, and 1885.

Acknowledgments

FIRST AND FOREMOST, we'd like to thank the current and former Harvard and Yale players and coaches. Without their stories this book wouldn't exist. Special thanks to Harvard head coach Tim Murphy; Harvard players Neil Rose, Carl Morris, and Ryan Fitzpatrick; Yale head coach Jack Siedlecki; Yale defensive coordinator Rick Flanders; and Yale players Jason Lange, Alvin Cowan, and Jeff Mroz. Their honesty and cooperation with answering our questions allowed us to gain insight into the rivalry.

Harvard graduate John Powers '70 of the *Boston Globe* and longtime *New York Times* sports writer and Yale alum Bill Wallace '45 served as the chief consultants for this project from the get go. Their extensive knowledge of all things Harvard and Yale, and the football rivalry in particular, proved invaluable. We thank them.

In addition to the players and coaches, several people from each school assisted us with our research. We owe a mountain of gratitude to them. From Harvard: Bob Scalise, athletic director; John Veneziano, former assistant director of athletics for sports information; and Chuck Sullivan, currently holding that post; Steve Staples, assistant director of athletics for external relations; Kristi O'Connor, director of marketing; Bob Glatz, Harvard Varsity Club director; Marvin Hightower, senior writer and archivist in the Office of News and Public Affairs; Bob Joyce, president of the Harvard Friends of

Football; Harvard football historian Dave Mitell '39; Geoff Movius '62, editor of the *Second H Book of Harvard Athletics;* and Mike Giardi, former Crimson quarterback and current radio color analyst. From Yale: Tom Beckett, athletic director; Steve Conn, director of sports publicity; Don Scharf, special assistant to the athletic director; Dr. Pat Ruwe, president of Yale Football Association; Dick Galiette, voice of Yale football; Carm Cozza, former coach and current radio color analyst; Sharon and Rich Lange.

The representatives of the Council of Ivy League Presidents provided specifics about the unique aspects of football in the Ancient Eight, especially Jeff Orleans, executive director.

We are grateful to the founding triumvirate of the Ivy Football Association for sharing their ideas and perspectives on the state of Ivy League Football. Thanks to Hank Higdon, Stanislaw "Stas" Maliszewski, and Bob Hall.

Athletic director emeritus Rocky Carzo and assistant athletic director Paul Sweeney of Tufts University shared with us the results of their research on the origins of football. Many thanks to them for helping us tell the story correctly. Also, thanks to Greg Kordic, New England Sports Museum curator Richard Johnson, University of New Haven professor Alan Sack, and Harvard Law School professor Paul Weiler for additional information on the beginnings of the sport. Sandy Smith from the modern military records office supplied us with information on Harvard and Yale war veterans.

Thanks to Paul McDonald of Leavitt & Peirce Tobacconist for opening a door into Harvard football history. Also, thanks to Bob Murgia, Brant Berglund and Phil Buckley, our crack filming and interview crew from The Game 2002.

We consulted the following invaluable resources during our research: *The Game: The Harvard-Yale Football Rivalry, 1875–1983* by Thomas Bergin (Yale University Press 1984); *The Beginnings of Yale 1701–1726* by Edwin Oviatt (Yale University Press, 1916); *Yale: A History* by Brooks Mather Kelley (Yale University Press, 1974); *The Second H Book of Harvard Athletics,* edited by Geoffrey Movius

(Harvard Varsity Club, 1964); *The H Book of Harvard Athletics*, edited by John A. Blanchard (Harvard Varsity Club, 1923); *The Yale Football Story* by Tim Cohane (G.P. Putnam's Sons, New York, 1951); *The History of Football at Harvard* by Morris A. Bealle (Columbia Publishing Company, Washington, D.C., 1948); *Big Time Football at Harvard, 1905: The Diary of Coach Bill Reid*, edited by Ronald A. Smith (University of Illinois Press); *The Blue Football Book* (Yale Banner Publications); *Crimson in Triumph: A Pictorial History of Harvard Athletics* by Joe Bertagna (The Stephen Greene Press, 1986); *Ivy League Football*, edited by John S. Bowman (Crescent Books, 1988); *Rites of Autumn: The Story of College Football* by Richard Whittingham (The Free Press, 2001); *Football: The Ivy League Origins of an American Obsession* by Mark F. Bernstein (University of Pennsylvania Press, 2001); *College Football: History, Spectacle, Controversy* by John Sayle Watterson (The Johns Hopkins University Press, 2000); *The History of American Football* by Allison Danzig (Prentice Hall, Inc. 1956); *The Harvard-Yale Boat Race and the Coming of Sport to the American College 1852–1924* by Thomas C. Mendenhall (Mystic Seaport Museum, 1993); *Ivy League Football Since 1872* by Jack McCallum (Stein and Day, 1977); *Anatomy of a Game* by Dave Nelson (University of Delaware Press, 1944); *Yale in the World War*, Volume II (1914–1918) edited by George Henry Nettleton under the direction of Lottie G. Bishop (Yale University Press, 1925), and *Ivy League Autumns: An Illustrated History of College Football's Grand Old Rivalries* by Richard Goldstein (St. Martin's Press, 1996).

Additional material reviewed included articles, game stories, and features from the *Boston Globe*, *Boston Herald*, *New York Times*, *New Haven Register*, *Harvard Crimson*, *Yale Daily News*, *Harvard Magazine* and *Sports Illustrated*.

Our agents, Frank Scatoni and Greg Dinkin of Venture Literary, believed that the story of the Harvard-Yale football rivalry was worth telling and convinced a premier publishing company to print it. We also owe a great debt to Pete Fornatale for battling for this book.

Thanks to Boston Channel 56's Mike Ratte, Jim Norton, and general manager Vin Manzi, and Jim Clark for helping to spread the word about this book and the Harvard-Yale rivalry. Also, thanks to Fritz Mitchell and Wendy Yamano of Lake Champlain Productions for showcasing the Harvard-Yale rivalry on ESPN's sports documentary series *Timeless.*

Special thanks to our editor, Shana Wingert Drehs—the third time was indeed a charm! Shana expertly guided us through the process of writing this manuscript. We couldn't have done it without her. Thanks also go to Campbell Wharton, Jill Flaxman, and Brian Belfiglio of the publicity and marketing departments at Crown for all their help in promoting the book, as well as designers Lenny Henderson and Jennifer O'Connor, production editor Jim Walsh, and production manager Suzanne Schneider.

Finally, thanks to our friends and families for their support and encouragement during the course of this project, especially Fay Corbett and the very patient Tracy and Sam Simpson.

Index

About the Authors

BERNARD M. CORBETT is a sports broadcaster, writer, and researcher based in Boston. He is the author of fourteen books, including *The Beanpot: Fifty Years of Thrills, Spills and Chills*, *Harvard Football*, *Boston University Terrier Hockey*, *On the Court with Grant Hill*, and *On the Ice with Wayne Gretzky*. Corbett has been published in several regional and national publications, including the *Boston Globe*, *Beckett Football*, *Sport Boston*, *Baseball America*, and *New England Sport Magazine*. He has been the play-by-play announcer for Harvard University football for eight years and Boston University Terrier hockey for twenty years. He lives in Stoneham, Massachusetts.

PAUL SIMPSON began his writing career covering high school sports for the *Stoneham Independent*, a local weekly newspaper. He has since worked part time as a researcher on seven of Bernard Corbett's book projects, including *The Beanpot: Fifty Years of Thrills, Spills and Chills*. He has also coauthored a *Boston Globe* feature and an article for *Hockey* magazine with Corbett. He resides in Wakefield, Massachusetts, with his wife, Tracy, and two sons.